DOING SUPERVISION
AND BEING SUPERVISED

Robert Langs

DOING SUPERVISION AND BEING SUPERVISED

Robert Langs

Foreword by
Theodore Dorpat

London
KARNAC BOOKS

First published in 1994 by
H. Karnac (Books) Ltd.
58 Gloucester Road
London SW7 4QY

British Library Cataloguing in Publication Data

Langs, Robert
    Doing Supervision and Being Supervised
    I. Title
    616.8914

    ISBN: 1 85575 060 0

Printed in Great Britain by BPC Wheatons Ltd, Exeter

CONTENTS

FOREWORD

Theodore Dorpat

D r. Robert Langs has presented a stunning and original work on supervision of psychoanalytic psychotherapy which, in my opinion, should become a standard textbook and a classic in its field. Not only is it the most comprehensive book thus far written on supervision, it also includes important topics that have been neglected or overlooked in the writings of others.

In what follows, my purpose is to discuss the significance of five major contributions the author has made in this book towards both the theory and the practice of supervision.

First, to the best of my knowledge, this is the only book on supervision based on contemporary knowledge of the mind and psychopathology as summarized in the early sections of this volume. The traditional models used for psychotherapy, psychoanalysis, and supervision have a restricted and narrow definition of the unconscious, limited to unconscious instinctual sexual and aggressive drives and defences against them. There is much, much more in the unconscious than Freud or many other analysts who followed after him knew about. We are now aware that higher-level cognitive functions, meaning analysis, perception, judgement, decision making, and a host of other complex mental functions can be carried out *unconsciously*. Any system of psychotherapy, psychoanalysis, or supervision should be based, as this book is based, on a contemporary view of mental functioning. Langs compares the communicative model of supervision with the traditional or classical model of supervision, and he correctly faults the traditional theory for its failure to comprehend the deeply unconscious nature of the therapeutic interaction.

A second important contribution of this volume is its knowledge about and emphasis on the interactional perspective in psychoanalytic treatment and in supervision. As Langs states, "Supervisory work is always cast in the framework of an active, ever-present, spiralling conscious and unconscious interaction between patient and therapist . . . the deep unconscious system is always centred on this interplay and its implications and ramifications". One of the major defects in the traditional model of supervision as well as in classical clinical theories about psychotherapy and psychoanalysis is that they are, for the most part, limited to the intrapsychic point of view. In contrast, the author includes both intrapsychic and interactional perspectives. This book emphasizes the necessity for the supervisor to monitor constantly the nature of the interaction between therapist and patient. In the past, many psychoanalytically oriented therapists and analysts have had a collective blind spot for interactional factors in psychoanalytic psychotherapy and psychoanalysis, and it is only in recent years, with the advent of the various object relations theories, self psychology, and the communicative approach, that some clinicians have begun to overcome this blind spot. The importance of interactional factors is also shown in Langs's emphasis on the second unconscious system of the emotion-processing mind as being focused on the individual's immediate interactions. That is to say, the patient's unconscious mind is constantly monitoring, analysing, and representing the nature of the individual's interactions with the analyst or therapist, and derivatives of this unconscious, highly intelligent process are manifested in the patient's communications.

A third and unique contribution Langs makes in this path-breaking book is his scholarly presentation about the supervisory frame, conceptualized as a system of ground rules, conditions, and boundaries necessary for effective supervision to take place. Today there exists an almost complete ignorance on the part of most supervisors about supervision-frame issues. Although many clinicians attempt to follow rules of privacy and confidentiality in psychoanalytic therapy, they seldom adhere to these rules regarding their conduct of supervision. Langs points out the importance of frame management and the supervisor's major responsibility for continually monitoring both the supervisor–supervisee frame and the therapist–patient frame. Because almost all of the training of psychotherapists and psychoanalysts occurs under deviant-frame conditions, it is extremely important that the dynamic importance of the frame be taught to all who do supervision. Securing the frame, as Langs indicates, requires understanding, strong motivation, and effort. Frame-management work is not a consequence of one's natural inclinations and takes much effort and vigilance. The author discusses the fixed frame of supervision, including the set time, set fee, set hours, and a set place, a private office, for ensuring privacy. Langs says, "Given that approaches to supervision universally tend to be even more undisciplined than those towards therapy, we are dealing with aspects of the supervisory experience that are in need of major reconsideration and change".

A secure supervision frame should include strict confidentiality and privacy. Perhaps the most common set of modifications of the supervisory frame has to do with privacy and confidentiality, and such frame deviations often occur in training programs. A particularly egregious example of the violation of the rule of supervisory privacy and confidentiality occurs under the aegis of The American Psychoanalytic Association. At periodic intervals, all of the institutes of the above organization are inspected by a site-visit team for the purposes of accreditation. As a part of this inspection, two site-visit members sit in with the institute supervisors while they supervise their candidates' work with psychoanalytic patients. As this has happened to me first as a candidate and later as a supervisor, I can bear witness to the disruptive effects it has first of all on supervisor–supervisee relations and secondarily often also on supervisee–analysand interactions.

In Langs's view, one of the most abused ground rules of supervision is the one concerning the relative anonymity of the supervisor. Supervisors who would never discuss personal issues, feelings, or experiences with their patients feel somehow free to discuss these extraneous issues and disruptive matters with their supervisees. The supervisory frame should include relative neutrality and anonymity similar to the rules in psychotherapy practice. The supervisor's lax management of the supervisory frame damages not only supervisees, but also indirectly sometimes the supervisee's patients. The need for a stable, well-secured, fixed frame is common to both therapy and supervision, as are the requisites for total privacy and confidentiality.

Now we come to the fourth major contribution made by Langs in his creative contribution to the neglected field of supervision. He provides a set of procedures and principles for supervisors to use, as well as clear guidelines about how supervisors should conduct supervisory sessions. Many, perhaps most, psychiatrists and psychoanalysts wrongly assume that graduation from a psychiatric residency program or from a psychoanalytic institute signifies that the graduate is not only competent to do psychotherapy or psychoanalysis, but also competent to supervise those activities. The truth is that the skills, techniques, methods, and knowledge necessary for doing psychotherapy or psychoanalysis are not the same as those necessary for carrying out effective supervision. The knowledge and skills required for one to conduct competent psychoanalytic psychotherapy and/or psychoanalysis are necessary, but not sufficient, for attaining supervisory proficiency. Currently, there is almost a total lack of training, establishment of standards, and accreditation for clinicians either to learn about supervision or to practise it. Langs has, in part, remedied this disorganized situation by establishing a system of procedures and principles for the conduct of supervision.

The standard model for supervision developed by communicative therapy has to do with trigger decoding. Trigger decoding is done by extracting the relevant theme from the manifest stories of the patient and linking them to their adaptation-evoking triggering events, most often constituted by some action, frame violation, or other intervention by the therapist.

This is the heart of the method supervisors and therapists use to formulate what is going on in the treatment. As Langs says, "The [supervisor] listener must trigger decode the patient's narrative material in the light of the prevailing adaptation-evoking interventions of the patient's therapist (and his or her supervisor) and thereby draw upon the wisdom of the deep unconscious system". The goal of supervision is to teach the techniques of psychotherapy; issues of formulating and intervening should be at the forefront of supervisory work. Langs clearly points out and differentiates the responsibilities of the supervisor as well as supervisee for the conduct of the supervision. Another original contribution is a discussion of supervisory crises, and the author presents some important heuristics and guidelines for how crises can be studied, managed, and remedied.

Finally, Langs's most important contribution to the development of an effective discipline of supervision is probably his informed overview of the basic principles and methods used for validation. A prime test for competency in doing supervision is how well the supervisor teaches the process of validation to supervisees. Though learning a system of validation is one of the most important tools necessary for doing psychoanalytic psychotherapy and supervision, it is almost entirely neglected in most training institutions. There is a widespread misconception that validation stops when the therapist or psychoanalyst intervenes. Most clinicians wrongly assume that they are carrying out some process of validation while they are listening to their patients and constructing their hypothesis and tentative interpretations. They have the false belief that they have silently validated their proposed intervention by weighing the evidence for and against it *before* they have intervened. Few seem to understand the simple truth that validation comes from examining how the patient responds to an interpretation or other intervention. I am not referring here to the patient's conscious agreement or disagreement, since neither is usually helpful for confirming or disconfirming a clinician's interpretation. Validation requires evaluating the patient's unconscious communication. Validation is attained by an examination of the stories, images, primary process derivatives, affects, and so on of the patient *following* the clinician's intervention. To be considered valid, a supervisory intervention must be confirmed through examining the patient's derivatives. A process of validation provides necessary feedback information for the clinician not only to know what is going on in his or her therapy sessions, but to understand the effect he or she is consciously or unconsciously having on his or her patients. Where validation is not carried out, there is a tendency for therapists to use stereotyped approaches and for treatment to become stalemated or corrupted into a process of indoctrination.

The validation system that Langs recommends is practical and pragmatic. Practitioners should follow the maxim, "By their fruits shall ye know them" — a heuristic slogan I use with supervisees to underscore our interest in understanding the effects of our interventions. No interpretation — no matter how brilliant, empathic, timely, tactful, or whatever — is any good unless it does something constructive for the patient. We cannot know whether any intervention has a healing or constructive effect until *after* the intervention is carried out. Then the therapist or supervisor can perform the process of validation by checking the patient's primary process derivatives as information needed for validating either the supervisor's formulations or the therapist's interventions with the patient.

My over 30 years of experience in teaching and supervising psychoanalytic psychotherapy supports Langs when he states: "Perhaps the most common form of present-day misalliance between supervisor and supervisee involves the offer of unprincipled suggestions by the former and their uncritical acceptance by the latter — all of it without a search for unconscious validation in the material on hand from the supervised patient".

Though much work and investigation remains to be done to develop and maintain a contemporary discipline of supervision of psychoanalytic psychotherapy, Langs has provided some excellent foundations for such an enterprise.

DOING SUPERVISION AND BEING SUPERVISED

Introduction

There is at present a lively interest in the supervisory process and its explication. Courses in the principles of supervision abound, and the critical role of supervision in the development of a psychotherapist is widely acknowledged. It is for these reasons that we need a comprehensive and critical book on the subject, one that would, of necessity, be addressed to both supervisors and supervisees. Such a volume would present the essentials of supervision, pay close attention to the conditions and ground rules within which it is conducted, establish validated principles of teaching and learning, define a series of optimal supervisory precepts, consider some of the basic issues in this often difficult arena, explore the supervisee's responsibilities and entitlements as well as those of the supervisor, and carefully re-examine the standard models of supervision with an eye towards the evolution of supervisory practices into new and more effective paradigms. Such are the immodest aspirations of the present book.

Given the vagaries of psychotherapy itself, the supervisory process has, in general, been treated in a rather casual and at times cavalier fashion, rather than in terms of confirmed pre-

1

cepts. It is well established that the work of a psychotherapy supervisor must be intuitive, inventive, and highly sensitive to the needs of both the supervisee and the supervised patient or client whose sessions are under review. But supervisory work also should be principled and properly framed, and sufficiently consistent and well defined to assure the supervisee the best possible supervisory experience and the supervisor a situation with as little possibility of crisis and untoward reactions, and as much reward as possible.

Communicative studies have shown that both conscious and unconscious communication and processing are continuous activities of the adaptive mind. It is therefore essential to recognize that there are two levels of experience — two distinct dialogues — that transpire between the two parties to individual supervision (I will leave group supervision for the main text).

The first level of exchange is *directly stated and conscious*; it is organized around the two most basic *cognitive goals* of supervision: first and foremost, the education of the supervisee in regard to the valid techniques of psychotherapy and their theoretical underpinnings; and second, the development of the best possible therapy for the supervised patient. These intentions are realized, by and large, through manifest supervisory comments made in response to the presentation by the supervisee of process-note case material. While undoubtedly there is a strong unconscious influence on these teaching and learning activities, these deeper factors are seldom, if ever, addressed in what I call the *standard models of supervision* (see chapter three).

While this surface interchange is unfolding, there is, however, a second level of communication and experience that also is taking place. This level of interaction is *expressed indirectly and is deeply unconscious*, and it unfolds outside the awareness of the two members of the supervisory dyad. In this realm, there is a series of highly sensitive, unconscious communicative exchanges between supervisor and supervisee that largely centre around the *framework or structure of the supervisory situation*, and secondarily, around the unconscious implied and encoded messages that each imparts to the other. Remarkably, the encoded aspects of these unconscious communications are disguised within many of the surface exchanges that occur between the supervisory partners.

The unconscious messages of a supervisor and supervisee are conveyed through a variety of communicative vehicles. They are crudely carried in their body language and in certain behaviours, in the implications of their respective manifest comments, as well as in a supervisee's choice of case material for presentation (Korn & Carmignani, 1987) and a supervisor's responsive comments and silences. But the most common and compelling means of unconscious expression is, however, encoded within *the coincidental narratives and stories* — personal, professional, and otherwise — told quite spontaneously by either party to supervision. These anecdotes, which depart from the central teaching and learning tasks of the supervision as it is focused on the process-note case material, are, as we will see, heavily laden with unconscious meaning.

This second and immediate realm of experience, *which pertains to the supervisory interaction itself,* has, of course, both conscious and unconscious components, although the unconscious aspects are far more powerful than their conscious counterparts. Dealing with this critical aspect of the supervisory interaction — and it has a strong impact with many experiential and behavioural consequences for the work and lives of both parties — is one of the most important and generally unrecognized problems confronting today's supervisors and supervisees, whether they are psychodynamically oriented or not. Indeed, as we pursue our investigation of the supervisory process, we will come upon a series of fresh considerations of the evolved, adaptive design and architecture of the emotion-processing mind that will compel us to focus on and clarify the deeper nature of the supervisory experience — and bring us to some unprecedented insights and recommendations as well.

In essence then, the principles of supervision that will be developed in this book will fully take into account not only the conscious experience and needs of both supervisor and supervisee, but also will be strongly guided by their all-important unconscious experience and needs as well — many of them in conflict with conscious inclinations. Ultimately, however, the *unconscious realm* will be afforded the greater say in regard to shaping and confirming the techniques and rules of supervision, and their underlying theoretical substructure. In this way, we will be acknowledging and dealing with motives and forces in the emotional domain that have by far the greatest power over the results of how we do psychotherapy—and conduct its supervision.

At first glance, it may seem that there is little that is new to be said about principles of supervision. However, this impression proves to be the consequence of conscious-system naiveté and defensiveness, and of the natural inclinations of the conscious mind to minimize or ignore the many nuances of emotionally charged experiences—it is a system that is, as we will see, relatively insensitive to the richness of human emotional transactions. The conscious mind tends defensively to pursue lax supervisory situations where it can gratify inappropriate needs, sustain its powerful and costly psychic defences, and justify maladaptive departures from much-needed secured settings and frames.

Folklore has it that the psychoanalyst works with "purity" in the formal psychoanalytic situation and is more "flexible" and loose—more non-interpretive and frame-deviant—in doing psychotherapy. Supervision is the last rung on this misguided ladder—a situation in which all too often any semblance of principles and decorum is lost. Indeed, in the extreme, reports of seductions of supervisees by their supervisors are far more common than those of patients by their therapists. And even when the infractions are less blatant, the negative impact of this lack of precepts and discipline on both the supervisee and the supervisor is, of course, quite extensive—even as it is, as a rule, consciously denied or ignored.

Psychotherapy supervision requires a sound framework and structure; it cannot be left to vague principles or chance. Conscious thinking is a treacherous basis for developing principles of supervisory practice, and thus the supervisory couple must utilize *encoded or unconscious confirmation* to establish the validity of all supervisory interventions and the theory on which they are based. We are forewarned, then, that we will need a method of indirect or encoded validation in addressing the structure of the supervisory situation and in teaching a supervisee how to conduct effective forms of psychotherapy. There is no place in supervision for teaching by fiat or authority, or for operating naively in the conscious domain, when the single most basic tenet of dynamic psychotherapy gives honour and power to *unconscious* processes and forces.

These considerations imply that there are, indeed, correct and incorrect, valid and invalid, interventions in both therapy and its supervision. This principle, which is impossible to affirm consciously but is abundantly in evidence unconsciously, places major demands on both supervisors and supervisees. Nevertheless, it speaks to the true nature of the supervisory process and facilitates the development of techniques designed to ensure the best possible experience for a supervisee and an optimal outcome for the supervised psychotherapy. The essential arbitrator of the validity of an intervention, be it from a supervisee or a supervisor, lies with the deep unconscious system of the emotion-processing mind — and with the encoded evaluative messages emitted by that system's profound and remarkable intelligence.

The ultimate supervisor in supervision is the therapy patient, who can be relied on to carry out, albeit *entirely without awareness*, a variety of effective teaching and healing activities through encoded narratives and directives — the patient's unconscious mind is the ideal supervisor for a psychotherapist and his or her supervisor (Searles, 1975; Langs, 1975, 1978, 1979). The supervisory situation must first be secured as a safe and reliable, consistent space for the revelations of the supervisee and his or her patient, and then imbued with a spirit that sees unconscious validation as its essential guiding feature.

Another relatively neglected aspect of supervision materializes with the realization that the supervisor and supervisee comprise an *S/S system* in which the supervised patient — who is a member of the patient/therapist (P/T) system in his or her therapy with the supervisee — is a non-present third party who helps to create an unusual tripartite system, the *S/S/P system*. These considerations introduce a variety of systemic, interactional, bipersonal, adaptive, and communicative factors that deserve full attention in the practice and theory of supervision.

The importance of systemic thinking can be especially appreciated at moments of supervisory crisis when the P/T, S/S, or S/S/P systems are overloaded with disruptive information and meaning that neither the supervisor nor the supervisee — nor the supervised patient — is able to cope with or metabolize. Finding the means to resolve these emergency situations often depends on adopting a systemic approach, because this way of conceptualizing the issues requires that each member of the system be held accountable for the crisis — whatever the proportions of responsibility might be (and supervisors must accept their full share). Quite naturally, there are both individual and systemic dynamic factors in supervision — each must be addressed and accounted for at all times.

Given that psychotherapy supervision is the backbone of a trainee's development, we need to forge a sound in-depth picture and conception of the supervisory process — its vicissitudes, issues, best methods, and the like. And we must address the sometimes conflicting needs and viewpoints of all three parties to the supervisory situation — the supervised patient, the supervisee, and the supervisor. The present volume attempts to offer this kind of balanced and thoughtful perspective. It does so with full cognizance of the needs of both supervisees and supervisors. And it proceeds with a deep dedication to both teachers and their students in the hope of advancing their professional and personal understanding, growth, and competency — and their ability to offer better forms of psychotherapy to their patients.

CHAPTER ONE

Issues in supervising psychotherapy

An idealized picture of psychotherapy and its supervision will teach us little; a realistic and perhaps troublesome picture, as Freud argued, will teach us a great deal. Psychotherapy is an uncertain and emotionally charged field where mistakes, large and small, are inevitable and commonplace — though often unrecognized. It therefore is reassuring to know that one inevitable way of learning and growing as a psychotherapist, supervisor, or supervisee is through a deep understanding and rectification of the errors of our ways.

A TALE OF SUPERVISION

I will begin our journey into the world of supervision with an embellished true story, based in part on a published report. Let us ask, as we follow it along, what is constructive and what seems bothersome about this picture of supervision? What are the signs of trouble and where did they come from? What can we learn from this at times grim tale?

The supervisee was a young man who was a trainee at a psychotherapy institute, who was being supervised by his boss, also a man, for whom he does research. There is no established time for the supervision because the supervisor's schedule is full; they meet on a catch-as-catch-can basis. Most often they talk in the dining room of the institution where they work, less often in either person's office. Whenever a batch of process notes, written during the sessions with the patient, have been transcribed by his secretary, the supervisee sends them via inter-office mail to the supervisor.

The supervisor reads the material in advance of meeting with the supervisee, and when they get together he offers his general impressions of the supervisee's work and a discussion will ensue. At times when notes are unavailable, the supervisee will simply present some issue or problem with which he needs help — little or no specific case material is used. Supervisory discussions are typically intermixed with talk about work, social relationship, gossip about other members of the department, and whatever else one or the other person happens to bring up. Finally, although the supervisee is unaware of this, the supervisor is presenting the work of this supervision to the institute's study group on supervisory practices.

Truth is stranger than fiction — especially in psychoanalysis and psychotherapy.* Without making a formal analysis of this supervisory situation, we may attempt to empathize with both the supervisor and the supervisee. The former is likely to have conscious feelings of guilt for secretly appropriating the supervisee's material for presentation to other therapists —

---

*This book is about the supervision of dynamic forms of psychotherapy. It is, however, illuminated by psychoanalytic understanding. Therefore, no effort will be made to distinguish psychotherapy from psychoanalysis proper because the principles developed in the book apply to the supervision of all modes of treatment, including formal psychoanalyses.

and the guilt will affect not only the supervision, but his own work as a therapist and even his daily life outside his profession. Furthermore, his awareness that his efforts are under scrutiny is certain to influence and bias his supervisory interventions.

The supervisor also is likely to be concerned about his mixed relationship with the supervisee; its three components — work, social, and supervision — are bound to be sources of confusion and conflict. The supervision will be affected by the two other realms of contact, and, in making his supervisory interventions, the supervisor undoubtedly will modulate his comments depending on what has happened between himself and the supervisee elsewhere — sometimes making his remarks more critical than otherwise, sometimes less so. In all, the supervisor undoubtedly will lose some of his necessary concerned detachment and neutrality because of these contaminating factors.

The irregularity of the supervision might well give the supervisor pause for concern should anything go awry with the supervised case. As the recipient of notes in advance of the supervisory discussions, he might well over-intellectualize the supervision because the preview will deprive the supervisory process of its spontaneity and excitement, and of the constructive uncertainty that accrues when a supervisee presents fresh process note material in the sequence in which the session had unfolded. Doing supervision in the dining room also could spoil this supervisor's appetite and create many guilt-promoting distractions.

Without further speculation, it seems probable that this is a treacherous and by no means entirely gratifying situation for the supervisor. We can suspect, too, that many of the effects of the erratic and poorly defined structure of the supervisory situation will go unnoticed and exert their influence outside his awareness — a setting ripe for neurosogenesis. A framework of this kind, filled with contradictory inputs and sources of anxiety and guilt, is quite poor in its holding qualities and could well drive the supervisor crazy (Searles, 1959).

* * *

What then of the supervisee — the much-neglected partner to these arrangements? It is easy to imagine his anxiety in presenting his work to his boss and the many dreaded consequences he would conjure up should his work be judged inadequate or, worse still, as harmful to the patient. And what if the supervised patient did poorly or experienced a symptomatic exacerbation or severe regression, for example? The sense of vulnerability, so common among supervisees, is likely to be compounded to levels that might well be beyond endurance and containment. The basic worry over being viewed as a competent psychotherapist is also exaggerated under these circumstances. And what if the supervisor developed grave doubts about the supervisee's ability to be a psychotherapist — what then?

Think too how this supervisee must have felt not knowing when he would have his next supervisory session and yet knowing that, in all probability, it would take place in the dining room where others could hear what was being said and recognize what was going on. The authoritarian position of the supervisor, reinforced by the fact that he also is the supervisee's boss at work, is certain to make questioning and doubting his supervisory interventions a very difficult position to adopt — and unusually risky as well.

These difficulties are compounded by the absence of a clear and fair, *unconscious* means of validating the supervisor's efforts. In particular, making supervisory pronouncements from notes read in advance of the supervisory session precludes *prediction* and the use of *encoded validation* in the material from the patient that follows a supervisory proposal regarding technique and the like. We must raise serious questions as to how effective teaching and learning can be under these strikingly arbitrary and frame-deviant conditions.

And what about the secret reporting being done by the supervisor? While the supervisee is not likely to be consciously aware of this situation (unless he inadvertently finds out — imagine that), it is highly likely that he will unconsciously perceive the presence of these intruders — psychotherapy patients always do so. This unconscious experience will have extensive ramifications for his professional work and personal life without his knowing or being able to do anything about their source. Were the supervisee to become dramatically paranoid in his work or social life, he would be seen as regressing and as ill, and the unconscious and interactional sources of the syndrome would go unrecognized.

What can we learn from simply empathizing with the two parties to this supervisory situation? Given that this vignette involves a supervision that received official sanction, it seems fair to say that, by and large, there are no perceptible ground rules, frames, boundaries, or precepts that are in common use among today's psychotherapy supervisors. A review of your own experiences as a supervisee, and, where applicable, the work you have done as a supervisor, will reveal many departures from common sensibility, the absence of clearly defined frames, and little in the way of validated principles of supervisory practice.

It is disconcerting to acknowledge the arbitrariness of the conditions and means by which the vital experience of psychotherapy supervision is presently conducted. We can only, for the moment, try to imagine the career-long adverse effects that these uncertainties and their traumatic qualities have on today's supervisees — and their supervisors as well. There is a conscious-system tendency among psychotherapists to avoid the direct realization of the price they are paying in emotional dysfunction and self-harm, and in harm to their patients, for these ill-defined approaches to supervisory work.

There are so many complex factors in emotional life, and in the sources of emotional difficulties, that we are seldom aware of the critical triggers or roots of emotional regressions and grief — whether in supervisees or their patients, or in their supervisors. Nevertheless, unconscious influence is an ever-present and exceedingly powerful part of professional life in the emotional domain. The effects of unconscious experience in situations like psychotherapy supervision are quite real, whether they are recognized as such or not — and especially when they are not.

Returning to our vignette, through empathy we can sense too that the lack of a stable structure for the supervision must have been disquieting for all concerned. The anxieties and pressures of learning how to do dynamic psychotherapy are enormous. The situation challenges our cherished, much-needed, and evolved psychic defences which we are obliged to modify or surrender in the service of helping patients become aware of and benefit from accessing deeply unconscious experiences — the ultimate source of emotional dysfunctions. As if this were not daunting enough, many of the repressed, encoded images in a supervised patient's material are extremely unflattering to the student — and often to his or her supervisor as well; nevertheless, they need to be trigger-decoded and consciously realized by all concerned. Adding superfluous and unneeded sources of anxiety and disequilibrium to these basic apprehensions can only be harmful on all sides.

In a global but affecting way, this opening vignette hopefully has motivated us to re-examine the supervisory situation and the practice and process of supervision. The story raises many questions about supervision that are as yet without satisfactory answers. It seems reasonable to believe that it is possible to fashion more stable, secure, and constructive settings and ways of doing supervision and being supervised than we have seen here. Let us begin that pursuit forthwith.

SOME BASIC SUPERVISORY ISSUES

We will, of course, examine more specific and detailed vignettes as we proceed. Still, this broad introduction can serve to alert us to the kinds of supervisory issues that we will need to address in the course of this book. Here then are the main questions we will try to answer:

1. How is supervision to be established and structured? Does it require a clear framework or can it be loosely defined? If a frame is needed, what are its proper and validated attributes? Indeed, if a frame is important, what role do the ground rules and boundaries of the supervisory situation play in the experience, enlightenment, and growth of a student — and of a supervisor?

2. How is supervision to be conducted? Is there a basic paradigm? When, if ever, should that paradigm be abandoned? Are written process notes needed for supervision, and, if

they are, should they be written during or (soon) after a given therapy session? And should they ever be offered to the supervisor in advance of a supervisory hour, or should they simply be reported in sequence during the meetings between the supervisee and his or her supervisor? And finally, is there any place in supervision for recorded sessions — or are they essentially harmful and counterproductive?

3. What are the basic goals and fundamental precepts of sound supervision? What are the respective role requirements of both supervisors and supervisees? And what are the essential responsibilities, entitlements, and satisfactions of each?

4. While all parties to supervision must be respected and treated with utmost sensitivity and grace, to whom does the supervisor have the primary commitment — the supervised patient or the supervisee? What should be done when the needs of these two individuals are in conflict?

5. What should a supervisee expect from his or her supervisor? How can the supervisee assess the supervision that he or she is receiving? And what should a supervisee do when he or she is dissatisfied with the work of a particular supervisor? When is it appropriate to change supervisors or to terminate supervision when it is going badly?

6. What are the main issues that can arise between supervisors and supervisees, and what are the types of supervisory crises that also may occur? How are these conflicts and problem situations best resolved?

7. What are the potentials of supervision and what are its limitations?

8. How long should supervision last, and when and how should it be appropriately terminated? And after termination, what is the position with respect to future contacts between a supervisor and supervisee? How should the search for further supervision for the terminated supervisee be handled, and what about the task of engaging in self-supervision?

9. How does supervision interdigitate with the psychotherapy

of the supervisee? Must the two situations be in different hands, or is there some means and advantage to their being done together?

As you can see, there are many pertinent unresolved issues related to the structure and nature of the supervisory process. The wide scope of these questions, and the uncertain response that many of them evoke in most readers, tells us that supervision is a territory that is, as yet, poorly explored and only vaguely mapped. The overall goal of this book is to give supervision the clear definition it deserves, while allowing as much room as possible for the individuality and inventiveness of both supervisors and supervisees.

The firmer the principles of supervision, the greater the opportunity for effective teaching and learning. Teaching activities do not go well when they are conducted within unstable conditions or with inconsistent techniques. Ill-defined efforts of that kind tend to generate schisms and contradictions between conscious and unconscious experience that disrupt the learning and growth of the supervisee.

The goal, then, is to identify ways that supervision can be conducted within a constructive, stable holding environment, with consistent yet sensitive and individually applied techniques, and in a manner that is consonant with both conscious and unconscious needs and experience. To do this, we need a validated methodology and a set of confirmed teaching principles. While these can be developed from observations within supervision itself, it is helpful to begin by exploring what clinical experience in the psychotherapy domain can offer as a guide and background to these efforts. This, then, is the subject of the next chapter.

CHAPTER TWO

A clinical foundation
for supervisory practices

To fulfil the promises of this book, we must establish a sound theoretical and clinical basis for the definition of effective and validated supervisory interventions and the underlying principles that support their use. To do this, we must redefine the parameters of supervision in light of recent insights into the nature of conscious and especially unconscious communication and processes, and make use of our newly acquired understanding of the evolved architecture and adaptive resources of the emotion-processing mind (Langs, 1986, 1987a, 1987b, 1988, 1989, 1992a, 1992c, 1992e, 1993a, 1993b, in press b, in press c). Let us turn to these tasks at once.

SOME BACKGROUND ISSUES

As Goodheart (1992, 1993) has cogently argued, psychoanalysis is a folk psychology that operates via global observations and draws general conclusions in the form of broad, high-level

15

theoretical constructs that lead to rather uncertain technical precepts for the conduct of a psychotherapy — and its supervision. We are not surprised, then, that writings on principles of supervision are scarce and that there is no consensus as to how supervision should be carried out — and no validated precepts of supervisory practice. Teach as you were taught and were analysed is the credo — a simple, down-to-earth approach that lacks guiding discipline or structure.

But there is yet another problem that besets today's supervisory practices. There is considerable evidence that psychoanalysts have retreated from a strong and clear position on the definition of its most basic proposition — the existence of a powerful *unconscious* domain with respect to communication, perception, fantasizing and remembering, and processing and adapting to incoming information and meaning. Characteristically, existing ideas are global and nondescript, so that anything that lies beyond someone's awareness at the moment is defined as unconscious. These elements may be processes, unnoticed patterns of behaviour, trends and actions, needs and motives, and the like. There is, however, virtually no conception of an organized *unconscious system* of the mind, one that embodies strong processing capacities and a deep intelligence. Nor is there a systematic approach to *unconscious communication* and to the means of defining and accessing *unconscious meaning*.

With regard to *adaptation*, the conception of this aspect of mental functioning is similarly vague. It is recognized that human beings strive to cope with emotional impingements and conflicts, but the means by which this is done and the specifics of our adaptive capacities are only vaguely stated — *the weak adaptive position* (Langs, 1992e, 1993a, 1993b). In the main, adaptation is defined in terms of *conscious* responses to broadly defined, *known stimuli*. The concept of *unconscious adaptation* to specific and repressed triggers — *the strong adaptive position* — is not in evidence.

Another problem lies with the continuing intrapsychic focus in psychoanalytic thinking, which downplays the role of external reality as it interacts with and arouses inner coping responses. As a consequence, the immediate interaction between the patient and therapist is relatively neglected. And even now, as this interaction draws more attention, it is usually misrepresented as being a reflection of the imagination of the patient or a situation in which the patient appropriates the therapist to express his or her inner needs, plans, tests, or fantasies. Missing still is a clear view of the therapeutic interaction as a situation in which a patient's adaptive responses, conscious and unconscious, say as much about the stimulus from the therapist as they do about the response from the patient.

These more global and often unreal views of the therapeutic interplay have led to a relative neglect of the therapist's real impingements on the patient and of the intricacies of these very human emotional interchanges. Missed too are the nuances of their *unconscious* communications and experience — a domain of great import in emotional life and in psychotherapy. Connected with this failure to appreciate the nature and functions of unconscious or *encoded* communication is a blind spot regarding the overwhelming importance in both therapy and its supervision of a therapist's or supervisor's establishment and maintenance of the ground rules and frames of each situation.

The prevailing conceptions of supervision — *the standard or classical model of supervision*, as I will call it (see chapter three) — typically takes these errant attitudes to an extreme. The focus almost exclusively is on the presented work of the supervisee, and, unless a supervisory crisis materializes, little attention is paid to the interaction between supervisor and supervisee; its unconscious aspects and frame are especially neglected. Nevertheless, as noted, the conscious and unconscious systems of the mind are at all times affected by the *immediate situation* in which the two parties to supervision find themselves. Given the emotionally evocative nature of psychotherapy, its supervision undoubtedly evokes powerful unconscious responses in both parties — and in the supervisee in particular. How, then, can we justify the relative neglect of this issue?

The first rejoinder to these arguments and the questions that they raise may well be the claim that the unconscious interaction between a supervisee and a supervisor is not especially important in the scheme of things. The main issue in supervision is the education of the supervisee — the unconscious aspects of the supervisory interaction belong in the supervisee's own therapy (and, separately, in the supervisor's treatment, if he or she is so occupied), or to their respective efforts at "self-analysis". Communicatively, this process has been revised and is called *self-processing* (see chapter fourteen).

Efforts of this kind, however, are usually reserved for the exploration of identified countertransference problems in a supervisee as reflected in his or her work with the supervised patient and for the much more rarely recognized errors and countertransferences of the supervisor. The ongoing unconscious aspects of a supervisory experience are not the subject of a personal therapy unless a clear emotionally charged issue happens to come up. The exquisite details of the continuous conscious and especially the unconscious exchanges between supervisor and supervisee, and the effects of the supervisor's management of the ground rules of supervision and the supervisee's own frame impingements, are all but ignored. Nevertheless, these aspects of supervision actually have deeply powerful effects on both parties to a supervisory encounter.

A second rejoinder to the question, "How can we justify the neglect of the unconscious interaction between supervisor and supervisee?", argues simply that it is impossible to access the unconscious experience of either party to supervision because neither of them free associates or communicates the kind of material through which such an exploration could be accomplished. Even if attempts were made in that direction, there is insufficient time in a supervisory session to work with both the supervisee's unconscious experience of the supervisor's efforts and the material from the supervised patient.

Are we left then with a seemingly irresolvable dilemma — the existence of powerful unconscious forces in the supervisory interaction in a setting where we lack the means to access their nature and to see to it that they enhance rather than disturb the supervisory process and experience? To provide a satisfactory response to this question, I examine in this chapter the nature of emotionally charged interactions, whether related to therapy or to supervision. Then, in chapters thirteen and fourteen, I return to this problem and discuss it more fully — and offer a solution to the conundrum it poses.

LANGUAGE AND THE DESIGN OF THE MIND

We need first to glimpse the architecture of *the emotion-processing mind*— the adaptive organ that evolution has fashioned to enable hominids to process and deal with emotionally charged impingements. While these insights into the design of the mind evolved from a listening process soon to be described (see below and Langs, 1988, 1992a, 1992b [1978], 1993a; see also Dorpat & Miller, 1992), it seems advisable to lay out the blueprint of the human psyche first. To do so, I turn first to the psychotherapy situation and reserve for later discussion the applicability of these concepts to the supervisory situation.

The communicative approach to psychoanalysis and psychoanalytic psychotherapy has long argued for the importance of *unconscious* communication and adaptation in human emotional life and in psychotherapy. It has stressed the need to base psychoanalytic theory and its technical precepts on a grounding derived from *moment-to-moment clinical observations and the use of encoded or unconscious confirmation* from patients as a guiding test of the validity of a therapist's interventions (Langs, 1992a, 1993a).

Once this methodology is adopted, we discover that a patient's *conscious* assessments of, and responses to, a therapist's interventions are exceedingly defensive and self-defeating, and that they are quite unreliable and misleading as a guide to sound and uncompromisingly helpful psychotherapy. In contrast, *unconscious* appraisals prove to be non-defensive, accurate, incisive, highly adaptive, and in general, quite sound. We need therefore to examine both the conscious and unconscious aspects of the therapeutic interaction in order to get our bearings.

The communicative approach has discovered that human language, the most critical emergent capacity of *homo sapiens sapiens*, is capable of conveying two distinctive types of messages. The first is a *single message form* that by and large is restricted to manifest contents, to surface meanings and their implications — evident and concealed, conscious and unconscious. These messages can be identified by their highly intellectual, non-narrative, and abstract qualities, as seen in communications that involve analyses, speculations, assessments, commentaries, and interpretations.

The second use of language involves a *double message* form that embodies both manifest meanings, with their implications, and *displaced and disguised (encoded) meanings* as well. These messages typically are configured as dreams and stories of any kind — essentially, they are *narrative expressions.*

In general, manifest meanings and their implications are dealt with through one system of the mind — *the conscious system,* which has a *superficial unconscious subsystem* for the processing of the *repressed but rather evident implications* of surface messages. In contrast, *encoded meanings and the more intensely repressed implications* of surface messages are perceived *subliminally* and processed by a different system of the emotion-processing mind — *the deep or second unconscious system.* This system has, in turn, two subsystems — a *wisdom subsystem* and a *fear/guilt subsystem.* In general, manifest meanings and their evident implications fall into the conscious realm, while the encoded meanings and deeply repressed implications contained in the same (narrative) messages fall into the deep unconscious realm.

Human language, however, does not exist as an isolated, autonomous entity. Language is, as are all primary biological functions, a means of *adaptation* — a way of coping primarily with environmental stimuli or triggers, human and non-human. To comprehend the remarkable meanings embodied in human language, then, the *adaptation-evoking stimulus* for the *communicated response* must be apprehended. Just as we cannot fathom how a liver actually *functions* without knowing the chemical stimuli to which it is reacting, we cannot know how language *functions* without knowing the meaning stimuli to which it is a response.

THE TWO SYSTEMS
OF THE EMOTION-PROCESSING MIND

Attempts to study human expressiveness, however, quickly come upon several complications. In our great complexity as humans, we have evolved a set of remarkable emergent mental and language capacities, but we also are called upon to adapt to emotional impingements that are far more complicated and weighty than those dealt with by any other species. Indeed, the incoming load — and especially the part that is emotionally charged — is more than can be handled by one system of the mind.

The emotion-processing mind therefore has evolved into a *parallel-processing, two-system entity* — each with its own sensitivities, *modus operandi*, and constraints (Langs, 1992e, 1993a, in press b, in press c). By evolved design, then, the conscious system and its perceptive apparati are selectively responsive to particular types or sets of adaptation-evoking stimuli and relatively insensitive to other kinds of impingements. In general, the triggers to which the system is most responsive are survival-related and consciously known — and their implications are quite evident.

On the other hand, the second unconscious system, which operates on the basis of *incoming subliminal or unconscious perceptions*, is keyed in on a very different group of stimuli. These are, by and large, attributes of people, actions, and the world about us that are screened out and relatively unimportant to the conscious mind. They centre on matters of *ground-rule and frame issues*, and secondarily on issues of the *level of meaning* that is being expressed and/or addressed and on the *helpfulness or failings of caretakers* — including psychotherapists and supervisors.

In a given situation, then, the conscious system will be focused on a particular set of triggers and a given constellation of meanings. All the while, the second unconscious system will be concentrated on either a different set of stimuli or on the meanings of those triggers that do register in awareness that are very different from those that have been cathected consciously. The conscious system is, by and large, activated by life-threatening and other physically dangerous triggers, gross needs for safety, self-protection, and defence, and by the task of living on — individually and as a species. It is designed to enhance the quests for food, shelter, safety, companionship, procreation, and the like — and the system is sensitive to stimuli related to fulfilling these needs. In contrast, the second unconscious system is activated by emotionally charged triggers that involve *the contexts or frames of these otherwise conscious experiences* and by traumas that cause noticeable psychological danger and damage — including the more disturbing emotional components of realistic perils.

In all, then, an emotionally charged incident or message will have two distinctive levels of meaning. This *dual input* configuration is received by a mental apparatus with a *dual processing system*— and a *dual output system* as well (manifest and encoded). Indeed, each system of the mind has its own perceptual apparati, locus of concentration, defences, need-subsystems, self-observing capacities, allowable inputs, intelligence and coping mechanisms, preferred modes of adaptation, and form of reportage or expression. In a general sense, it could be said that each system has its own ego, superego, and id (Langs, 1992c). We experience the world on two planes, in two very distinctive ways that often radically diverge from each other and are in conflict.

A PROPOSED EVOLUTIONARY SCENARIO

Over millennia, the emotionally charged inputs that hominid minds were compelled to cope with increased enormously in complexity and power. Humans have by far the greatest amount of emotional information and meaning to deal with among the animal species — for example, extended bonding, child-rearing, communal living, an intricate social structure, cultural pressures, ageing, awareness of personal death and the implications of illness and injury, and so forth. As a result, the conscious system evidently became overtaxed by these emotionally charged concerns — dealing with both survival and emotional life was more than that evolved mental system could manage (Langs, in press b).

The problem of maintaining well-functioning conscious adaptive resources escalated over time, mainly because social, cultural, and technical advances evolved at a pace that is far faster than the evolution of the human organs designed to cope with these changes. In response, it appears that, at first, nature selected for human minds that expanded their superficial unconscious subsystems so that relatively evident but anxiety-provoking inputs could be processed outside of awareness — thereby sparing the conscious system some of the enormous pressures on its coping mechanisms. The output results of this kind of processing are encoded messages that are simple in structure and easily trigger-decoded — for example, an allusion to an angry teacher that encodes a reference to an angry therapist. Conscious awareness is spared the experience of the teacher's hostility, and the stability and energy of the system are safeguarded. All the while, the incoming impression has been subjected to superficial unconscious registration and processed by that subsystem which then generated a simplistically disguised image that is easily deciphered for its camouflaged meaning.

However, this development apparently was insufficient to safeguard conscious functioning because emotionally charged inputs so easily disturbed and impaired its coping mechanisms. The conscious system therefore was afforded by natural selection a series of additional protective mechanisms for dealing with its continuing overload of emotional impingements — defences like denial, avoidance, and repression; perceptual and other forms of distortion and obliteration; vague and global ways of experiencing the world; pseudo-stupidity and the like. While these measures safeguarded the equilibrium and adaptive capacities of the conscious system, they did so at considerable cost. The system became prone to error, misperception, overly biased responses, and unresolvable uncertainties. These failings, especially as they related to emotionally charged stimuli, created severe limitations in our capacities for learning and coping in the emotional realm. A vitally necessary attempt to protect conscious and direct adaptational skills led to compromised evolutionary solutions that were very costly to the total organism because of their many maladaptive features.

To deal with the still dangerously overloaded state of the conscious system of the emotion-processing psyche, nature appears to have selected for a second line of protection, an additional form of perception that occurs entirely *without awareness — unconsciously or subliminally.* A primary function of this intake mode appears to be the diversion of especially disturbing emotional impingements and their meanings into a special and deep processing system that is entirely divorced from awareness. This design moved these emotionally traumatic inputs further away from conscious registration and processing, and away from easy access to awareness, and thereby added a new line of natural defences to the existing protection for the conscious system designed to keep it from being overwhelmed and from malfunctioning.

Attached to *unconscious perception* is, as noted, a *second or deep unconscious system of the mind* that develops in each individual via *unconscious experience* from infancy on. This unconscious adaptive system includes an incisive and remarkably intelligent processing subsystem — *the deep unconscious wisdom subsystem* — which is an invaluable guide to human emotional coping. Indeed, in the emotional realm, *conscious learning and adaptation* is impaired by the enormous need of the conscious system for layers of defence. In contrast, *unconscious learning and adaptation* is unencumbered and defences seldom are activated. They are quite unnecessary largely because deep unconscious processes are safeguarded by an important and unexpected feature of the emotion-processing mind, namely, that *the contents and adaptive solutions or insights of the second unconscious system have no direct access to awareness.*

The meanings processed by the second unconscious system involve just about everything that is intolerable to the conscious mind. As a result, the second unconscious system has evolved in a way that precludes awareness of its distinctive world of experience; indeed, the conscious registration of these perceptions and meanings would render the conscious system dysfunctional. But rather than simply shutting off these potentially painful inputs from any kind of registration, these stimuli are received and acknowledged unconsciously and processed without awareness interceding. And then, rather than simply letting the end products of these unconscious efforts disappear into the nether reaches of the mind, the deep system reports its perceptions and processing in *disguised or encoded form.*

With great consistency, the deep unconscious system makes use of two-tiered, narrative messages — storied expressions of all kinds — to convey camouflaged images and themes that embody the system's adaptive responses to incoming emotionally charged stimuli or *triggers*. The conscious mind has no awareness of this level of meaning in its own messages which it fashions according to conscious needs for communication and adaptation. Nevertheless, encoded messages simultaneously reflect two levels of coping — one conscious and the other unconscious — and, as I have pointed out, each is a response to very different impingements or to different meanings of the same stimulus.

Communicatively, the only means by which the conscious mind can gain access to its own deeply unconscious processes is by decoding the thematic material in the narratives it produces in light of the adaptation-evoking triggers to which the encoded images are a response. This process, which is termed *trigger decoding*, is the window into the world of deep unconscious experience.

One other subsystem of *the deep unconscious system* must be identified because it is fateful for emotional life and for the therapy and supervisory situations. This subsystem is called the *fear/guilt subsystem* and it is the embodiment of two terrifying entities: first, our deepest fears of personal annihilation, of death; second, a universal and compelling sense of guilt and need for punishment and suffering that is empowered in all humans by crimes real and fantasied — and infractions borrowed from others such as parents and spouses.

The conscious system is *not* directly affected by the deep unconscious wisdom system, thereby creating a great loss of adaptive resourcefulness. Instead, this sensitive part of the deep system exerts its effects via displacements onto situations other than those to which its primary response has been directed. Thus, the system is activated in one sphere in the immediate moment, but its behavioural outputs fall into a different situation at another time. As a result, the latter reactions are misplaced and inappropriate to the interaction of the moment, and therefore they have distinctly maladaptive qualities. The evolved architecture of the emotion-processing mind is strangely configured indeed.

Many of these misplaced and "neurotic" responses are a consequence of the additional strong unconscious influence of the fear/guilt subsystem on conscious-system functioning. As a result, many conscious behaviours and choices — in therapy, supervision, and elsewhere — are unknowingly motivated and driven by unconscious needs to deny personal death and/or to unwittingly seek self-punishment and self-harm. Trigger decoding the activated images from the second unconscious system is the only presently known means of bringing these processes into awareness so as to allow for insight and correctives. In principle, then, trigger decoding is the essential process through which we can access and appropriate the workings of the deep unconscious system. This procedure therefore should, of necessity, be a vital aspect of teaching and learning in the supervisory situation.

SOME CRUCIAL ATTRIBUTES OF THE HUMAN PSYCHE

Several features of the two basic systems of the emotion-processing mind are important for our investigation of the supervisory process. The first relates to the attitude of each system to *rules, frames, and boundaries*. Under the influence of death anxiety, of the need to suffer, and of basic defensive inclinations, the conscious system is both frame insensitive and inclined towards frame modifications. Violations of rules, frames, and boundaries, which often go unnoticed consciously, abound in conscious-system choices and behaviours. These frame modifications afford the frame-breaker unconscious illusions of omnipotence and immortality — defying a rule ultimately implies defying the basic, existential ground rule that life is framed by death. This action form of denial is, however, quite harmful to all concerned and is effected at considerable but usually denied cost.

The second unconscious system, on the other hand, advocates adaptation via frame-securing efforts — adherence to *unconsciously validated* ground rules and boundaries — and the system deeply appreciates the holding, containing, ego- and self-enhancing, and growth- and health-promoting attributes of secured frames. In both therapy and supervision, the deep unconscious system will derivatively (unconsciously) confirm all frame-securing interventions, whether they come from a supervisor, supervisee, or supervised patient. On the other hand, the system's encoded images consistently invalidate and point to the deeply harmful effects of all frame-deviant interventions and behaviours — for example, holding a supervisory session in a public place, changing a supervisee's fee, and so on (see chapters three to seven).

In addition to the striking split in the emotion-processing mind regarding frame issues, there is another unexpected feature to this sector of the human psyche. As you know, we have a *deviant-frame danger signal in the form of anxiety* — all threats of harm involve some frame infringement. But we lack a comparable *secured-frame anxiety signal* and therefore fail to appreciate the intensity of secured-frame entrapment and annihilatory anxieties, and the unconscious motivational forces that are unleashed at secured-frame moments — despite their distinctly powerful healing qualities. Secured-frame anxiety is the silent plague of the emotional world — an unseen enemy that wreaks havoc with both psychotherapy and its supervision.

Another critical difference between the two systems of the emotion-processing psyche involves a telling attribute of the systems' perceptual capabilities. In addition to the already noted differences in the focal issues for each of these systems, there are basic differences in how each system functions or operates. The conscious system is designed to cope directly with known, immediate survival-related, adaptation-evoking stimuli, but it also can effectively scan and attempt to deal with past, present, and future issues. Through imaginative manifest images, the conscious mind can explore these distinctive temporal domains and arrive at adaptive solutions — in preparation for what lies ahead, in retrospect regarding the past, or as they pertain to current problems.

Consciously, then, an immediate therapeutic interaction can be ignored, set aside, or taken for granted, in favour of explorations of relationships outside the treatment setting. This is, of course, exactly what is done in the standard model of supervision in that precedence is given to the enlightenment of the supervisee based on his or her work elsewhere with the supervised patient. As a result, the focus of the supervisory effort, and its conscious explorations and adaptations, is on transactions outside the supervisory setting — most often, on events in the supervised therapy that usually have occurred prior to the moment at hand (and, at times, that are anticipated in a future session). Except for minor matters of procedure or supervisory crises, the relationship and interaction between supervisor and supervisee falls into the background and is not dealt with consciously or directly. This approach is similar to much present-day psychotherapeutic work where the patient–therapist interaction receives far less attention than the patient's outside relationships and life.

Nevertheless, the attentive focus of the second unconscious system — unconscious perception — has very different attributes from those just described for the conscious system. Firstly, the eyes of second unconscious system are always fixed and centred on the immediate situation — they do not wander away from that focus into the past or future except for events and frame issues that are activated by, and related to, the present stimulus. Secondly, as noted, this here-and-now concentration is primarily fixed on current transactions related to the ground rules and framework of that situation — including recent and intended impingements in this domain.

This second system also pays a great deal of attention to the level of meaning being communicated and addressed at each contemporaneous moment — whether these meanings pertain to manifest contents and their implications alone, or also include encoded meanings. This issue also is one of virtually no concern to the conscious system. *The second unconscious system, then, is always focused on the transactions of the immediate interaction, though there is some secondary extension into related concerns from that centre.*

For example, a psychotherapy patient's deep unconscious system will focus its cathexes on a therapist's recent or anticipated frame-related interventions — for example, a recent or planned change in the time of a therapy hour. Deep reactions to frame-related interventions are often sustained for some weeks before and after such an impingement. However, during the supervision of such a session, the second unconscious system of the treating supervisee will *not* be addressing the frame problem in the supervised psychotherapy. Thus, even as the supervisee and the supervisor are giving their full conscious attention to the material of the presented session, the deep unconscious systems of both remain focused on working over their own immediate impingements on each other within the framework of the supervisory situation.

The differences in the concentrations of the two systems of the emotion-processing mind are especially clear in the supervisory setting. No matter how much conscious discussion is being afforded the supervised case, the second unconscious system is continuously processing the conditions under which the discussion is taking place — and, secondarily, the level of meaning that is being explored and, for the supervisee, the extent to which a supervisor is correct or incorrect (in terms of *unconscious* assessment) in his or her supervisory interventions.

Given the evidence for the enormous power of deep unconscious experience in emotional life and in the work of a psychotherapist, our exploration of the supervisory process must, of necessity, be informed by these new insights into the architecture of the emotion-processing mind. These considerations belie the power of supervision conducted solely in terms of the supervised case and communications restricted to manifest contents and their implications (the standard model). They also raise questions about the *standard communicative model of supervision* which, although it requires the encoded validation of the interventions of both supervisors and supervisees or therapists, nonetheless also is cognitively cast and concentrated on the supervisee's work with his or her patients.

We must, then, begin to think of possible ways that the powerful conscious and, especially, unconscious interaction between supervisor and supervisee can be accessed, trigger-decoded, and mastered so as to yield deep insights into these neglected processes. The supervision of psychotherapy is a two-levelled experience with a conscious focus on the supervisee's presented material and direct teaching on the first level, and, on the second, implicit teaching conveyed by the unconscious communications and behaviours of the supervisor as he or she interacts with the supervisee, and especially as he or she manages the ground rules and frame of that interaction. In essence, both conscious and deeply unconscious teaching and learning occur in supervision, and it is critical to keep track of the transactions within both domains and to see that they are consonant with and reinforce each other — and essentially constructive as well.

With all this said, in order to introduce the clinical concepts of listening and formulating, let us turn now to a case vignette.

The listening process: a clinical excerpt

Dr. Harper,* a male student psychologist, was in supervision at a clinic with Dr. Banks who also was male. The patient he was presenting, Mrs. Johnson, had asked for a change in the time of her next appointment because she was scheduled to see her dentist at that exact time. With little exploration, Dr. Harper had made the requested change. In that session, Mrs. Johnson began by expressing her gratitude to her therapist for accommodating himself to her needs. She had gone to her dentist as planned, but he had messed up her mouth. He really didn't seem to know what he was doing. She had asked him for gas, which he never uses, and he administered it in a way that gave her a lot of trouble; she had nearly choked to death. If he knew it would be harmful to her, he shouldn't have done what she had asked him to do.

To discuss this small excerpt, let us first consider the *manifest contents* of Mrs. Johnson's material. There is a direct indication of appreciation that her *therapist* had changed her hour

---

*With due respect for the privacy and confidentiality of the supervisory situation, the vignettes in this book are fictional narratives that nonetheless are faithful to reality. As is true of all clinical excerpts, they are offered solely as illustrations of the ideas presented in the book. Any reader who adopts the methods of listening and formulating of the communicative approach will quickly discover the incredible world of the second unconscious system that is at the heart of this book.

and a story of a *dentist* who had done a poor job and who, when she requested an anaesthetic, had nearly killed her. The surface message, then, shifts from a positive response to the therapist to a negative reaction to her dentist. There is little sign of neurosis, although one might speculate about the implications of the story about the dentist: does it reflect the patient's jaundiced view of men, her sense of victimization, her fantasies of oral incorporation or penetration — or is it simply a description of an unpleasant encounter? For dynamic psychotherapists, the question also might be raised as to whether the narrative contains a conscious or unconscious transference fantasy or wish — possibly to incorporate the therapist's phallus, a fantasy that is seen as dangerous in some way.

These formulations belong to the realm of *the conscious system and its superficial unconscious subsystem* — they are centred on the manifest message and its possible ramifications for the mental life of the patient. The seemingly unconscious meanings and implications of the surface material are matters of speculation with little certainty. As for the therapeutic interaction, only the surface is touched on — the therapist had changed the patient's hour and Mrs. Johnson is appreciative of his having done so. In terms of *conscious triggers*, the main adaptation-evoking stimuli are the change in hour, which is seen as a helpful move, and the behaviour of the dentist, which is seen as harmful.

Is there, however, a *repressed, unconscious* trigger and encoded message here as well? The answer is, of course, in the affirmative, although the main trigger that has activated the deep unconscious system is identical to one of the triggers that also activated the conscious system — the therapist's change in the time of the patient's session. However, where the conscious system sees the trigger as a kindly favour, the second unconscious system sees it as a dangerous frame alteration (encoded in the image of the dentist using a near-fatal anaesthetic that is not part of his usual armamentarium) which the therapist should not have acceded to (*a corrective or model of rectification* that is encoded in Mrs. Johnson's comment that the dentist should not have given in to her request because it was not his usual practice and was dangerous) and as an entrapment (encoded in her nearly choking to death).

We can specify these unconscious perceptions via *trigger decoding*. This is done by *extracting* the relevant themes from their manifest stories and *linking* them to their adaptation-evoking trigger, constituted by the therapist's frame-modifying intervention. Thus, the extracted theme of a dentist — a kind of doctor — acceding to a request that caused harm to his patient is formulated as a valid unconscious perception of a meaning or implication of the change in the time of a patient's session — a meaning to which the patient is *selectively sensitive*. This type of theme — here, reflected in the allusion to acceding to an unusual request — is termed a *bridging theme* in that it is an image that *connects the manifest contents to their encoded latent contents via a shared or common thread of meaning.*

The incident with the dentist, which is not part of the immediate interaction, is *not* a meaningful trigger for the second unconscious system. It is instead a survival-related event that mobilized conscious-system responses. Communicatively, however, the incident also served admirably as a vehicle for simultaneous unconscious expression — it is a conscious tale that embodies a series of unconscious perceptions of the therapist, the processing of their deep meanings, and the corrective needed to re-secure the frame of the therapy (don't deviate when a patient asks you to do so).

The vignette shows how manifest-content formulations lead to one picture of the emotional world, and of psychotherapy and its supervision, while trigger decoding affords quite a different picture. Trigger decoding is therefore the key to doing both therapy and supervision in terms of the critical realm of deep unconscious experience. The entire shape of supervision and of a supervisor's interventions is different depending on whether the fundamental listening–intervening process is geared to manifest contents/implications alone or includes trigger decoding in its basic armamentarium.

To return to the clinical material:

Dr. Banks offered his opinion that changing the time of the session seemed unnecessary and he questioned his supervisee about his reasons for doing so. Dr. Harper became quite defensive. He said that other therapists at the clinic frequently changed the time of their patients' sessions, and he recounted an incident in which one of the student therapists had had the clinic secretary call all of her Monday patients in order to change the day of their sessions with her to a Tuesday. Having a third party impose that kind of sudden change in hours was, he added, a far more insensitive and cruel thing to do to patients than changing an hour at the request of a patient in a session. In fact, he concluded, the student simply should not have done that to her patients.

There are, as I have indicated, two levels of interaction of relevance to the supervisory situation. The first involves the P/T system formed by the supervisee and his or her supervised patient. Whatever other conditions and ground rules are met or altered in that setting, it is inherently frame modified because of the creation of process notes and the presence of the supervisor, usually as a remote, unseen observer of the therapy (even when, as is proper, the notes are written after the sessions and the patient is not informed of the supervision).

The cognitive teaching of the standard models of supervision is centred on that interaction, and in the communicative model the ground rules and frame of the therapy play an essential role. The latter proves to be necessary because frame impingements activate the deep unconscious system which emits the encoded derivatives that are subjected to trigger decoding to reveal the nature of a patient's unconscious experience. This in turn facilitates the alleviation of his or her emotional dysfunctions, which have their roots in the patient's unconscious perceptions and their inner elaboration. The teaching that Dr. Banks was doing around the change in Mrs. Johnson's session, which was being offered without communicative understanding, was on this cognitive, manifest-content level.

It is accepted wisdom that the transactions within supervision have a variety of effects on the therapeutic situation — the second level of interaction relevant to supervision. Some of these effects are conscious matters of the supervisee's learning from the teachings of his or her supervisor — or reacting against those teachings. But much of this influence occurs without the awareness of the supervisee.

These unconscious effects are of two kinds: first, those that come from the implied meanings of a supervisor's comments of which the supervisee is unaware; second, those that come from any encoded narrative that the supervisor happens to tell and from the supervisor's management of the supervisory frame (an activity that cannot be avoided — even a failure to define any ground rules for a supervision is a frame-relevant intervention). These latter interventions are relatively unrecognized sources of a supervisee's experience in supervision and a strong unconscious influence on what he or she learns from a supervisor. Access to the exact nature of these latter effects can be made only through trigger decoding a *supervisee's* narrative images when they are available in a supervisory session.

This last segment of the supervisory interaction we are considering demonstrates that unconscious communication often does transpire in the supervisory setting and that the unconscious messages so contained are typically of great import. The story told by Dr. Harper about the other students at the clinic is an example of a two-tiered communication. On the *surface*, the adaptation-evoking stimulus was, of course, the supervisor's criticism and questioning of his supervisee because he had changed the time of this patient's session. The supervisee's conscious response was adaptive, defensive, and self-justifying — manifestly and by evident implication. The supervisee was defending his status as a student at the clinic.

But there also is a *repressed or unconscious trigger* that Dr. Harper's second unconscious system was working over, and it lies within the supervisory interaction itself. This level of deep processing is reflected in the *latent encoded* aspects of the story about the other students. The *key bridging* themes in these narratives are that others modify frames all the time and that some, with the help of calls from the clinic secretary, even change their entire schedule without advance notice.

Extracted themes reflect adaptation-evoking triggers. What, then, is the trigger for these encoded images? Communicative principles tell us to look at the immediate interaction between the supervisor and supervisee because the second unconscious system responds to contemporaneous stimuli, and to look to the supervisor's frame-management efforts in particular. Yet, to this point in the supervisory session there had been no direct mention of the supervisor or the supervision. Thus, this postulated trigger is at the moment under conscious-system repression — probably for both the supervisor and the supervisee. What then could it be?

The mystery is solved when we learn that ten days before this supervisory session, Dr. Banks had asked the clinic secretary to call all of his supervisees to change the day on which he held their supervisory sessions. He had made a new commitment that would take him away from the clinic on the Wednesdays he had set aside for his supervisory work there. Dr. Harper had been called and had agreed to see Dr. Banks on a new day. He also knew that several of his peers had changed their supervisory hours with Dr. Banks as well. Indeed, the supervisory session that I am describing was their first meeting at the new time.

Having discovered the *repressed trigger* within the immediate supervisory interaction, we can see that *encoded* into the story of the *student* who had asked the clinic secretary to change her patient's hours was a valid unconscious (displaced and disguised) representation and perception of the *supervisor's* frame alteration. The theme of the secretary changing people's hours is the *bridging theme* that links the manifest and latent, conscious and unconscious, aspects of this story. Dr. Harper also encoded his criticism of his supervisor's change as inconsiderate and cruel — and he added a disguised suggestion for securing the frame in the comment that the student should not have done what she did.

We can see, then, that unless a supervisor or supervisee happens to introduce an encoded narrative, and unless one of them searches for and finds a pertinent (frame-related) adaptation-evoking trigger within the supervisory interaction, the unconscious experience of the supervisee (and supervisor) will go entirely unrecognized and untouched. The importance of this gap is seen when we realize that at the very moment that Dr. Banks is admonishing his supervisee for breaking the frame of the supervised psychotherapy, he himself has broken the frame of the supervision. His manifest-content/conscious-system message is the exact opposite of his unconscious behavioural message — a communicative split that can only confuse Dr. Harper and compromise his opportunity to learn the sound techniques of psychotherapy—including how to manage a therapeutic frame. It is only by knowing when and how to trigger-decode that it becomes possible to reveal and work through the second level of unconscious experience. Yet triggers within supervision, especially those that are frame-related, exert an enormous influence on the supervisee, so a great loss is suffered.

Consciously and unconsciously, then, a supervisee is caught in the middle of two interactions, each of which affects his unconscious experience and ways of doing therapy. The first lies within the supervised psychotherapy, and, through communicative supervision, it can be readily brought into awareness largely because much of it is reflected in the encoded narratives of the supervised patient. The second occurs within the supervision itself and is, intermittently, encoded in the extraneous or coincidental narratives and storied comments and explanations of the supervisee. Capturing these meanings and effects requires trigger decoding in light of the frame-management efforts of the supervisor.

The unconscious effects of the frame management and deep experience of the supervisee in the two situations are, of course, under mutual influence. These effects may flow in one or both directions, although the most common pathway leads from the supervisory situation and the supervisor's frame-management efforts to the supervised therapy and the supervisee's frame-managing interventions. A full understanding of a supervisee's work therefore requires an in-depth understanding of the unconscious aspects of the supervisory interaction.

The vignette shows that the consequences of a supervisor's frame deviations are not restricted to narrative communications from the supervisee. There are, as well, real behavioural/action effects—especially with respect to how the supervisee manages the frame of the supervised psychotherapy. It may well be that if Dr. Banks had not modified the framework of the supervision, Dr. Harper would not have altered the framework of the supervised psychotherapy and would not have evoked the disturbing unconscious perceptions and experience that Mrs. Johnson was then compelled to endure.

The illustration also shows the dramatic differences between conscious and unconscious experience and thinking.

With regard to the former, Mrs. Johnson had felt appreciative of her therapist's change in her hour and Dr. Harper saw little harm in making the change — he thought that it might even help the patient to see him in a good light. Dr. Harper also actually welcomed the change in the day and time of his supervision in that the new hour was easier for him to use. Dr. Banks thought of the change as necessary and relatively unimportant in the grand scheme of things. Nevertheless, unconsciously, both the supervised patient and the supervisee saw the frame alterations as damaging and hurtful. The supervisor's frame modification set the stage for the change made by his supervisee — the effects of one situation on the other seem clear.

In all, then, the vignette illustrates the striking differences between conscious-system and deep unconscious system responses to the same situations and triggers. It also shows the intricate tapestry that weaves together the supervisory and supervised situations, consciously but more especially unconsciously. The supervisee is the pivotal middle person — taking in from the patient, conveying it to the supervisor and then taking in the supervisor's responses and carrying them back to the therapy setting and to the supervised patient. An enormous part of these effects transpires without the awareness of any of the three people involved. Indeed, the most critical aspects of these unconscious communications and transactions can be brought into awareness only by trigger decoding — deciphering the themes in reported narratives in light of their adaptation-evoking, usually frame-relevant, emotionally charged stimuli. Doing so is a service to all concerned — and needs to be a vital part of the supervisory effort.

CHAPTER THREE

Models of supervision
and unconscious validation

To broaden our purview, it will help now to identify the prevailing models of supervision and their main attributes. With this done, we can then continue our pursuit of a sound listening process for the supervisory experience and develop a clear and incisive validating methodology.

There are, it would seem, three loosely defined basic models of supervision. To introduce them here, they are:

1. *The standard (psychodynamic or psychoanalytic) model*

This terms refers to the many loosely related dynamic forms of supervision. While the model has many variations, its main distinguishing features are:

a. The presentation in some form by a supervisee of a description of therapy sessions with one or more patients.

b.   The supervisor's offer of loosely structured comments on the supervisee's work and on issues of theory related to that work, as well as a variety of extraneous comments on a wide range of possible topics.

c.   The use of some form of psychoanalytic theory as a foundation on which the teaching is based.

d.   The concentration of the teaching on the reported material from supervised therapy.

e.   The relative neglect of the ground rules and frame of both the supervised therapy and the supervisory situation and, overall, a loosely configured student–teacher relationship.

f.   Manifest-content/implications formulations of the material from the patient and the intermittent use of surface methods to confirm the interventions of both the supervisee and the supervisor.

In general, this model offers little in the way of established or agreed-upon ground rules for the supervisory situation; reliance is placed mainly on common sense and flexibility. The teaching is centred on the supervisee and his or her patient, but the supervisor's comments may wander far and wide from there; professional and personal self-revelations are not uncommon — allusions to a supervisor's own patients are a prime example. Only rarely is attention paid to the supervisory relationship or interaction *per se*, and this is done mostly at times of crisis and virtually always in terms of manifest communications and their implications. The authority of the supervisor is an evident force in this model, which is also lacking in specific criteria with which to test the validity of the supervisee's interventions and the supervisor's teaching efforts — by and large, the teacher's word is law.

Overall, this model of supervision is especially wanting in two basic ways: first, in its failure to comprehend the deeply unconscious nature of the *therapeutic interaction* and the importance of its frame; second, in its neglect of the *supervisory interaction* itself, especially in respect to its frame-related and unconscious aspects.

2. *The standard communicative model*

This model is a variation on the standard psychodynamic model, and it has several features that afford it a distinctive and more valid cast:

a.   The requirement that the student present process-note case material written after each session and that the material be presented in specific detail entirely in the sequence in which it unfolded.

b.   Supervisory comments are cast in adaptational/interactional terms, and they are given a predictive cast. They are focused on the case material and issues in the technique of psychotherapy — and, secondarily, on relevant theoretical underpinnings. Extraneous remarks, especially those that are personally or professionally self-revealing, are excluded or kept to a minimum.

c.   The communicative approach is the background theory that informs the supervisory work. This includes a stress on unconscious communication and processing — and on trigger decoding.

d.   The consistent use of trigger decoding leads to a deep appreciation of the nature and functions of the ground rules of the supervised psychotherapy and a more variable appreciation of the ground rules and framework of the supervisory situation. There is a structure to the supervision, although the principles through which the supervisory frame is established and maintained are not consistently defined, nor is access made to the supervisee's encoded communications — except, at times, when a supervisory crisis materializes.

e.   The case material is formulated in terms of both the surface and its encoded meanings. Use is made of *encoded or derivative validation* for all interventions of the supervisee and supervisor.

This model of supervision is based on a specific definition of the unconscious domain from which its techniques and theory are derived. There is, however, a single glaring limitation to this model — it fails to allow for the full expression and integration into the teaching situation of the supervisee's unconscious experience of the supervisor's establishment and management of the supervisory frame and of his or her interventions to the student. Nevertheless, this *cognitive communicative teaching model* will be developed extensively in this book because it offers the most complete and unconsciously validated approach to a supervisor's efforts to teach the techniques of psychotherapy to his or her students.

3. The self-processing supervision model

This model is a radical departure from the prior two models in that it is structured as a supervisory situation that allows for the expression of both process-note case material from a supervised patient and personal material from the supervisee — thereby providing the means to access every significant level that a supervisee experiences in supervision. This model embraces all of the features of the standard communicative model of supervision, but adds the following features (see chapter fourteen):

a. Full attention is paid to the transactions between the supervisor and supervisee, and to the framework of the supervisory situation — including the supervisor's management of that frame.

b. Before presenting process-note case material, the supervisee engages in *self-processing exercises* that facilitate the revelation of his or her own unconscious experience of the supervision.

c. The development and use of trigger-decoded insights as they relate to the supervisee's unconscious responses to both the teaching and frame-managing interventions of the supervisor.

This last model addresses the two essential features of the supervisory experience: first, the *cognitive education* of the supervisee via the supervisor's direct teachings; second, the student's essential *unconscious interactional education* via the supervisor's frame-securing actions and his or her success-ful trigger decoding of the supervisee's unconscious experience of the supervisory interchanges. Both conscious-system and deep unconscious system perceptions, effects, processes, and needs are addressed.

There is, in all, a definitive effort to integrate a supervisee's conscious and unconscious experiences within this super-visory modality so that the two levels of experience are each and together effectively helpful, non-contradictory, and well integrated. This paradigm leads to the development of the best possible holding/educational environment for the supervisee, maximizes his or her learning capabilities, and allows for an ideal opportunity to learn through conscious knowledge and unconscious example.

THE PROCESS OF VALIDATION

The evolved design of the emotion-processing mind has some rather important implications for how supervision should be conceptualized and carried out. Perhaps no point is more basic than what this architecture tells us about the fundamental *validating process* in supervision. Indeed, the design of the emotion-processing mind speaks strongly to the means by which all matters of intervention, discussion, formulation, and technique are to be confirmed as sound and helpful — or re-jected as incorrect or invalid — whether introduced by the supervisee (either in the supervised therapy or in the supervi-sion) or the supervisor. The features of this architecture indicate that the choice of validating methodology lies between *an entirely unreliable conscious-system method of confirmation and a highly trustable, deep unconscious system method* — that is, that there is, indeed, only one sensible and effective means of validation and it must rely on unconscious/encoded com-munication.

As we have seen, our theory and techniques of supervision are based entirely on how we observe both the supervised clinical interaction and the supervisory process itself — and derive postulates and conclusions, however tentative or firm, on that basis. Ultimately, every aspect of this process, whether it is a theoretical construct or a point of technique — and whether it is related to therapy or supervision — must be confirmed in some unbiased *unconscious* (indirect or encoded) manner.

TWO METHODS OF VALIDATION

Let us look again at the listening process in psychotherapy since it serves well as a model for comparable efforts in supervision. As I have pointed out, most work in psychotherapy at present is based on attending to the manifest contents emitted by the conscious system and to their consciously and superficially unconsciously registered implications. Patterns of behaviour are identified in this way, as are supposed unconscious needs for mirroring or idealization and fantasies of sexuality or aggression — and much more. Since many implied meanings of communicated messages, such as the contents of free associations, are outside the awareness of the patient, this work is viewed as psychoanalytic in the sense that configurations and tendencies of which the patient is unaware are interpreted to him or her: something that previously was unconscious is made conscious.

What means of validation are used in this model? Since the realm of communication and experience that is monitored in this paradigm primarily is conscious and expressed directly, or with little disguise, confirmation usually is a matter of direct agreement by the patient, to which may be added a surface comment that extends or elaborates upon the interpretation made by the therapist. At times, there is a disguised, supportive response, but it *breaks through into awareness whole-cloth and its meanings are relatively transparent — it is a reaction from the superficial unconscious subsystem and therefore also part of conscious-system responsiveness.*

For example, Mr. Wilder, a male patient, was seeing Dr. Penn, a woman therapist, in psychotherapy. In one session, he reported a dream in which a woman lures him into her bedroom with a trail of one-hundred-dollar bills; she then has sex with him. In associating to the dream the patient thought of his parents' bedroom, and this led the therapist to interpret that the dream revealed a repressed unconscious sexual wish to sleep with his mother. Mr. Wilder responded that the intervention made sense, and he then added that he suddenly remembered that he had once dreamt of being in bed with his mother in a very cheap hotel room.

Dr. Penn then proposed that her patient was having sexual fantasies about her too. Mr. Wilder responded by saying that he never really thought of his mother as attractive; she used to hound him until he did things her way, and more often than not she was wrong about what she forced him to do. You couldn't talk to her, he added, she never wanted to know the truth about things.

This sequence as dealt with by Dr. Penn is primarily conscious and manifest, although there is an undoing of a minimal disguise in the interpretation that the woman in Mr. Wilder's dream represents his mother and, then, his therapist. This kind of slightly disguised, easily translated image is the product of conscious-system defence and reflects repressed images and memories that lie within the superficial unconscious subsystem of the conscious system. Characteristically, the image is treated as an unconscious entity lying within the mind of the patient, and there is no call for a dynamic-interactional-adaptive cast — the images are seen as mental products rather than a reflection of coping responses to a specific emotionally charged stimulus.

As for the issue of validation, Dr. Penn took the patient's agreement with her intervention and the recovery of the repressed dream as full support for her interpretation. In the classical models of psychotherapy and supervision, both responses — direct agreement and the *emergence whole-cloth* of a directly supportive recollection — are taken as confirmatory responses to therapists' interventions. And there is truth value to this contention — conscious-system repression has indeed been modified to allow a forgotten memory to emerge from unconscious storage. Nevertheless, the sequence remains *without an adaptive cast* and therefore is lacking in a critical dimension of the living and coping human mind.

In this model, Mr. Wilder's failure to agree directly with Dr. Penn's so-called transference interpretation and his remarks about his nagging and wrong-headed mother would be seen as reflections of defence and resistance caused by anxieties connected with the conscious realization of sexual feelings towards his mother — and therapist. There is, then, no definitive means of *non-validation*: even a direct disagreement with or repudiation of a therapist's interpretation is seen mainly as a resistance — as in this instance, where the defensiveness was thought to have been mobilized by unconscious incestuous and transference-based anxieties.

The psychotherapist who uses the standard psychodynamic model does not seek out specific adaptation-evoking triggers, nor does he or she engage in trigger decoding. The grave consequences of these omissions are seen in the present clinical material when we learn that there was a *repressed trigger* that unconsciously was motivating these communications from the patient: at the request of her patient, in the previous session, Dr. Penn had reduced her fee. It seems likely that this same trigger unconsciously was driving the therapist's interventions as well, largely because they kept the trigger and its ramifications outside of awareness for both patient and therapist. Indeed, this formulation actually is encoded in the patient's comment that his mother never wanted to know the truth about things.

It is largely through the discovery of a repressed trigger that the weaknesses of confirmation via either direct agreement or the emergence of thinly disguised supportive images can be appreciated. *Weak forms of validation* abound in psychotherapy and they have some value, but they support insights and therapeutic work that are of only minimal importance to the psychic economy and to the unconscious basis of emotional and interpersonal dysfunctions.

Even more serious is the realization that the interventions that find support via conscious-system confirmation primarily serve as ways of avoiding the critical ramifications of repressed triggers, usually in the form of frame-related interventions by a therapist — or supervisor. The superficial validation of these non-adaptive interventions therefore functions to support avoidance and falsifications of the most critical issues and conflicts to which a patient (or supervisee) is reacting in the immediate moment. There is a spurious and hurtful quality to the entire effort which unconsciously is driven by defensive needs in both patients and therapists, supervisors and supervisees — needs that help to explain the absence of an adaptational cast to these approaches.

If we consider the emotionally charged trigger to which Mr. Wilder was adapting through his dream and associations, we arrive at a very different formulation of this material from the one his therapist saw as validated. The fee reduction is the frame-relevant trigger, and the dream of the seductive woman who uses a trail of money to seduce the patient clearly encodes an unconscious perception of an unconsciously registered implication of the therapist's intervention. The *bridging theme* that links the manifest dream with its latent trigger is that of the *money*, and the seduction portrays an implied meaning of the fee reduction, to which the patient is reacting in light of his own selective sensitivities, needs, and issues.

In this light, the association to the patient's mother is a genetic link to the present rather than the representation of a detached unconscious memory or wish. That is, the therapist has in her own way behaved seductively as had the patient's mother in the past. The purported *transference wish* is more properly formulated as an *encoded perception* of the therapist's actual seductiveness and self-depreciation via the lowered fee — the latter encoded through the patient's allusion to the cheap hotel. Encoded images reflect responses to currently active frame-related triggers and to the implications of the immediate interventional efforts of the therapist as well — virtually all of them occurring outside the patient's and the therapist's awareness.

We have here an example of *encoded non-validation* via the images of the mother who was persistent but wrong and afraid of the truth. At this same juncture, the therapist, who was using the standard model of therapy, believed that her interventions had been validated. Nevertheless, her form of validation extends her own and the patient's defensiveness, while the encoded form of validation would recognize that the responsive material was non-validating — a realization that would compel the therapist to reconsider her intervention and reformulate the material, a very necessary step in this situation.

In principle, we must distinguish between support for an intervention that comes from the conscious system and support that comes from the deep unconscious system. In the first case, which largely serves defensiveness and falsification, there is either direct agreement or the surfacing, whole-cloth and without significant disguise, of a repressed memory or fantasy. But in the second case, direct agreement is not given serious thought (although direct refutation usually is taken to imply that indirect or disguised refutation also will follow). On this level, the images that are studied for confirmation or its lack are in the form of disguised or encoded narratives. The meanings and implications of these stories are taken as encoded or unconscious assessments of, or commentaries on, the therapist's intervention. In substance, a patient's stories with a positive cast are seen as confirmatory, while those with a negative cast are not.

While non-validation is difficult to come by in the conscious-system realm, it is readily identified in the realm of the second unconscious system. But for those therapists who fail to appreciate and search for repressed triggers, this second world of experience, with its enormous unconscious power over emotional life and psychotherapy, is lost. And the loss is a significant one for both patients and therapists, who are left to work with conscious systems that are so devoted to defence and pathological satisfactions that they allow for grave deceptions and pathological forms of acting out that harm everyone involved. The supervisory work in this book will, of necessity then, be founded on tests of *the encoded forms of validation* — it cannot be otherwise.

Validation: a clinical excerpt

To help us precisely define the nature of encoded validation, let us turn to another clinical vignette.

Ms. Green was in therapy with Dr. Martin, a male psychologist who was presenting her case to Dr. Lester, a woman psychologist. In one session, the patient told her therapist that her boss was stealing money from the petty cash box — wasn't that just like a man to get away with something like that? Dr. Martin interpreted this material as containing his patient's projection onto her boss of her own greedy and dishonest needs, and he pointed as well to her hostile and jaundiced view of men.

In supervising this hour, Dr. Lester intervened at this juncture (an intervention by a supervisee is an opportune moment for supervisory comment; see chapter eight). This was her first session with Dr. Martin, and the supervisee was working on the basis of the standard model of psychotherapy and had only a rudimentary understanding of the communicative approach. On the other hand, the supervisor was using the communicative model exclusively.

In commenting, Dr. Lester first discussed principles of listening, formulating, and intervening with her new student. Next, she ventured that communicatively, in terms of the responses of the deep unconscious system, her student's effort would *not* obtain encoded validation (communicative-model supervisors consistently make predictions about the validity of the supervisee's interventions in terms of the unfolding interactions within the sessions that they supervise). She indicated that she was making this prediction because the intervention was arbitrary and focused entirely on the patient as if she were not interacting and adapting to her relationship with her therapist — the comment lacked a necessary adaptive cast. The intervention also was concerned only with manifest contents and their purported implications and was not based on trigger decoding.

Dr. Lester suggested that both she and her student listen carefully to the material in the session with the patient that would now follow her supervisory comment. They would do well to keep two issues in mind: first, whether the supervisee's intervention in the therapy session would obtain encoded validation; second, whether her own expectation of non-validation would be confirmed by the same material and its images.

We may note as an aside that a supervised patient can be expected to confirm a supervisor's valid assessment of a supervisee's intervention because unconsciously the patient is working over the essential attributes of the supervisee/therapist's efforts. If a supervisor is correct in his or her evaluation, his or her predictions will be borne out in the encoded realm by the patient who *unconsciously* is working over the same features of the intervention that the supervisor has identified *consciously*. This type of prediction is not possible in the standard model of supervision because the effort involves adaptational/interactional assessments in realms not touched on by that model; it also requires the use of trigger decoding — in this case, deciphering the patient's disguised material in light of the supervisor's intervention, namely, her evaluation of the supervisee's comment.

Returning to the supervised session, Ms. Green next said that she was unaware of projecting any of her own feelings into her boss and that she also was tired of hearing about her nasty picture of men. Despite all that, she guessed that her therapist must be right. She feels she's really stupid and dense when it comes to these matters; people tell her that she's always pointing fingers at the faults of others when she should be taking a good look at herself. She must be a mess psychologically.

Dr. Martin took his patient's agreement with his interpretation as a validating response and saw her added comments as further indications that his intervention was correct. Dr. Lester expressed her scepticism and asked him, as an alternative, to *trigger-decode* his patient's response as well. The supervisee paused to reflect and then said that his intervention must be the trigger for the material that followed it — here he began to feel anxious and surprised — and that the images the patient reported of herself must be encoded perceptions of him in light of what he had said.

"It's not a nice picture", he added, "It says that I was being stupid and accusatory of my patient when I should have been looking at something I had done." Dr. Martin now realized that his supervisor's prediction of non-validation had been confirmed — the images were negative and spoke to error and blindness rather than understanding and insight.

We can see, then, that the test of encoded confirmation had repudiated the supervisee's effort, while at the very same time it had supported the comments and prediction of the teacher. This *dual search for encoded validation* in the material from a supervised patient as it pertains to the interventions of both supervisee and supervisor is one of the most distinctive features of the communicative model of supervision.

To return to the vignette, Ms. Green next said that something was annoying her about Dr. Martin, but she couldn't put her finger on it. Buoyed by his patient's direct acceptance of his interpretation, and commenting in light of the allusion to himself, Dr. Martin went on to interpret that in addition, the thievery image indicated that in the transference, in her relationship with him, Ms. Green wanted to rob him of his penis in envy of his being a man with power.

In brief, Dr. Lester saw this intervention as having the same arbitrariness and failings as the previous one, and as even more attacking of the patient than before. She again predicted non-validation, as well as a strong negative image of some kind in response to the assaultive qualities of this purported interpretation.

In the session, Ms. Green responded to her therapist's comment by saying that his interpretation was a lot of nonsense — it was *his* fantasy, not *hers*. Dr. Martin suggested that her denial was proof of his point in that it was an attempt to resist his interpretation and destroy the very power in him that she envied so badly. Ms. Green began to cry and conceded that at times she must be a hostile and castrating woman. She thought of a girlfriend

who always put down men, but then added that her
behaviour was understandable because she had once been
date-raped.

Many manifest-content therapists take conscious agreement as affirmation, and disagreement as resistance — a
no-win situation for the patient that is all too familiar in our
field. We see again that the standard model of therapy allows
therapists to invoke the mechanisms of disguise and displace-
ment in a way that is neither adaptive nor interactional. Thus,
the so-called transference interpretation implies that the
patient's boss, via disguise, represents her therapist. In this
connection, the stealing is seen to represent the patient's own
impulse and wish as directed towards her therapist. The underlying psychoanalytic theory sees the patient as a mental entity
with global inner needs that are projected unconsciously onto
others — here, the therapist. As pointed out, the sense of a
patient's immediate adaptation to, and interaction with, the
therapist and his or her real inputs is entirely absent. The
therapist is treated instead as a shadowy figure who innocently
and without need or impact on the patient is available for his or
her projections — all the while contributing little else.

Interventions made on the basis of this theory and its
variants uniformly *fail to obtain encoded validation*. If the
therapist's comment is especially assaultive, there often is
conscious disagreement from the patient, and if the therapist
persists, as Dr. Martin did, the unconscious (and at times,
conscious) experience of attack is quite strong. This valid sense
of harassment is an implication of the therapist's intervention
that is experienced by the patient unconsciously, and only
rarely consciously. The unconscious component is processed
by the deep unconscious wisdom subsystem and results in
personally selected, valid encoded perceptions of the therapist
in light of his or her errant comment.

In this instance, as predicted by Dr. Lester, the therapist's
insistence and unfairly isolated focus on the patient and her
purported problems were experienced unconsciously by Ms.
Green as a rape. This image again disconfirms the supervisee's
intervention, while confirming that of the supervisor. The principle of guidance through encoded themes from the supervised

patient in response to interventions by either party to supervision holds up very well here.

As a rule, a supervisor's comments and predictions are tested out in the subsequent material from the patient in the same way that unconscious confirmation of a therapist's interventions is sought for in a patient's material in therapy sessions. To clarify this point, an essential task of a communicative supervisor is to attempt to articulate directly and *consciously* the patient's *unconscious* experience of the supervisee's interventions. If the supervisor does so correctly, the themes and images that the patient will encode in response to the supervisee's comments can be formulated with great accuracy. It is this fact that makes encoded validation of a supervisor's interventions possible — and an absolutely essential foundation of sound supervisory work.

The ideal type of *confirmatory response* from a patient involves trigger-related, encoded imagery of well-functioning and helpful people (*interpersonal validation*), and narratives whose encoded meanings add new perspectives to the interpretation or formulation at hand (*cognitive validation*). These types of encoded affirmation, which stem from adaptive assessments made by the patient's second unconscious system, are the only reliable guide to effective psychotherapy available to us today.

MORE ON ENCODED VALIDATION

To return again to the vignette, we have seen that there was no allusion to a specific manifest or repressed trigger in the therapist's comments. Leaving manifest triggers aside for the moment, we may again ask if there was a *repressed trigger* that had prompted or activated the encoded material that we have heard from the patient. The question is naive in that repressed triggers are ever-present, especially in the world of psychotherapy and its supervision. Ms. Green therefore unconsciously must be reacting to the (probably frame-related) interventions of her therapist — it cannot be otherwise. The question is not whether a repressed trigger exists, but whether we can identify it and account for its effects.

This situation proved to be no exception to this rule.

In the previous session, Dr. Martin had handed his patient his bill and it had contained an overcharge for one session more than had been held. Consciously, Ms. Green had thought the bill seemed odd, but she was not aware of why; she had written a cheque for the amount she had been charged, but then left it at home.

Despite her *conscious* defensiveness and obliterating efforts, through *unconscious perception* her second unconscious system undoubtedly had perceived the error and processed its implications. But if this is the critical repressed trigger for this material, how do the images decode as adaptive responses to this frame violation and its ramifications?

We can formulate that Ms. Green had, through the image of her boss, revealed an encoded perception of her therapist as stealing from and exploiting her. In this light, we can see that the therapist's interpretation of his patient's projections and her castrating transference are of little dynamic import at the moment — and that they are substantially erroneous and defensively distracting in light of the therapist's prevailing interaction with the patient. Indeed, Dr. Martin's interpretations turn reality upside down: at the very moment he is in reality attempting to steal from and harm his patient, he is accusing her of wanting to steal from him.

Patients often encode their unconscious perceptions of their therapists through allusions to themselves. When this occurs, the manifest-content/implications therapist will hold the patient accountable for dysfunctional behaviours and fantasies that actually belong primarily to himself or herself — a common means through which therapists deny the unconscious implications of their interventions and attack their patients for failings that primarily are their own.

These problems with the standard model of therapy bridge over to the standard model of supervision where there are even fewer safeguards against error and harm than exist in the treatment situation. The danger of a supervisor projecting his or her issues and pathological needs into a supervisee, and of a supervisor's use of unrecognized denial and other defences, is enormous. The only currently available check against these inevitable tendencies of the conscious mind lies with the requisite that supervisory and therapeutic interventions not be accepted as sound unless they are followed by encoded validation in the process-note material from the case under scrutiny.

To complete the vignette, when Ms. Green mentioned that she had forgotten Dr. Martin's check, he began to sense that something was amiss, and he started to mull over the bill that he had given to his patient. Meanwhile, Ms. Green's associations went to a department store bill that had been in error because it contained a charge for merchandise she had returned; the nice thing about it was that the store corrected her bill as soon as she brought the error to their attention.

At this point in the session, it suddenly struck Dr. Martin that in the previous month, one of Ms. Green's sessions had fallen on a legal holiday. There had been no session that day, but he had forgotten the holiday and had charged her for the hour. Now at last, unconsciously directed to the missing trigger by the patient's derivative (encoded) images — a trigger that both he and his patient had repressed — Dr. Martin was able to trigger-decode some of the patient's earlier material, and he prepared to intervene.

With the therapist still silent, Ms. Green's next association was to a newspaper story about a man who had seduced a woman and stolen her money. Dr. Martin then spoke up and pointed out that Ms. Green had forgotten her cheque and was talking about billing errors and overcharges, as well as men who steal from women. This seemed to suggest that there was a problem with the bill that he had given to her and, from her imagery, it seemed to have something to do with his overcharging her.

In the supervision, Dr. Lester congratulated her student on his intervention — it dealt with a powerful frame-related trigger and decoded the patient's thematic images as encoded perceptions of himself in light of his lapse. Dr.

Lester tentatively predicted that Ms. Green would respond to this intervention with a partial encoded validation. Her hesitation was based on the fact that Dr. Martin had not as yet rectified his error — indeed, until his specific mistake was directly stated by the patient and brought into the material, he could not do so (i.e. at this point in the session, this was not a failing on his part). Without frame rectification — here in the form of correcting the bill — otherwise sound interpretations either fail to obtain encoded validation or are confirmed in some minimal and incomplete way. When a frame is modified, both interventions — *a correct interpretation and frame-securing efforts* — are essential.

In the session, Ms. Green laughed and said that she had had an uneasy feeling that there had been an error made on the bill, but she hadn't been able to locate it. "Had Dr. Martin charged her for a session on the holiday last month when they hadn't met", she asked aloud. In her head, she calculated the correct amount she owed her therapist, remembered the amount she had been billed for, and concluded that that was exactly what had happened. Dr. Martin then acknowledged his error and indicated that of course, Ms. Green should pay him only for the sessions that they had held.

With rectification now accomplished in response to the patient's conscious and encoded material (recall that the department store had corrected its error immediately), Dr. Lester indicated that her supervisee's intervention was now complete — it had used trigger decoding for both interpreting the patient's material and securing the frame. This effort met the criteria of a sound intervention according to the principles and theory of the communicative approach. Dr. Lester indicated her belief that validating imagery would follow.

In the session, Ms. Green responded by first saying that of course, she wasn't about to pay for a session that had been cancelled. Her mind then shifted again into the associative mode and she thought back to an incident that her father had been involved in when she was a child. It seemed that someone had discovered that he had hired a former convict to work in his dress-manufacturing plant. Some of the employees had information that her father had known the former criminal in connection with some shady dealings that both had been involved in years earlier. These employees had been upset and had expected trouble, but the man proved to be quite honest and an excellent worker. The doubts about her father also had disappeared.

Without pursuing the clinical material further, we see here an example of how a patient's images can simultaneously offer encoded validation of interventions that were made by both a therapist and his supervisor. This correspondence occurred, of course, because both had agreed on the most cogent formulation of the patient's material and both were correct in their assessment — according to the patient's responsive encoded narrative. The tale of the reformed criminal nicely encodes the therapist's reformation via his last intervention — his change from a thief to an honest, frame-securing worker.

The patient's response also introduces her father into the material, and he appears to have been the significant genetic figure related to this frame-deviant/frame-securing sequence. Current triggers activate conscious and unconscious memories of past incidents of a related nature. Her father in the past had been dishonest and had then reformed, much as the therapist had done. To state this another way, the therapist, in his error, had repeated in a particular form a past pathogenic trauma from the patient's father. Only interpretation and frame rectification could change this picture for the patient — as it did in this session. Technically, Ms. Green had rewarded Dr. Martin with both forms of validation — *interpersonally*, through the images of reformed and well-functioning figures, and *cognitively*, by introducing the genetic link between the therapist's error and a childhood incident with her father.

We have now established *a basic listening–formulating process* that centres around adaptation-evoking stimuli, some of which are conscious and evoke manifest, conscious-system responses, while others are repressed and unconscious and stimulate reactions in the deep unconscious system that lead

to encoded messages fraught with camouflaged adaptive solutions of great value. We have seen, too, that the repressive
defences that keep the critical triggers that activate the second
unconscious system outside awareness operate in two ways:
first, by effecting the total repression of a given stimulus or
trigger; second, by repressing selected but powerful meanings
and implications of known triggers so that some aspects reach
awareness, while others of greater impact do not. These defences are psychobiological mechanisms that operate by virtue
of the evolved design of the mind and deep but costly needs for
self-protection, and they are seen in patients and in therapist/
supervisees and their supervisors. The differentiation here is
that therapists and supervisors should use these obliterating
defences less often than their patients and supervisees, respectively, and should be capable of detecting their operation when
they are, as is inevitable, activated from time to time under
stress.

It has been emphasized too that these repressed triggers
almost always involve the management of ground-rule conditions, whether in therapy or in supervision, and that interpersonal and psychodynamic conflicts unfold from these
repressed and denied triggering or adaptation-evoking experiences. We have also put into place a method for obtaining
encoded validation for all interventions as our criterion of the
soundness of the work of both supervisee and supervisor.
Throughout this book we refer to this effort variously as *the
search for unconscious confirmation (or its lack); the quest for
encoded, derivative, or unconscious validation; the unconscious
validating process* — or *encoded validation*, for short. With this
methodology in place, we turn now to the details of the supervisory process, beginning as you might expect with the ground
rules and frame of that great teaching situation.

CHAPTER FOUR

Frames and systems: contexts for supervision

Throughout animate and inanimate nature, the frame or boundary conditions of an entity or system are a major determinant of the functioning and survival of that entity. The supervisor/supervisee (S/S) system is, of course, no exception to that rule. Indeed, each S/S system is established within a framework, however well or poorly defined, and that frame exerts a strong influence over the conscious and unconscious experience and the functioning of the two members of the system. The paradox is that even though conscious experience is deeply affected by the frame, it has little appreciation of those effects — they tend to be written off or overlooked. Indeed, the symptom complexes that are frame-driven tend to be accounted for in other, erroneous or secondary, ways. In structuring a supervisory situation, it is essential to afford the systemic aspects and ground rules of the experience their full due.

THE INFLUENCE OF THE FRAME

The effects of the frame of supervision are everywhere. The ground rules of supervision establish the role and responsibilities of each party, the scope and limits of acceptable behaviour, the means by which the supervisory process is to unfold, the quality of the inherent hold and support of the supervisor for the supervisee and the appropriate ways that the supervisee secondarily can hold and support the supervisor (e.g. by preparing proper process notes, attending supervision regularly, listening attentively, etc.), and a host of other contextual considerations.

The frame also influences the *communications* between the supervisor and supervisee. It delimits the range and nature of what can be said by each party — the material asked of the supervisee, the interventions that can be offered by the supervisor (e.g. ideally, that they be based on the case material, be as predictive as possible and open to encoded validation, be confined to the essentials of teaching, preclude self-revelations, etc.), and the allowable responses of supervisees (e.g. framing the means by which he or she can legitimately challenge the supervisor's comments on the basis of non-validation in the supervised patient's material).

There is more still. Frame management is an ever-present behavioural dimension. That is, the supervisor is at all times either creating, maintaining, or modifying aspects of the ground rules of supervision, and the supervisee is always adhering to or defying them — or suggesting rules of his or her own. It is naive and erroneous to suppose that ground rules are established at the outset of a supervision and that they fade into the background thereafter. It is also in error to postulate that since supervision is not therapy, the ground rules need not be made explicit and the situation can be managed loosely and flexibly. These attitudes deny the ever-present power of deep unconscious influences in all emotionally charged situations and support the conscious system's inclinations towards uncertain and easily modified frames — and the pathological defences and gratifications that they provide. Such thinking also fails to appreciate that *deeply unconsciously*, both supervisor and supervisee wish for and validate a well-defined frame for their work together, and that, furthermore, through trigger decoding, the specific nature of that frame can readily be stated.

Recognized explicitly or not, frame management is a continual activity of the supervisor and, to a lesser extent, the supervisee, and frame issues are remarkably common in supervision. Typical examples include requests to change the time of a supervisory session, a report from a supervisor to an education committee of a training program, a lapse by the supervisor who mentions one of his own patients to the supervisee, etc., etc. As an ongoing behavioural input, then, the supervisor's frame-related attitudes, decisions, and actions exert powerful effects on the second unconscious system of the supervisee and in turn on his or her therapeutic work — and personal life. A supervisor may consistently intervene with frame-securing interventions, may be consistently frame-modifying, or may alternate between the two polarities of frame-securing and frame-modifying. All these inputs are taken in by a supervisee's deep unconscious system and processed in terms of his or her personal selection of particular but real unconscious implications of these interventions. Virtually every lapse by a supervisee has at least one source in a frame-related — usually frame-modifying — intervention of his or her supervisor.

SECURED AND MODIFIED FRAMES

The *ideal or secured frame* is defined, as noted earlier, by the *encoded* reactions of the person towards whom the frame-related interventions are directed. In therapy, this individual usually is the patient; in supervision, it is the supervisee. More rarely, therapists and supervisors will be obliged to react to the frame-securing or frame-modifying efforts of a patient or supervisee, respectively.

Without exception, frame-securing interventions are derivatively confirmed by patients (and supervisees when the responsive narrative material is available); they do so via displaced and disguised, encoded stories of safe and creative spaces, well-functioning individuals, and the like. In contrast, frame alterations evoke non-confirmatory images of unsafe places, ignorance, assault, seduction, exploitation, and such. These evoked, adaptive, displaced narratives are the only reliable guide to frame-management efforts. Indeed, as we have seen, the conscious system tends to be frame-insensitive and inclined towards frame alterations, which accounts for the relative neglect of this vital dimension of therapy and supervision in the standard psychoanalytic model.

In their own right, *frame-securing* efforts are constructive, holding, and containing, a means of establishing a favourable ambience for efficient learning, growth-promoting, and ego- and self-enhancing — yet they always evoke a measure of *secured-frame anxiety*. As a result, the reaction of a supervisee to a secured-frame intervention from his or her supervisor is typically biphasic. On the one hand, the intervention unconsciously will inherently be highly supportive and will promote the use of secured-frame interventions by the supervisee and strengthen his or her interpretive and other skills. But on the other hand, there will be unconscious reactions to the sense of entrapment and the death anxieties aroused by securing a frame.

These anxious secured-frame responses are usually confined to communicated derivative images and do not spill over into defensive frame alterations and other forms of acting out. However, when the anxieties are over-intense, they may do so. For example, in reacting to a supervisor's frame-holding intervention — for example, not reducing a supervisory fee when asked to by a supervisee — the student will experience a positive introjective identification with the frame-holding supervisor and will benefit in various ways, but may then have a dream of being trapped in an elevator. More rarely, the supervisee may be late to the next supervisory session.

In contrast, a supervisor's *frame modifications* — for example, changing a supervisory hour, increasing or decreasing the fee, seeing the student in the context of a training program (remember, nature is nature), and so forth — consistently have a series of detrimental effects on the supervisee. Frame-deviant actions by supervisors disturb the learning capacities and therapeutic work of their students and implicitly encourage and sanction their use of frame-altering interventions as well.

This touches on an unrecognized problem for the entire field of dynamic psychotherapies in that almost all of the training of psychotherapists occurs under deviant-frame conditions and thereby creates an unconsciously transmitted heritage of frame-deviant proclivities passed on from its older to its younger practitioners. This situation renders almost the entire field frame-insensitive and inclined towards frame-modifications. These attitudes are buttressed by the failure to use trigger decoding in attempting to understand the material from patients and supervisees, and a phobic-like avoidance of the investigation of the unconscious implications and behavioural consequences of frame-altering interventions. The situation is in need of intense efforts at trigger decoding and frame exploration — most certainly, this would lead to a major shift towards more frame-secured therapies and supervisory situations.

A supervisor who ignores frame issues or deals with them in a perfunctory manner and in terms of manifest contents and their implications will be inclined to support frame alterations in his or her supervisee's work, and in the supervision itself he or she is likely to create a deviant-frame setting for, and cast to, his or her teaching efforts. Learning to do psychotherapy is impaired under these frame-modified conditions because the teaching situation itself is unstable, the unconscious introject of the supervisor by the supervisee is toxic and disruptive, and the supervisor's frame-deviant interventions *unconsciously* are correctly perceived as invalid and essentially misleading and confusing.

A supervisor who teaches a supervisee the value of secured-frame interventions, but who then modifies the framework of the supervision, is self-contradictory. Mixed messages of this kind — a type of double-bind in which the supervisor says one thing and does the opposite — tends to drive a supervisee crazy (Searles, 1959) and greatly destabilizes the supervisory situation. At times of supervisory crisis, the first line of investigation should be directed towards the status of the supervisory frame.

The supervisor's frame-management interventions are *unconsciously empowered teaching inputs*, and their implications are introjected by the supervisee as a model for his or her therapeutic and daily life behaviours. The effects range far and wide. Frame modifications inherently contradict and undermine all genuinely and otherwise valid efforts by the supervisor, while securing or maintaining the supervisory frame supports the best of his or her teachings. The very way a supervisor's verbal messages are understood and responded to is exquisitely influenced by the frame conditions of the work. *The supervisor's handling of the ground rules of supervision arguably is the most critical intervention that he or she makes — its unconscious ramifications are extraordinary.*

THE SUPERVISOR/SUPERVISEE SYSTEM

Before turning to the details of the ground rules of supervision, it will help to develop a sense of the extent to which it is of value to think of the supervisor and supervisee in systemic terms as a way of *supplementing and clarifying, but not replacing, the usual two-person psychodynamic approach to the situation.* In much the same way that it has proven enlightening to think of a patient and therapist as a two-person (P/T) system (Langs, 1992e), it is illuminating to think of the S/S system as an entity in its own right.

A given supervisor develops a somewhat different interaction and relationship with each of his or her supervisees. The systemic viewpoint stresses the distinctive features of each S/S system and recognizes contributions from each party to the system. Among the systemic attributes that prove useful to consider are the *stability* of the system — some S/S systems appear to be consistent and well-regulated, while others are erratic and unpredictable. Another useful systemic concept is that of *system overload* — situations in which there is, as a rule, a supervisory crisis because the S/S system is overtaxed and unable to metabolize and resolve issues and conflicts in the supervised therapy or the supervision, or in both.

Systemic thinking implies that all of the events in supervision and all of their effects on the supervised therapy receive inputs from both parties to supervision — *shared responsibility* for all successes and failures is the rule. In addition, systemic thinking calls for a careful investigation of the ground rules, frames, and boundaries of the S/S (and P/T) systems because of the critical role played by these dimensions for all systems in nature. Had psychoanalysts thought *both systemically and dynamically* from the inception of the field, ground-rule and frame considerations would long ago have been appreciated for their importance. After all, every system is defined by its frame and boundaries, which are *per se* critical components of the system they define.

The adaptations and functioning of a S/S system are strongly influenced by its frame — systems tend towards dysfunction within poorly secured frames and operate optimally within secured frames. In addition, every S/S system is obliged to metabolize or *adapt to its own frame conditions* — indeed, this proves to be a primary adaptive task. In studying supervision, then, we will do well to maintain a systemic position in that all dysfunctions within a supervisory situation and the therapy being supervised, whether located in the behaviours of the supervisor, supervisee, or patient, will be examined for their systemic attributes.

In establishing this basic systemic principle, however, let us be mindful that the supervisor is the teacher and senior person in these systems (i.e. he or she constitutes the most responsible subsystem). The supervisor therefore must bear the greater onus and accountability for the framework and transactions of the supervisory experience — and their consequences. However, the supervisee is not thereby excused from accountability, but must retain his or her sense of responsibility for his or her actions as well. This encourages the supervisee to ask for the unconscious validation of a supervisor's recommendations in the case material from the supervised patient and, with all due respect, to think judiciously for himself or herself as a relatively autonomous person (subsystem) within the S/S system — he or she is both systemically bound and separate.

Finally, there have been some writers, including myself (Langs, 1979), who have advocated including the supervised patient in the S/S system, making it a three-person system — an S/S/P system. There are both advantages and disadvantages to this conception. On the positive side, the idea of a tripartite system does justice to the fact that through the process-note material the supervised patient does enter into the S/S system as a third member of the system. Certainly, the supervised patient has an influence on the supervisory interaction, and a supervisory crisis, for example, may be fuelled by the patient's actions, mental state, and communications. This three-person accountability with the patient held least responsible yet culpable is a sound and useful idea. Each supervised patient does indeed affect each S/S system in a distinctive way — a shift from working with a difficult to a relatively easy case shows this quite clearly.

The main problem with the tripartite system idea is that the frame of that system is exceedingly complex and difficult to characterize and study in a productive manner. We would, of necessity, be obliged to include two separate, though interrelated, frames and settings — one for the therapy, the other for the supervision. The two settings share a great deal with respect to their ideal secured-frame ground rules, but there are notable differences as well. And while the role and functions of the patient and supervisor are relatively fixed, the supervisee shifts from being the therapist–intervener and frame manager to being the student who is the recipient of the supervisor's interventions. Indeed, as this analysis shows, *the supervisee has the most difficult role in supervision* (see chapter eleven).

In all, then, the two distinctive settings, the shifts in the functions of the supervisee, and the differences in role assignments for a patient and supervisor allow for only a limited use of the three-system model. It may well be more fortuitous to invoke a model that focuses on the interaction between the two interrelated systems — P/T and S/S — and their frames, and to think of the supervisory case material as needing to be processed and metabolized by the S/S system within the framework of the interaction between supervisor and supervisee.

FURTHER PERSPECTIVES ON FRAMES

Returning now to the ground rules and boundaries of the S/S system, the second unconscious system is extremely sensitive to every nuance of a supervisor's frame-related interventions. With due respect for the inordinate power of this system to influence the professional and private lives of a supervisee, we will examine each ground rule of supervision in careful detail.

The principles that will be generated here through trigger decoding have been validated unconsciously through derivative material again and again.

In delineating the ideal ground rules for supervision in the two chapters that follow, we are, in essence, speaking for human need and about human nature. Just as we need oxygen to breathe and state that requirement in absolute terms — there are no known substitutes — there are essential emotional needs in a supervisee (and supervisor) that must be met to allow for his or her optimal functioning as a therapist (and person). When these needs are satisfied, the supervisee flourishes; when they are frustrated, there is damage and suffering. We must not be misled by conscious-system denial and repression. Nor should we be deceived by the fact that the conscious mind far more readily accepts phenomena it can experience directly and in simple terms than it does phenomena for which the evidence is indirect and a matter of decoded but logical conclusions.

The needs for safety and holding and for a stable, uncontaminated relationship are not matters of rigidity. Their satisfaction is of utmost necessity and the entitlement of every supervisee — and supervisor. It is the primary responsibility of the supervisor to learn how the supervisory situation is properly configured and to transform these principles into everyday practice.

In general, frames are clearly demarcated, and the exact nature of a secured-frame choice can be precisely defined. There are, however, some situations and ground rules that fall into that inevitable gray area between clearly secured and clearly deviant frames. The fee a supervisor charges a newly practising supervisee is a common example of this uncertain realm. How much can a supervisor reduce his or her usual fee for a novice who has a small income without causing a major frame-deviant disturbance? Every reduction in fee is, of course, a frame modification — even when the supervisee is not told that the fee is a departure from usual practice (that particular self-revelation would only intensify the effects of the frame alteration on the supervisee). The main question lies in the balance between the necessity for the fee reduction so supervision can take place and the fact that such a reduction modifies the supervisory frame — nature is nature, and the effects are seemingly subtle but nevertheless unconsciously powerful.

One of the great advantages in dealing with frame-related, adaptation-evoking triggers is that they are as a rule far more easily defined and their implications far more readily grasped than is the case for what are called *impression triggers* (Langs, 1993a) — conscious opinions of and feelings about a super-visor's non-frame interventions, such as his or her advice, interpretations, side comments, and the like. In practice, the validity of these latter impressions — and they range from being quite vague to exceedingly strong — must be tested by means of narrative messages that encode the supervisee's *unconscious perceptions* of these same, more uncertain triggers. Only the second unconscious system can assess fairly the non-manifest attributes of a non-frame intervention.

As we examine and develop each of the many components of the ideal, secured frame of supervision, our first response to a given unconsciously validated ground rule is likely to be domi-nated by conscious-system needs and defences. We will think that some of these tenets are absurd or extreme, and we will try to pretend we can cheat nature because there is little or no obvious conscious protest against a frame-deviant situation. Yet anyone who engages in the kind of self-processing super-vision to be described in chapter fourteen will be astounded to discover the incredibly strong unconscious and real influence that every nuance of the frame has on the supervisee (and the supervisor as well).

Seemingly minor frame alterations that are taken for granted consciously appear in the encoded material of a supervisee as horrendous assaults, betrayals, and seductions. The world of deep unconscious experience is forever surprising to the conscious system. It also is far more demanding than the conscious world of experience in what it asks of both supervisor and supervisee — and yet far more consistent and rewarding as well. It is quite humbling to experience these compelling derivatives and what they tell us when they are linked to their frame-deviant triggers. Without entering this second domain, we helplessly and defensively tend to wonder what the fuss is all about. Still, it is well to strive to sense and appreciate the qualities of the ideal frame and, at the very least, attempt to validate unconsciously all frame-related interventions in the course of a supervisory experience. Doing so can help us to appreciate the power of frames and the need for secured frames if one is to function well and wisely.

Another counter-argument to the contention that frames are a critical aspect of supervision revolves around the well-rationalized and sometimes necessary exceptions to each specific ground rule which tend to leap to mind when an ideal rule is presented. Indeed, it is impressive to see how often exceptions to these unconsciously validated ground rules materialize in the real world of psychotherapy supervision. Hopefully, the accumulated evidence for the harmful effects of frame alterations will motivate us to re-investigate the framework of supervision and move it towards its rightful secured-frame state.

There are, of course, some frame alterations that cannot be rectified given the accepted conditions and practices in today's world of psychotherapy. Psychology interns, social work students, and psychiatric residents will in many cases need to be supervised in the clinic or hospital where they are working — and by supervisors with whom they have interactions and relationships outside the supervisory hour. It is therefore essential to realize right off that both supervisors and supervisees must make a fundamental choice between frame-securing and frame-deviant values and approaches — there is, as a rule, no stable middle ground (situations tend to veer in one direction or the other). Thus, these frame alterations can lead to a proliferation of other frame breaks or, instead, be surrounded by an otherwise secured frame — the differences between these two choices are fateful for all concerned.

Along different lines, we must come to terms with the fact that a frame deviation is a frame deviation and that it has inevitable conscious and unconscious consequences — frame modifications can be denied, ignored, or argued away consciously, but none of this mental self-deception eliminates the unconscious impact of transactions in this realm. Thus, an understanding of the importance of secured frames should motivate supervisors to strive to create the most ideal frame possible under the circumstances of the supervision. As noted,

it is vital to eliminate the plethora of unneeded frame alterations that exist in private teaching and clinic supervisory
settings.

Finally, it is advisable to maintain a watchful eye for the
effects of seemingly necessary frame deviations in order to
process their harmful effects by bringing their unconscious
consequences into awareness and keeping them to a minimum.
It is essential to learn from personal experience that every
human being deeply needs and wishes for secured frames, yet
also suffers from silent secured-frame anxieties. Each of us
exists with an evolved conscious system that is designed to
adapt through frame-breaks and denial (however costly), more
so than by securing frames and foregoing defensiveness. In
supervision, then, all parties, as humans beings, inevitably
will find themselves mired in, or creating for themselves —
deliberately or inadvertently — all manner of frame alterations.
Securing frames requires understanding, strong motivation,
and effort — they are not a consequence of our natural inclinations.

In this light, we can see that modifying a frame is one way of
being human; but to re-secure that fractured frame is to be a
devoted and effective supervisee or supervisor. As therapists,
we must accept our inevitable lapses and personal frailties and
work to manage them as best we can. Frame breaks cause
harm and evoke unconscious and more rarely conscious guilt
in their perpetrators. Indeed, *unconscious guilt* is the prime
disease of psychotherapists who *unconsciously monitor* the
error and harm of their ways and suffer unknowingly for their
injurious doings. Modulated guilt for a frame break is a
healthy, constructively motivating response, but undue guilt is
disturbing without being helpful. If we have a well-reasoned
perspective on these issues, we can strive to secure the best
possible supervisory frame available under whatever the
circumstances of supervision happen to be, and work through
the unavoidable lapses. We must tolerate our limitations and
inclinations as poorly evolved human beings and learn and
grow from the error of our ways.

With these perspectives in mind, let us move now to identifying the specific dimensions of the ideal framework of a
supervisory situation.

CHAPTER FIVE

The fixed frame of supervision

We are now ready to spell out in detail the ideal, secured frame of supervision. The goal is slowly to build a picture of the supervisory framework as *unconsciously validated by supervisees*, and, indirectly at times, by their patients, and to develop a full appreciation for the functions and power of that frame. This exposition will serve the needs of supervisors and supervisees alike — for the supervisors, it spells out their responsibilities; for the supervisees, their rightful expectations and what they should in principle accept as the best conditions for their education and growth.

I will begin by identifying what are potentially the most stable aspects of the supervisory frame — the fixed attributes that can stand as relatively unchanging aspects of the conditions of supervision. In doing so, it should be borne in mind that the supervisor has the primary mandate for managing the frame, but the supervisee also has a responsibility to accept and adhere to the secured frame and to monitor the supervisor's interventions in this basic area — and to intervene if possible if a frame is altered because the situation usually is of crisis proportions.

THE FIXED COMPONENTS

The *fixed frame of supervision*, as it is called, optimally includes the following principles and components:

1. *The setting for supervision should be the private office of the supervisor and should be maintained as such for the life of the supervision*

In this respect, the supervisory frame is similar to the psychotherapy frame. It is clear that private supervision should take place in the supervisor's office, but what of the supervision of a trainee, an employee of a clinic or hospital — is the ideal setting in the institution or in the supervisor's private office?

This is an example of a class of situations in which *there is a basically frame-deviant element inherent to the conditions of the supervision*, and thus a choice must be made as to *the least deviant arrangement* available under existing conditions. There is in these cases a compromise with the ideal frame whichever way the supervisor turns. As for the dilemma of the student in a training setting, an argument can be made that the supervisee should be seen within the setting in which he or she works — that this choice respects the overall conditions of the supervision. This proposal, which is frame-deviant in that it is a departure from the ideal of using the supervisor's private office, must, however, be safeguarded by using the *supervisor's office* and not the supervisee's (which would be a further frame modification — *the office for supervision should be that of the mentor* and not of the student), and by assuring maximum privacy and confidentiality (again, as much as conditions permit) and using *the same office for all of the supervisory sessions*.

Nevertheless, this particular choice of locale almost always involves some loss of confidentiality and privacy — the supervisee is likely to be seen entering the supervisor's office by a variety of other people. In addition, there is a great likelihood of inadequate sound-proofing, in that clinics and other teaching settings generally do not attend to such matters as sound-proofed offices. Indeed, these settings typically are beset with many unnecessary frame alterations — for example, supervisory conversations held in hallways and other places outside the supervisor's office, records that are available to third parties, and so forth. The net result is that supervision held under these conditions is secured by keeping the work within its appropriate teaching context, but deviant because of the many contaminants inherent to these conditions.

These departures from the ideal frame have extensive, unconsciously transmitted consequences. Despite the possible inconvenience, then, it seems that under these circumstances, the use of the private office of the supervisor will in most cases be the better choice. That particular setting can be properly managed to ensure an otherwise ideal frame for the supervisory experience by affording the supervisee both privacy and confidentiality — and more (see below).

In principle, *the setting for supervision should be established and sustained for the entire span of the supervisory work. The office should be sound-proofed and private, without third-party access.* A supervisor must try to avoid common and usually unnecessary departures from the ideal setting, such as the use of excessively deviant spaces like a relatively open institute classroom, a colleague's office, and, especially, the supervisee's office or a supervisor's apartment, home, or home–office.

Any mixture of home/personal life and professional space, no matter how well the office is set off from the living space, is strongly frame-deviant. Settings of this kind violate the necessary privacy of the supervisory situation and expose the supervisee to family members and others; they also modify the relative anonymity of the supervisor. In addition, the lack of a clear professional setting is self-contradictory in that supervision is a professional activity that is belied by a social context.

This type of arrangement often sets the stage for other frame deviations, such as contacts between the supervisor and supervisee outside supervision and engagement in a social relationship as well. It is well to realize, then, that supervisees tend to react to this group of frame modifications by defensively and automatically looking away from them consciously, and by ignoring the devastating derivative perceptions they inevitably produce in reaction to these fixed-frame deviations. Incidents like a major run-in with a family member "somehow" almost never get mentioned in a supervisory hour, and the encoded imagery, if it does materialize, is exceedingly difficult to trigger-decode — especially when the trigger is deeply repressed by both student and teacher. All the while, these frame alterations are having profound but *sub rosa* effects on both members of the supervisory dyad.

The standard model of supervision provides no consistent or established means of accessing the dynamics of these issues and their unconscious ramifications. Serious inputs go unrecognized and are played out without awareness interceding in either party to the supervision. While a communicative supervisor would be aware of the deviant aspects of these situations, he or she also would have little means to explore the specific ramifications of such frame-altered interludes — only self-processing supervision is designed to do such work (see chapter fourteen).

The rule of a fixed private setting for supervision implies that *the contact between a supervisor and supervisee should be confined to the supervisor's private office — and to the agreed-upon time for the sessions.* This ground rule is honoured, however, more through violation than adherence. Contacts between a supervisor and a supervisee outside the supervisor's private office abound — most often they occur at professional meetings and parties, and in social settings. To the conscious system these contacts seem innocuous and even inviting, but the attraction is unconsciously motivated by pathological frame-deviant needs that will make these frame alterations costly in the long run.

The supervisee's (and supervisor's) second unconscious-system processes all of these contacts outside the supervisor's office as frame-deviant and recognizes that they are seductive and assaultive experiences — as they are even consciously at times. The ideal ground rules of supervision are limiting and constraining, so we need to remember that they also are remarkably health-giving and growth-promoting as well.

A supervisory vignette

Dr. Packard contacted Dr. Tyler, his former teacher at a psychotherapy training program, for private supervision. They reviewed possible hours and found that they could not find a suitable time to meet. Dr. Packard knew that Dr. Tyler lived near his home and suggested a Saturday morning supervisory hour at his teacher's residence; Dr. Tyler agreed.

The supervision was carried out in Dr. Tyler's living-room. Family members kept out of sight, although on the occasion of the first supervisory session, the supervisor did introduce his supervisee to his wife, who was with him in the kitchen when the student first arrived.

Once in the living-room, Dr. Packard introduced the case he had prepared to present. But he quickly interrupted himself to ask Dr. Tyler if he could mention a problem that had come up the day before, even though he hadn't planned on discussing it. Dr. Tyler said that of course he could, and the supervisee then told his story.

It seemed that Dr. Packard was seeing a young woman whom he had met at a dinner party and who had called him for therapy. A bit uncertain about what to do, but very much in need of patients, he had agreed to see her. The patient was a rather attractive woman, and the problem was that she has been having open sexual fantasies about dating and sleeping with Dr. Packard, and he was having trouble handling the material because he found her appealing too. He tried explaining to her that maybe their outside contact was making therapy impossible, but she simply disagreed and insisted on continuing to work with him.

The worst of it was that she didn't seem to accept his interpretations and recently had begun to threaten suicide. She seemed confused about the nature of their relationship and was unable to grasp that it was no longer social, but entirely professional. She even called him at home one night and spoke to his wife because he was out at the time. He wondered what he should do to set things straight. His inclination was to terminate with her.

A supervisor working from the standard model of supervision would answer this supervisee's question in one of several ways depending on his attitudes towards rules, frames, and boundaries. Some mentors would see the contaminated relationship as precluding therapy and would suggest a referral to another therapist. Some might even suggest themselves as the recipient of this transfer, thereby simultaneously securing one frame and modifying another — ideally, *supervising a case precludes a supervisor from treating the supervised patient.* Other supervisors would recommend that Dr. Packard continue to see the patient and work through her fantasies and seemingly "intractable transference reactions". His patient would be seen as borderline and unable to sustain the so-called transference illusion — and in need of help to do so. Still other standard model supervisors would trivialize the contamination as inconsequential and simply recommend that Dr. Packard continue to interpret the transference until the problem was resolved.

A supervisor using the communicative model of supervision would be in a quandary. He or she would recognize that the contaminated frame described by this supervisee — Dr. Packard's prior social contact with his patient — is the trigger for the patient's deviant behaviours and sense of confusion. Therapists' frame modifications beget frame modifications from their patients and also disturb their sense and grasp of reality (unconsciously, the unanswerable question persists — is the therapist really a therapist or is he or she a friend, or both, or what?). *In the conscious system, for a patient a person can be both therapist and friend, but in the deep unconscious system, once a friend, never a therapist. Unrectifiable frame alterations* of this type preclude effective therapy and call for work directed specifically towards the constructive termination of the therapy *based on the patient's derivative material* as it directs the therapist towards both this ultimate frame-securing measure and trigger-decoded insights.

However, had a communicative supervisor agreed to work in this type of supervisory setting — and doing so runs counter to communicative principles — he or she might well recognize that the supervisee's story about his contaminated relationship with his patient encodes a series of unconscious perceptions of his supervisor in light of the supervisory frame that he had created. Dr. Packard's tale of woe encodes his woeful perceptions of his supervisor in light of the frame-deviant conditions of the supervision.

While a communicative supervisor might eventually answer this supervisee's question about his patient directly, the first order of business certainly would be to *trigger-decode this narrative* in order to identify the supervisee's unconscious adaptive processing of the supervisory frame — especially the setting and the more benign but still deviant prior contact between the supervisor and supervisee. It would be essential to both interpret these unconscious perceptions and suitably rectify the contaminated frame as much as possible. The recommendation about terminating with the patient has its parallel in the *ideal* recommendation about the supervision — as demanding as this may seem, it is nevertheless the optimal choice. However, moving the supervision to the supervisor's professional office, if it is a private and uncontaminated setting, might secure the supervisory frame sufficiently to allow effective supervisory work to follow. However, some continuing deep effects of this initial frame break and of their prior relationship would continue to play themselves out for a long while.

To clarify these comments, let us first note that *under deviant fixed-frame conditions, a supervisee will always encode his or her unconscious responses to the frame modification. Doing so reflects a psychobiological adaptive function* — acute frame breaks universally evoke unconscious perceptions and processing, and encoded reactions, in their recipients. Thus, a supervisor needs to be on the alert for encoded narratives under such circumstances. Conversely, *when a supervisee chooses to tell a coincidental story, a search should be made for the repressed (usually frame-deviant) trigger that has prompted the encoded narrative communication.*

Under these circumstances, the supervisor must be prepared to depart from the primary cognitive teaching task in order to explore and interpret the supervisee's unconscious communications and rectify the altered frame to the greatest extent possible. To ignore these tasks under these conditions is to allow an insidious unconscious process to do damage to the supervisee and his or her ability to learn and become an effective psychotherapist.

The supervisee will find the means to communicate in disguised form his or her unconscious experience of an altered frame, usually by one of two means, or by both. The first is through *the case material selected for presentation*, while the second and more compelling vehicle involves the telling of *a coincidental or marginally related story* — a narrative other than the prepared case material.

In principle, the central responsibility of the supervisee is to present a chosen case for supervision. As we will see, the selection of a patient for presentation to a supervisor is under strong unconscious influence from the actual and/or anticipated frame of the supervision. That is, the case will be selected for both *conscious reasons* (e.g. that he or she is a difficult or interesting patient) and *unconscious reasons* (e.g. that the patient admirably communicates material or is involved in a frame situation that will allow the supervisee to express in encoded fashion his or her own unconscious experience of the conditions of the supervision).

Every narrative told by a supervisee (and supervisor) that departs from the case that is being presented should be recognized as an encoded out-of-context or marginally related story. These tales always convey unconscious messages in response to frame-related triggers created by the supervisor — or, more rarely, the supervisee. It is, of course, with this mode of unconscious communication that, unconsciously, Dr. Packard chose to express himself in this instance.

Before trigger decoding his narrative, let us examine Dr. Packard's *conscious* appraisal of the supervisory framework and setting. His conscious feeling was that he wanted to work with Dr. Tyler because he admired his teaching abilities and wished to benefit from further work with him — the frame-deviant aspect, which is small yet notable (see below), never occurred to him. In addition, he felt that Saturday mornings were not too inconvenient. There even was an advantage to having supervision on that day — it kept his weekday work hours free to see patients. Consciously, then, Dr. Packard was contented with his choice of supervisor, who had advocated the proposed arrangement, and he gave it his full support. He also enjoyed meeting Dr. Tyson's wife, which he took as a sign of acceptance by his mentor.

What then was Dr. Packard's *deep unconscious* response to this same set of triggers? While his conscious mind was focused on the convenience and congeniality of the situation, without a thought of the frame, the focus of his second unconscious system is revealed in his exquisitely wrought two-tiered story about his woman patient. The narrative is a lovely communicative condensation and compromise formation in that it does, of course, tell a consciously intended tale of a therapeutic dilemma, but it also tells an unconsciously intended tale as well — the story of the supervisee's experience of and adaptive responses to the supervisory frame.

We must engage in *trigger decoding* to capture this second level of experience and meaning — there is no other avenue of access. The key stimuli here are the prior teaching contact, the home setting for the supervision, and Dr. Tyson's introduction of his wife to his student. These triggers are well represented through *encoded bridging images*: the prior teaching contact is disguised as the prior-to-therapy (outside of the frame) social meeting; the supervisory setting is disguised in the allusion to the dinner party (having contact outside a professional office); and the introduction of the supervisor's wife to the supervisee is encoded in the reference to the patient's talk with the supervisee's wife. There is as well the theme of a mixed relationship, one that is both social and professional, which alludes to doing supervision in the supervisor's home. In all, we have strong and clear bridging themes that give reason to argue that the story about the deviant therapy encodes the story about the deviant supervision.

What, then, are the *personally selected, valid unconscious perceptions* of this supervisory frame that Dr. Packard is conveying through his clinical story? Dr. Packard certainly had no awareness that this case material unconsciously pertained to the setting in which he found himself at the moment — a problem had popped into his mind and he had thought it worth pursuing, nothing more. Our job is to bring his unconscious experience into awareness through trigger decoding. This requires that we *lift or extract the themes from the manifest situation or context to which they directly allude and transpose or link them to the repressed contexts* — the prior contact, meeting the supervisor's wife, and seeing him in his home. Once we do so, *we can use the resultant images to create a new, unconsciously wrought narrative that begins with the repressed meanings of the frame-related triggers and delineates the student's perceptions of the implications of those triggers and his deeply unconscious adaptive responses to it as well.*

The story — Dr. Packard's *unconscious* tale of adaptation — roughly transposes as follow:

"You, Dr. Tyler, have agreed to see me in supervision even though we worked together in a different setting, something that confuses me in regard to the nature of our relationship. You also have agreed to see me professionally in your home, and you have introduced me to your wife. Unconsciously, I feel that you are creating a mixed relationship with me, one that is both social and professional — and I'm not sure which is the stronger. In fact, I'm quite confused about the actual nature of our relationship — is it social or professional? I feel that you're being quite seductive with me and, frankly, I'm attracted to you as well. I'm having difficulty in taking in your supervisory interventions because of the confusion I am experiencing as to how we are to relate — whether it is to be intellectually or sexually. I think the solution to this problems is that we should not be seeing each other at all — the situation is too sexually charged and unstable; mixing social and professional relatedness just doesn't work."

As you can see, the clinical narrative contained not only valid encoded perceptions of the unconscious meanings of this frame-deviant situation, but also a *model of rectification* — a corrective or adaptive solution, namely, that the supervision should be terminated. While this certainly is the ideal resolution to these contaminations, clinical experience has shown that for most supervisees, prior contact between a supervisor and supervisee need not preclude further supervisory work together even though the frame-alteration is unrectifiable. Because the contact was professional (and we assume that it was well managed), the deviant aspects are minimal — though real. Still, this is an extremely common source of supervisory talent, and while its deviant aspects may need processing in the supervision, they need not derail the teaching/learning experience (see below).

As we can see, the adaptive preferences of the second unconscious system are far different from those of the conscious system, which simply accepted this deviant frame without notice and took it as a matter of course. We can see too that the supervisory frame that Dr. Tyler created on the basis of his student's request and manifest-content/implications listening and formulating is very different from the one he would have fashioned through trigger decoding the messages from his supervisee's (or his own) second unconscious system. And you can be certain that the supervisory work goes far better in the secured-frame setting as compared to deviant-frame conditions.

One final point. Unconsciously, Dr. Packard had selected Dr. Tyler as his supervisor because of the inherently frame-deviant aspects of their working together — a need reflected too in his proposal of a deviant-frame setting for the supervision. These choices unconsciously were largely motivated by Dr. Packard's need to assuage his own unconscious guilt for the many frame modifications in which he himself had engaged — as a therapist and in his daily life — including a recent, messy affair with a married woman.

Unconscious guilt is a source of many frame-deviant and other *unconscious supervisory misalliances*. Supervisees often unwittingly seek out unconsciously harmful supervisors who are known to be lax and deviant with their frames in order to obtain unconscious sanction for their own frame-altering and often corrupt ways. Both supervisors and supervisees should be wary of basically frame-deviant supervisory contracts and of their inevitable inclinations to modify the fixed frames of supervision — and therapy.

2. *The time of supervision should be fixed, as should the length of the supervisory session and its frequency*

When establishing the *supervisory contract*, the supervisor should offer a specified forty-five- or fifty-minute session, and a time should be agreed upon and remain fixed throughout the supervisory experience. Much the same applies to the frequency of the meetings — ideally, they should be once weekly.

In respect to this last point, many supervisors will, under some circumstances, offer to hold supervision bi-weekly or even monthly. These arrangements should be understood to be frame deviant because the supervisor's setting aside time for the supervisee and meeting less often than weekly implies one of two likely possibilities — either someone else is present in the supervisor's office during the supervisee's time, or the supervisor is sacrificing income by seeing no one during the alternate hours.

As is true of therapy, *the supervisor should lease his or her hour to the supervisee* and the time should be set aside for the supervisory work. Missed hours are the responsibility of the supervisee unless, of course, the supervisor does the cancelling. In this regard, the latter should maintain a sense of his or her responsibility to be available for all scheduled sessions and should not cancel a supervisory session for anything but emergency reasons. Similarly, the ideal frame does not allow for changes in the time of the supervisory sessions, for make-up supervisory sessions, or for shortening or lengthening the duration of the teaching hour.

A set, sound-proofed place, and a set time, frequency, and duration of sessions — these are some of the essential elements of the physical and psychological fixed frame. They are easily overlooked as sources of impact and meaning, but their management has major consequences for all concerned.

Contrasting supervisory examples

Ms. Abel, a social work student, was in supervision with Mrs. Frank. The supervisor had had to attend a meeting of agency supervisors and therefore changed the time of the supervision. However, Ms. Abel missed the session because she forgot about the change. In her next regular meeting with her supervisor, she apologized profusely. She then asked if she could present a fresh case, and Mrs. Frank said that her doing so would be fine.

The patient was one with whom Ms. Abel had changed the time of a session because she, as a student-therapist, was obliged to be at school for a meeting. In the changed hour, the patient reported a dream in which she is locked out of her apartment. One association to the dream involved a time when the patient was to meet her boyfriend at his apartment but when she arrived, he wasn't there. It turned out that he was elsewhere with another woman. The patient was furious with him for deserting her and stopped seeing him — she could no longer trust him.

Here again the supervisee's selection of case material, however much constrained by reality, speaks for both the supervised patient and the supervisee. The patient's dream and association encodes her deep unconscious reaction to her therapist's request to change the time of her session and serves as well to convey the supervisee's unconscious response to a comparable trigger in her supervision. In both situations, the second unconscious system was conveying the following adaptive message: "Your change in my hour was experienced unconsciously as an abandonment and a turning to another lover. I can no longer trust you and should quit the therapy/ supervision (the corrective)." The frame insensitivities of training psychotherapy programmes cause considerable damage to many people — notably supervisees, their patients, and their supervisors.

While you may think that the adaptive solution proposed by the patient's and student's deep unconscious systems is extreme, it is well to realize that we have touched on but one of many frame deviations in both situations — both settings were frame-altered in many ways. But you will notice too that neither the patient nor the supervisee followed the adaptive advice of their second unconscious systems: neither quit their respective situations. This fact shows again that *deep unconscious processing does not lead to conscious adaptive responses* — essentially it is without awareness or behavioural influence (unless trigger decoding is brought into play).

On the other hand, staying in frame-damaged situations is unconsciously motivated in patients and supervisees by needs derived from the fear/guilt subsystem of the deep unconscious part of the mind. Doing so gratifies unconscious wishes to deny personal mortality (the frame-breaker is an exception to all manner of rules, including the one that states that life is framed by death) and to justify their own frame-deviant ways. Frame-altered settings and behaviours created by others assuage the unconscious guilt they feel for frame breaks that they themselves have engaged in, and also offer hurts and punishments for these transgressions. Frame alterations create deviant vicious cycles that go in circles from a supervisor to a supervisee's work with his or her patients and back to the supervisor, without end. They also are the basis for supervisory misalliances between teachers and their students whose pathological aspects go unrecognized unless the means is found to engage in trigger decoding narrative material evoked in response to a particular frame alteration. In the present situation, the supervisor's frame break became an unconscious model for the supervisee, who then acted out this identification by breaking the frame herself — and for a frivolous reason in that her presence was not required at the meeting at school. Again and again, frame-breaking actions beget frame-breaking actions — let the frame-breaker beware.

To turn to a different kind of example, Mrs. Ball, a psychology intern, was in supervision with Dr. Dunn, a woman psychologist. At one point in their work together, Mrs. Ball asked if the time of the supervision could be changed. She explained that she had very little library time and could get a ride to school the morning of the supervision and spend that time doing her article searches and readings. Dr. Dunn responded by proposing that they go on with their work as planned in order to give her time to see what comes up and to think about the request.

In the course of presenting her process-note case material, which involved a patient's complaint about a doctor who kept her waiting for two hours, Mrs. Ball interrupted her presentation to complain about Dr. Ayres, one of her teachers at the hospital where she was interning. "You know", she said, "I think you really ought to talk to Dr. Ayres for us. He keeps missing classes and rearranging their scheduled times. He's driving us crazy and nothing we've said to him has changed what he's doing."

Dr. Dunn took this out-of-context narrative as a story created by the conjoint efforts of her supervisee's conscious and deep unconscious systems. The *surface (conscious) trigger* was, of course, the irresponsible, frame-breaking instructor; the *latent and repressed, unconscious trigger* was what is termed an *anticipated trigger* — the expectation that Dr. Dunn would, as requested, change the time of the supervision. Whenever a supervisee requests a frame modification or a supervisor announces one for the future, the second unconscious system will work over the proposed deviation and encode its adaptive processing of the planned intervention. Something comparable occurs, of course, when a frame-securing intervention is sought out or otherwise anticipated as well.

Mrs. Ball's *marginally related story* encodes the following adaptive scenario: "If you change the time of my supervision you will, like Dr. Ayres, be irresponsibly messing up our schedule in a way that will drive me crazy; talk to yourself and don't let yourself do it [the frame-maintaining corrective]".

In the supervision, Dr. Dunn offered exactly that interpretation to her student and indicated that she would hold fast to the agreed-upon time for the supervision. Mrs. Ball responded almost without thinking, "You know", she said, "come to think of it, you don't have to say anything to Dr. Ayres. Dr. Field already has promised to take care of the situation. Dr. Field is really very sharp; everyone respects and listens to her — she knows what she's doing. I'm sure she'll set things straight."

This fresh *out-of-context story* encodes the *unconscious validation* of Dr. Dunn's secured-frame-maintenance intervention through a displaced allusion to someone who is in command and functions well and with respect — an example of *interpersonal validation*.

With that said, Mrs. Ball commented that it was stuffy in Dr. Dunn's office, she could hardly breathe; she then went on with the material in her prepared notes. This last remark is a reflection of Mrs. Ball's secured-frame, entrapment anxieties, mobilized by her supervisor's frame-holding intervention; her anxious response would need watching and dealing with if need be. Still, this is the typical reaction to a sound frame-securing intervention by a supervisor — encoded validation followed by some expression of secured-frame anxieties. Such are the ways of human nature.

3. *A single set fee to be paid at the beginning of each month for the previous month's supervisory sessions, with full responsibility by the supervisee for all sessions for which the supervisor is available — and the supervisor's firm commitment to hold sessions as initially agreed upon*

The fee structure of supervision should be comparable to that of psychotherapy, with the hour set aside for the supervisee and his or her acceptance of full responsibility for the time. It is common practice to create a supervisory frame that is loosely constructed with changes in the time of the session, extensions of the time when there is a therapeutic crisis, and the waiver of the fee when a supervisee misses a session because of another commitment — as when a supervisee takes a vacation that does not correspond to time off by the supervisor.

All such frame alterations are a disservice to the supervisee — and the supervisor. With supervisors who are using the standard model of supervision, these frame modifications further support the supervisee's deviant-frame inclinations. And with supervisors working from the communicative model of supervision, deviations of this kind generate disruptive mixed messages — a basically frame-securing teaching approach coupled with frame alterations with respect to the supervisory frame. This contradictory mixture confuses the supervisee and undermines his or her efforts to deal with personal secured-frame anxieties and to develop the skills of sound frame management in doing psychotherapy.

In stating his or her fee, the supervisor should propose a single, fair fee in keeping with his or her expertise — and within limits, the supervisee's ability to pay for supervision. The fee should be neither too low nor too excessive, nor should there be fee negotiations or a fee that is set with the idea that it will be increased later when the supervisee can afford to pay more. The many conscious and unconscious implications of deviations and manipulations in the highly sensitive area of payment for services render these kinds of frame-deviant manoeuvres quite harmful to both parties to a supervision.

As for the supervisor's vacations, the rules are that they should be announced well in advance and taken judiciously (at most, one or two weeks during the working months and three to five weeks during the summer). Interruptions should occur in the form of well-separated segments of time, and they should not be compensated for through make-up sessions.

A *vacation* is a frame interruption and therefore a frame break (the supervisee's *unconscious* expectation is that supervision will be continuous until he or she has completed his or her learning experience to a point of sufficient expertise and skill). But the failure of a supervisor to take vacations also is frame-deviant in that it creates an unbearable and unfair frame (the ideal frame requires periods of separation and the supervisee is entitled to have the opportunity to take a vacation without penalty — he or she must pay for time away when the supervisor is not on vacation). In all, then, a supervisor's prop-

erly announced vacation is a mixed intervention frame-wise —
it modifies the frame in one sense and secures it in another.
Overall, however, primarily it is a secured-frame intervention.

Another supervisory vignette

Dr. Postal was a psychiatrist who had recently completed
his residency and had called Dr. Clark, one of his
supervisors from the training program, to arrange for
private supervision. Dr. Clark offered to see him in his
office at the hospital, and Dr. Postal agreed because he
would be working there for much of the week.

At that initial session, Dr. Clark raised the fee issue by
asking Dr. Postal what he thought he could afford for his
supervision. The supervisee replied that his income came
from two private patients and his low-paying job at the
hospital, and that it might sound ridiculous, but twenty-
five dollars a week was all that he felt he could pay. Dr.
Clark responded by saying that his usual fee per hour for
a patient was one-hundred-twenty-five dollars and that he
generally saw supervisees for one-hundred dollars a
session.

When Dr. Postal's face dropped and he whispered that a
fee like that was out of his league, Dr. Clark asked just
how much higher he thought he could go. Dr. Postal then
said that forty dollars a session was a stretch, but he
might be able to do it. Dr. Clark then asked him if he
could handle fifty dollars a session, indicating that he
could see his way clear to working for that fee for now —
with the understanding that the fee would be increased as
Dr. Postal's practice grew. Relieved, Dr. Postal said he'd
try it for a while and see how it went; it would be a real
problem, but maybe he could handle it.

We will by-pass the remainder of this first supervisory
session and shift to the following one, which Dr. Postal
began with a shy look and by saying that he had had a
dream of Dr. Clark the night after their first meeting and
wondered if it would be alright if he told it to him. Dr.

Clark said that supervision really wasn't about supervisees' dreams, but if he needed to, sure, he could go ahead and tell him the dream.

"I dreamt", Dr. Postal began, "I dreamt that we were both part of Robin Hood's band. We were talking and you were telling me about some of the robberies you had committed before I joined the group. The other men in the camp could hear what we were saying and they began to laugh; I was furious with them. We all left camp and waylaid a traveller. When he realized we were about to rob him, he pleaded with us to spare his life and leave him some money. Ignoring his pleas, we took all of his money and goods. I felt he deserved to pay his dues, but I didn't like taking the money from him and being a criminal — we should have made him give the money to charity. It was then that I realized that we were all screwed up — we were in the wrong forest and needed to find our camp. I was cut off from the others and felt lost. I woke up quite frightened."

Working from his version of the standard model of supervision, Dr. Clark suggested that some rather hostile negative supervisory transferences had developed after their first session. He indicated that Dr. Postal should take them up with his therapist in his own therapy — all they could do in supervision was to make note of the dream and move on to the case material that the supervisee wanted to present.

In discussing this vignette from the vantage point of the communicative model of supervision, we may first note that there is a lot that is deviant and a reflection of poor supervisory practice in this situation. For one thing, *a manifest dream about a supervisor usually is a sign of a major frame break in the supervision* — one that has caused a breakdown in the supervisee's usual capacity to disguise and encode. The dream speaks for a likely supervisory crisis whose nature would need to be discovered.

Given the implied call for help regarding the supervision itself, it seems best for the supervisor to ask the supervisee to briefly associate to this kind of dream. The most compelling themes to emerge should then be transposed or linked to the active frame-related triggers in the supervisory situation. Without some measure of trigger decoding, an unconscious disturbance is left to fester, and the work with the dream in the supervisee's own therapy will in general not resolve the supervisory issues.

This type of dream conveys unconscious messages about both the supervision and the personal therapy of the supervisee. In the therapy, the active meanings will pertain to the therapist's frame-related interventions (this particular dream indicates that they are frame-deviant) and not to the supervisory situation; in the supervision, the reverse is true. In a sense, there are two danger situations, and each has to be dealt with on its own turf.

In the actual situation we are looking at, we have only the manifest dream to trigger-decode. To do so, we need to list the triggers in the supervisory situation that Dr. Postal was being called on to adapt to. To start with the *conscious triggers*, they include the beginning of the supervision — a vague and general conscious-system stimulus that evokes a series of broad and global responses. The fee also concerned Dr. Postal consciously in that he felt that it would deplete his meagre earnings; nevertheless, he saw the necessity of paying a decent fee. This was the limited extent of his conscious thoughts.

To pursue the deep unconscious system response, we must first extend our list of triggers to include the stimuli that Dr. Postal repressed in their entirety or the implications of consciously registered triggers that are exceedingly anxiety-provoking and therefore barred from awareness. This means that *both entire triggers and the most disturbing implications of known triggers are dealt with by the second unconscious system.* Here, then, with respect to the consciously recognized fee issue, the *repressed implication triggers (aspects of the stimulus whose ramifications went unregistered consciously)* include Dr. Clark's allusions to the fee he charges his patients and to his usual supervisory fee, his bargaining with the supervisee regarding the fee that was finally set, and his indicating that at some future date the fee would be increased. Each of these aspects of his fee setting was totally ignored by the conscious systems of both parties to these negotiations, even though we can be certain that their second unconscious systems were zeroed in on and processing these frame impingements with great intensity.

The supervisor's prior contact with the supervisee in the training program and the decision to hold the supervision in the supervisor's office at the hospital instead of his private office are additional, unmentioned (entirely repressed) frame deviations in the supervision. Typically, these frame alterations evoke a split response from the two systems of the mind — conscious-system acceptance coupled with *deep unconscious system* protests against the hurtful frame-deviant aspects of the decision (see below).

On the supervisee's side, his choice of a supervisor with whom he had had prior contact and accepting the deviant setting and participating in the fee negotiations were frame-altering actions. The same applies to telling a personal dream to a supervisor in a setting whose ground rules do not allow for doing so. The role requirements of the supervisee specify a restriction of his or her communications to the presentation of process-note case material and reactions to the supervisor's teaching efforts. The report of the dream therefore modifies the frame, yet, as noted, the deviation may be necessary because the dream report signals a supervisory crisis. Each of the two alternatives available to the supervisor is problematic. Keeping the frame secured by precluding the report of the dream allows the crisis to simmer, while allowing the frame-deviant dream to be told is likely to facilitate interpretive and frame-securing efforts, and lead to the resolution of the crisis.

Although it is always best in principle to maintain the frame, there is sufficient argument to justify an exception with respect to a dream that a supervisee wishes to report because it usually reflects an unconscious effort to repair a defect in the existing supervisory frame. This decision involves one of those relatively rare moments when the frame is altered in order to enhance its security — here, because of a probable supervisory crisis (see chapter twelve). Thus, the proposal by a supervisee to report a dream should alert the supervisor to the likelihood of a major deviant-frame issue. At the very least, working over the dream and a few guided associations to its elements can facilitate the identification of the critical trigger that has prompted the supervisee to alter the framework of his presentation responsibilities; the material is likely unconsciously to orchestrate the frame-reparative process (Langs, 1982).

The standard supervisory situations are not structured to deal extensively with the supervisee's encoded material, and, in general, it is difficult to modify the supervisory process to do so because it entails spending much of the hour with the dream and the supervisee's much-needed guided associations to it. As a result, it is unlikely that there will be sufficient time to deal with all of the process notes from the session in need of supervision — the secured-frame task. Still, the need to resolve a supervisory crisis must take precedence over all other adaptive tasks, and the presentation of case material may have to be limited or postponed until the following supervisory session. These issues touch on the limitations and constraints of the standard supervisory models and suggest a need for their modification (see chapters thirteen and fourteen).

Returning to the vignette, we may now take advantage of Dr. Postal's dream and see what we can learn of his deep unconscious response to the repressed triggers — the deviant prior contact between the supervisor and supervisee, the modified setting for the supervision, the self-revelations by the supervisor, and the bargaining over the fee. To trigger-decode the themes of this dream, we should begin again with *bridging themes* that reflect in disguised form the nature or identity of the stimulus; this is a useful way of establishing the link between the encoded images and their triggers. Being together in *Robin Hood's band* encodes their prior contact in the *residency training program,* while the allusions to the supervisor's *previous robberies* disguises his *self-revelations about his fees for patients and other supervisees;* being in the *wrong forest* encodes being seen for supervision in the *wrong office;* and the *robbery victim's bargaining over money* encodes the *supervisor's bargaining over Dr. Clark's fee.* (Recall that the decoding must first be stated as decoded unconscious perceptions of the supervisor and then as self-perceptions of the supervisee.)

The encoded adaptive narrative indicates that Dr. Postal unconsciously perceived his supervisor's selection of the hospital office as a mistake — placing them in the wrong forest or space — and as unduly exposing him to others (the men who could hear what was being said — the office was not sound-proofed and others could see the supervisee come and go). Adaptively, Dr. Postal's second unconscious system suggested the form that rectification must take — they should move to the right office (forest) to go properly about their business. The deep unconscious system consistently offers relatively ideal adaptive solutions; usually they are the very opposite of what the conscious system is inclined to do, but they are, as a rule, the most healthy and the least costly alternatives available.

As for the fee, Dr. Postal unconsciously experienced the way the fee grew larger and larger as an assault and robbery — he felt exploited. The prospect of eventually increasing the fee added to these perceptions. However, this last frame modification falls into a special class of frame alterations — those that actually secure an existing frame deviation. Thus, the reduced fee is a frame modification, and a suitable increase would secure the proper frame; nevertheless, the increase itself is a frame break in that the ideal frame includes an appropriate fee for the supervisor from the outset of supervision. In general, however, *any frame modification that permanently secures the frame of supervision is an advisable intervention to make.*

In this situation, moving to Dr. Clark's private office would modify the tenet of a single office for the entire super-vision and would also entail a change in the time of the session, but it would secure an important aspect of the frame — a setting constituted as the supervisor's private, unshared, sound-proofed office. Such are the wise and complex frame-related directives of the second unconscious system.

THE SELECTION OF A SUPERVISOR

The vignettes in the present chapter have raised the important frame issue of whom a potential supervisee should ideally engage as a supervisor. It has been necessary to allow the clinical material to point the way in this regard because not only is the subject relatively neglected, but also, in actual practice, the choice is almost always frame-deviant — and therefore generally ignored by the conscious system. Thus, the ideal preference should be for someone with whom the supervisee has had no prior contact; nor should he or she know anyone who has been in either therapy or supervision with the teacher. If we understand these contaminants to include reading the written work of the supervisor or hearing him or her speak at a professional meeting, we can readily appreciate how difficult it is to meet these ideal conditions of supervision.

Given the problems inherent in a search for a truly anonymous and uncontaminated supervisor, *a supervisee can only opt for the best possible available selection and be prepared to explore at some juncture the frame-altered aspects of his or her choice.* In general, then, it seems best for a supervisee to engage a supervisor with whom there has been no prior therapeutic or social contact, and with whom the prior professional interaction has been relatively frame-secured. Previous professional contact with the supervisor that has been well managed and relatively frame-secured (e.g. not especially self-revealing, preferably on a one-to-one basis, and without spill-over into social settings) or contact that has involved only professional presentations, papers, and/or books are likely to prove workable. However, a supervisor who has treated a family member or a close class-mate or colleague of the potential supervisee is best avoided.

In principle, any strikingly prior frame-modified relationship should preclude a supervisory association. Furthermore, because more workable contaminations are so easily overlooked by the conscious system, both the supervisor and the supervisee should be on the alert for indications that the frame-deviant aspects of their contact are causing some degree of disturbance — signs that the situation requires a measure of self-processing (see chapters twelve and fourteen). Finally, while these guidelines have been offered primarily for supervisees, supervisors should also be mindful of these tenets and refrain from accepting into supervision anyone with whom prior frame modifications are likely to disturb the supervisory work.

CONCLUDING COMMENTS

In all, then, I have introduced a number of critical and rather neglected aspects of supervision that must be dealt with in every supervisory situation. For supervisors, I have offered guidelines to the ideal relatively fixed aspects of the secured frame that he or she should offer to supervisees. For the student, I have described this frame as a guide to the process of selecting a supervisor and to his or her own responsibilities to adhere to the ground rules of supervision — and as a yardstick against which he or she can measure a supervisor's efforts in this realm.

As we will see, supervisory frame deviations should be interpreted when feasible, and certainly rectified if the supervision and supervisee are to flourish. These efforts may, at times, have to be initiated by a supervisee when his or her supervisor fails to see their necessity. These issues and their solutions will become increasingly clear as we extend our study of the framework of supervision in the next chapter.

CHAPTER SIX

Privacy and confidentiality

There are hosts of additional ground rules and boundaries that need to be established and maintained for an ideal supervisory experience. Among the most salient of these tenets, those related to the *privacy and confidentiality* of the supervision and to the *relative anonymity and neutrality* of the supervisor — and to some extent, the supervisee — are most vital.

As we approach these issues, let us be reminded again that without a sharp focus on rules, frames, and boundaries, these necessities escape notice on both sides of the supervisory equation. But unnoticed frame modifications have countless unnoticed but real consequences that extend from the supervisee's (and supervisor's) professional life into his or her daily living — unconsciously driven needs and defences are not left behind in a supervisor's office. Both supervisors and supervisees have a distinctive responsibility to safeguard the framework of their supervisory work together.

A look at today's practices of psychotherapy show an endless flow of frame modifications as they relate to the pivotal areas of privacy, confidentiality, and relative neutrality and anonymity. Disregard for these four dimensions of the secured frame in psychotherapy and supervision is rampant and on the increase each day — witness clinic records, insurance reports, governmental intrusions, the offer by therapists of personal opinions and directives, the use of home–office settings, and so forth. Given that approaches to supervision tend universally to be even more undisciplined than those towards therapy, we are dealing with aspects of the supervisory experience that are in need of major reconsideration and change.

Realistically, we must acknowledge that this desperately needed reformation will be extremely difficult to accomplish. There is a strong trend in psychotherapy towards laxness of frames and the denial of the consequences of frame modifications. On the practical level, economic pressures lead therapists to alter frames and violate the rights and healthy needs of their patients even when they sense that harm is being done — money corrupts, even in psychotherapy and its supervision. Furthermore, the intensification of death anxiety and of unconscious guilt in today's world leads both supervisors and supervisees unconsciously to ignore these dimensions of supervision, and to greatly prefer deviant to secured frames — attitudes rationalized consciously through many false and spurious arguments.

Communicatively, the problem is daunting because the conscious system and manifest messages are both frame-insensitive and inclined to sanction frame alterations. It is only the second unconscious system and its encoded narrative voice that cries out in protest over the damage being caused by alterations of the ideal frames. The conscious mind has a way of not decoding and not hearing the urgent and hopeful encoded messages of the deep unconscious system, and defensively the system fails to realize that disguised communications involve real events and perceptions that have real and often strong repercussions. In fact, unconscious experience is far more in touch with reality than conscious experience, which is so defended and distorted as to make emotional reality almost unknowable directly. It is with these humbling realizations that we now approach these most important aspects of the framework of supervision.

PRIVACY

With respect to privacy, the ideal ground rule states that *supervision is an entirely private matter between the supervisor and supervisee*. There is, then, no access to the supervisory experience by any other person — be it the supervised patient, an officer or committee member of a training program, peers of the supervisee (as occurs in group supervision), or readers of professional and other papers and books (i.e. no use is made of supervised material for purposes other than the immediate education of the supervisee).

Total privacy implies a *one-to-one relationship and a professional setting, a sound-proofed office, and the absence of observers or intruders*. It indicates too that neither supervisor nor supervisee will discuss the supervision with any third party whatsoever — professional or personal. The rule also means that the process notes used for a supervisory hour are destroyed after the consultation session and that neither party to the supervision makes notes during or after the supervisory hour. In this regard, the writing of process-note case material by the supervisee is the only necessary exception to this general principle of non-recording (see chapters eight and eleven). Supervision, like psychotherapy, should be an unchronicled experiential event whose psychological and emotional residuals build naturally and spontaneously within the supervisee — and supervisor — over time. It is a natural process that is stifled and damaged by any kind of record-keeping or note-taking.

CONFIDENTIALITY

The ground rule of total confidentiality is a complement to the rule of total privacy. Supervision is an emotionally charged teaching and learning experience in which the supervisee reveals much of his inner mind and soul, conscious and unconscious, and within which, as noted, unconscious experience, especially as it is frame-related, plays a major role. Teaching and learning of this kind can be done safely only in a totally secured space. Ideally, then, *there should be no release of information regarding a supervisory experience under any circumstances—full confidentiality should be assured.* Taken together, privacy and confidentiality close off the supervisory space from the outside world and give the supervisory situation the safety and containment it requires for openness of communication and non-conflictual teaching and learning.

COMMON FRAME-DEVIANT EXCEPTIONS TO THE RULES

Deep pathological and defensive needs buttressed by manifest-content/implications listening and formulating have created a rather large list of commonly accepted exceptions to the rules of total privacy and confidentiality for supervision. I will make note of some of the more common infractions to give us a sense of the scope of the problem. In general, these issues tend to evoke far more concern in supervisees as compared to their supervisors, even though the former mistakenly tend to be rather indifferent to the framework of their supervisory experiences. Clearly, both parties to supervision should have a major investment in a private and confidential supervisory space.

An office for supervision that is located in a clinic or hospital, or any other kind of general-access setting, violates the privacy of the supervision, as does any report on the supervisee and his or her work. So too does any note-taking during or after supervision or report of the clinical material or of the teaching experience to outsiders. Discussion of the supervision with third parties like peers, colleagues, relatives, or friends also violates these tenets. The same is true when a supervisor (or supervisee) uses supervised material or supervisory experiences for a professional paper or book on psychotherapy or supervision.

Many supervisors obtain a supervisee's oral or written permission to use aspects of the supervised case material in a publication, but even if the patient is suitably disguised, this does not make the frame violation any less compelling. Supervisees virtually always consciously consent to such requests, often with the fantasy and hope of currying favour with the supervisor. They also are burdened with fears of the negative consequences of not cooperating with their mentors. In addition, the supervisor who makes such a request is exploiting his or her authority and power, although this rather evident feature of these situations is often overlooked. Yet, as we would expect, the deep unconscious reaction to these frame-modifying requests is always very critical of the supervisor and negatively toned; the invasive and seductive qualities of this kind of frame break do not escape deep unconscious notice.

One of the more common violations of privacy — and of relative anonymity as well — is the use of an office at the location where a supervisor lives, whether in a house or apartment, and with or without a separate entrance for the supervisor's office. Arrangements of this kind expose the supervisee to family members and other third parties and violate the privacy of his or her contact with the supervisor. Along different lines, as noted, *group supervision* is inherently frame-deviant in that the situation lacks both total privacy and confidentiality. An invitation to anyone to observe a supervisory session similarly violates the privacy and one-to-one requisites of the ideal supervisory frame.

Any discussion that a supervisor or supervisee has with an outsider to the supervision is a modification of the total confidentiality of the situation, as is any report that is made to a third party — including those connected with a training program. A decision to taperecord or videotape a supervisory session or to record a therapy session for supervisory purposes entails blatant losses of both privacy and confidentiality. The supervisor who makes such requests and the supervisee who acquiesces to them are both parties to these violations — a S/S system with this type of modified frame often dysfunctions badly. Both supervisor and supervisee are mandated by the second unconscious system to safeguard these aspects of the supervisory frame.

A frame-related vignette

Dr. Horace was supervising Dr. Little in the context of his psychoanalytic training — both teacher and student were men. Dr. Horace was writing a paper on the obsessive compulsive syndrome, and the case that Dr. Little was presenting suffered notably from that difficulty. In the course of a supervisory session, Dr. Horace told his student about his paper and indicated that he would soon be presenting it to their analytic society. He asked permission to make notes from time to time over the next few weeks in order to use the supervisory case material for his presentation and writings. Consciously pleased by the interest of his supervisor, Dr. Little willingly agreed to his request and then took out his process notes in order to present them to his supervisor.

As he began to report the material, Dr. Little interrupted himself and asked if he could mention another case that he was finding difficult to handle. Dr. Horace agreed to this not-uncommon frame alteration and the supervisee said that the patient he was concerned about was a latent homosexual man whose homosexuality was now surfacing "in the transference". The problem was that the man felt that he, Dr. Little, was trying to seduce him, and no amount of denial and analysis had changed the patient's mind. In fact, the more they worked on the problem, the worse things got; last session the patient had reported a manifest dream of being cornered by Dr. Little and penetrated anally. The supervisee felt that he must be doing something wrong, but he had no idea what it was or how to correct it.

Naive to the communicative approach, and invoking the standard model of supervision, Dr. Horace simply advised his student to take up the matter directly with his patient and use confrontative techniques to show the patient his misperceptions — and to try to trace the childhood roots of this malignant transference reaction, which were likely to involve seductiveness by the patient's father.

Had Dr. Horace asked about the ground rules and frame of this man's therapy, he would have unearthed the critical *repressed trigger* that was creating Dr. Little's dilemma. In all likelihood, given that the story was being told to the supervisor, this missing trigger must have a counterpart in the frame of the supervisory situation. As discussed in the previous chapter, conscious sexual thoughts about and wishes towards a therapist are almost always unconsciously motivated responses to a major frame deviation by that therapist. In this instance, Dr. Little had become concerned that this man's therapy was foundering, and he had increased the number of sessions from one to three a week — the patient's homosexual feelings had surfaced very soon after the change.

For our purposes, however, we must move from the triggers and issues within the psychotherapy to *the repressed trigger in the supervision*. This was, of course, Dr. Horace's request to use Dr. Little's supervisory material for his own writings and presentation. The trigger itself was conscious to both parties, but they both repressed and denied its most disturbing (frame-related) unconscious implications. In addition, both had failed to realize that the out-of-context story presented by Dr. Little — the case material from the second patient — conveyed his personally selected, valid unconscious perceptions of his supervisor's frame-deviant trigger and the adaptive processing of its ramifications.

In essence, the supervisor's request for permission to use the supervisee's case material was perceived unconsciously as cornering the supervisee and seducing and penetrating him. There is truth to these images psychologically and emotionally, even though they do not allude to grossly seductive behaviours of the supervisor, but only to their implied and unconsciously experienced meanings.

The seductive and penetrating qualities of the request, operating deeply unconsciously, gravely affected the behaviour of the supervisee, who displaced his *uninterpreted unconscious perceptions* of his supervisor's request into his own therapeutic work with the primary patient whose case was being supervised. Thus, in the session that followed the supervisory hour that I have just described, Dr. Little had asked his patient to write out his early life history — informing him that he needed the material for a course on psychopathology that he was taking at his psychoanalytic institute. This unconsciously seductive and penetrating/merging intervention had many disturbing effects on that treatment situation, and both the patient and Dr. Little suffered as a consequence. Altering frames may well be thought of as a contagious disease with many ill-effects.

In supervising this next session, Dr. Horace criticized and reprimanded Dr. Little for his request to the patient, basing his critique on the patient's conscious objections to what had been asked of him — he had claimed that he did not have time to do it. For our purposes, we may note that this blaming intervention by the supervisor entirely overlooks and denies his own unconscious contribution to his supervisee's frame-deviant intervention. Without trigger decoding and a recognition of the S/S system that calls for accountability on both sides, these kinds of injustices flourish in today's supervisory world.

Finally, for his part, Dr. Horace had responded manifestly and in terms of conscious meanings to his supervisee's case material, not realizing that it encoded a response to his adaptation-evoking, frame-modifying trigger. But his own deep unconscious system unconsciously experienced the perceptions encoded within his supervisee's narrative and processed them silently and without his awareness. A dream of his own in which he was punished for a criminal act of plagiarism showed that, unconsciously, he had felt guilty for his hurtful frame-break even though he never gave it another conscious thought. Behaviour-wise, he later constructed his presentation to the analytic society in a way that drew avoidable criticisms — never once realizing that unwittingly and because of unconscious guilt, he had arranged his own undoing. In all, then, each member of an S/S/P system suffers when the supervisory frame is modified in any conceivable — and often, seemingly inconceivable — way.

SEEMINGLY NECESSARY FRAME ALTERATIONS

There are, of course, many situations in which the frame alterations that I have spelled out here appear to be a necessary part of the conditions of supervision. There are, however, several contingencies to these possibilities. First, there are many frame violations that are rationalized as inescapable that, upon examination, prove to be inessential and easily rectified. For example, we saw that Dr. Clark, mentioned in chapter five, had made a decision, approved by his supervisee, Dr. Postal, to hold their supervision in his hospital office because it was convenient for both of them (let the supervisee beware). While this seemed to be the only way that they could get the supervisory work under way, reflection showed that it was an unnecessary frame modification that easily could have been rectified. Had Dr. Clark been frame-sensitive, he would have found the time to see the supervisee in his private office.

There are many situations in which highly questionable conscious-system arguments are used to justify unneeded modifications in the privacy and confidentiality of supervision. It is well to realize, however, that even when a frame modification is entirely justified — if that ever is the case — there will be an intense unconscious reaction to the deviation. Necessity softens, but does not eliminate, the adverse consequences of frame alterations.

In substance, the assessment of the necessity of a frame modification depends on the extent to which a teacher or student understands and respects the power of the frame in psychotherapy and in supervision. As they begin to appreciate the impact of frame-securing and frame-modifying interventions, they are certain to view the supervisory situation through different lenses and with a different weighting of choices than they would without such sensitivities. They will come to value secured frames and to see the harm done by even the most well-intended frame alteration, and they will struggle mightily against all manner of conscious-system protests, defences, and deceptions in order to secure as much of the supervisory frame as possible.

Perhaps the most common set of modifications of the privacy and confidentiality of supervision takes place in training programmes in psychotherapy and psychoanalysis. There is classroom supervision, group supervision, peer group supervision, observers of supervision by various committee members, reports to committees and institute officers by the supervisor — and more. These are all modifications of the ideal frame, and they will exert unconscious effects on both the supervisor and supervisee — especially the latter. As a rule, they are an enormous and unappreciated source of grief, pain, and even physical illness among mental health professionals in training. A supervisor's attention to the narratives from a supervisee-in-training will direct him or her to secure as much of the frame as possible in these frame-altered situations.

Another altered frame

Dr. Marks was a young woman in psychoanalytic training who was being seen in supervision by Dr. Ball, a male analyst. Dr. Marks' analyst, Dr. Dutton, who also was a man, was on the education committee that oversaw and evaluated the supervision done under the aegis of the institute — both supervisee and supervisor were assessed. As part of this process, Dr. Dutton sat in on a supervisory session in which Dr. Marks presented case material to Dr. Ball. On the surface, while Dr. Marks felt anxious, everything seemed to go well, and her analyst even complimented her on her work at the end of the supervisory session that he observed.

The patient whom Dr. Marks presented was a young man who played the guitar professionally; he was in therapy because of a severe depression. In the session that followed the observed supervisory hour (of which *consciously* the *patient* knew nothing), the patient mentioned that he was performing at a small local concert hall, offering music that he had written and arranged; it would mean a lot to him if Dr. Marks could attend. He gave her a ticket to the performance and she took it, saying that she would think about coming to see him.

In the meantime, in her own analysis, in the hour after being observed by her analyst, Dr. Marks reported a dream in which her brother forcibly undressed her in her bedroom. He began to fondle her breasts, and she awoke from the dream with a start. Her associations to the dream brought her to a time when she was a young teenager and her parents went out for the night. Her brother had forced his way into her room and tried to have sex with her. She had fought him off and later had her parents put a lock on her bedroom door for her protection. She had been unable to tell them why she had asked for the lock — she felt that they wouldn't understand and that she'd be punished as the seducer of her brother instead of the other way around.

The night of the dream, Dr. Marks had become irrationally angry with her husband because, inadvertently, he had walked into the bathroom when she was on the toilet — they had had a terrible fight and she had slept in another room. Working with the standard model of classical psychoanalysis, Dr. Dutton's interpretations involved his patient's incestuous wishes towards her brother and her unconscious identification of her husband with her brother. He also suggested that she must have been having sexual fantasies about him in the transference, including wishes that he would fondle her. Dr. Marks responded to this seeming interpretation by castigating herself as insensitive, stupid, and evil. Her conflict about whether to go to her patient's performance did not come to mind in the session.

Dr. Marks did go to her patient's performance, stayed through the first intermission, and then left. When she reported her action to Dr. Ball, who worked on the basis of the standard model of supervision, he became annoyed with her. Without waiting for the material from the session that had followed her attendance at the performance, which should have been the basis for his supervisory comments, he criticized his student rather harshly. He told her that she had acted out some kind of voyeuristic, primal scene fantasy and suggested that she turn to her own analysis to explore what she had done. When Dr. Marks said that she felt that her patient would have experienced her absence as a narcissistic blow and rejection, and that she had acted in empathy with his needs for mirroring, Dr. Ball modified his criticism and said that she may well have done the right thing — but nevertheless she should be careful about becoming too involved with her patients.

In the patient's session, as later reported during this supervisory hour, he thanked his therapist for coming to hear him. The night after he had performed, he had had a nightmare. In the dream, a woman who looked a little like his mother was chasing him with a knife, screaming that she was going to cut his heart out. The dream led him to a recollection of his mother coming into the bathroom while he was in the tub as a teenager. She looked at him very strangely, began to soap his genitals, said some weird things about how easily they could be sliced off and then left as mysteriously as she had entered. A week later she had had a nervous breakdown over her husband's decision to get a divorce.

As Sir Walter Scott so wisely wrote, "Oh, what a tangled web we weave, When first we practice to deceive" — even when we do our weaving and deceiving entirely outside our awareness. One frame deviation begets another which then begets yet another still, and pity the poor supervisee who must bear the burden of blame and responsibility alone — a burden of guilt that is both personal and unconsciously borrowed from those who enact the very injustices for which she herself must give penance.

The intrusion of Dr. Marks' analyst into her supervisory space was a major frame modification twice over — it violated the privacy and confidentiality of both her supervision and her analysis. Given the driving power of a frame violation of this magnitude, and given that the unconsciously activated conflicts and perceptions went unrecognized and unresolved, Dr. Marks then unwittingly re-enacted her analyst's error and intrusive frame violation with her own patient. After doing so, she was prematurely reprimanded by her supervisor without proper use of the (encoded) supervisory material. We can speculate that his premature condemnation probably was motivated by his own unconscious guilt for participating in the original supervisory frame break. Furthermore, his acceptance of Dr. Marks' rationalization for this unconsciously driven act is typical of the standard model of supervision — manifest-content, conscious-system supervision is without firm principles.

The realization that Dr. Marks' behaviour was a maladaptive response to frame modifications in both her supervision and her analysis is not an aspect of standard model thinking. The trigger for her behaviour is missed, as are her deep unconscious responses. And blaming replaces fair accountability, which should have been apportioned to all three individuals involved — with the analyst (and the institute) getting the largest share, the supervisor next, and the supervisee last, but still bearing some responsibility of her own.

The process-note case material from the supervised case exquisitely but sadly reveals the patient's disturbed reaction to his therapist's attendance at his concert. There is at first a direct expression of appreciation, a denial-based conscious-system response of utter simplicity and defensiveness. But the encoded narrative material tells a dramatically different story. Dr. Marks' misguided frame break was perceived unconsciously as an incestuous, voyeuristic, strange and insane, seductive and violent act — one that repeated in its own way a psychotic behaviour of the patient's mother.

This decoded reading of the adaptive processing by the patient's second unconscious system of this frame deviation is true to the emotional and psychological meanings of his therapist's behaviour. Indeed, the patient reported that he had had an anxiety attack while performing the following night; this was part of the behavioural, symptomatic, and maladaptive consequence of his therapist's maladaptive frame-break — a reflection of *system overload* within the patient himself and the P/T, S/S, and S/S/P systems.

As for Dr. Marks, her own dream, associations, and behaviour revealed an encoded perception of her analyst as seductively and incestuously invading the privacy of her supervisory space — an experience that was sexualized for her because frame deviations universally are unconsciously perceived as instinctualized actions of seduction and violence. These unconscious perceptions were acted out in her going to see her patient's performance, which was, of course, a re-enactment of her therapist's frame deviation in which he went to see his analysand perform in her supervision. Dr. Marks did, however, unconsciously offer a *model of rectification* — lock the door and keep the incestuous intruder (the analyst) out.

Lacking the proper interpretations of this complex interlude and lacking deep insight of her own, Dr. Marks fell victim to the

frame-violating acting-out of her supervisor and analyst. Even
if consciously she had felt that there was something wrong
with her analyst's intrusion into her supervision, her plight
is poignantly expressed in her inability to complain to her
parents — they would not understand and would hold her responsible for what her brother had done. Unfortunately, the
dream proved to be prophetic in this regard.

Analysts and therapists who accept this kind of frame break
as institute policy usually do not and cannot understand the
unconscious ramifications of the frame modifications inherent
in most of today's teaching situations. They tend to blame
the patient/supervisee for errant actions and interpret the
supervisee's behaviours as an acting out of his or her inner
fantasies and memories — interventions laced with injustice
and misconception. The only means of avoiding this kind
of problem is, of course, the use of trigger decoding and the
adoption of a systemic approach to supervision. In accounting
for a supervisee's behaviour as responses to his or her supervisor's triggers, the communicative approach creates a fair and
balanced appraisal of a supervisee's dysfunctional actions that
does justice to all concerned. With this in mind, we turn now to
two more essential components of the secured supervisory
frame — relative neutrality and anonymity.

CHAPTER SEVEN

Relative neutrality and anonymity

Probably no ground rule of supervision is more abused than the requirement for the *relative anonymity* of the supervisor — the rule of *no deliberate self-revelations*. Given the collegial and relaxed attitudes that pervade most private supervisory situations and the urge to help a supervisee-in-training to identify with his or her mentors, there are any number of rationalizations for unneeded and inappropriate personal revelations by supervisors. All manner of self-revealing biases are communicated by today's teachers of psychotherapy, and seldom are their frame-altering aspects recognized consciously — though they are, of course, worked over by the supervisee's (and supervisor's) second unconscious system with great intensity and perspicacity.

Linked to the relative anonymity of the supervisor is the much-misunderstood ground rule of the supervisor's *relative neutrality*. There is of course no such entity as a totally neutral supervisor, in that it is impossible to teach without a viewpoint and a background theory that serves to order and give meaning to the hugely complex data of a psychotherapy session. However, these inevitable orienting principles should not imply a

111

rigid approach that is arbitrarily prejudiced or refractory to new ways of ordering the data — and to fresh ways of thinking and doing both supervision and therapy.

Relative neutrality is impossible without a supervisor's use of encoded validation — a requisite that ensures balance and fairness. More fundamentally, this tenet requires that *the supervisor at all times should intervene solely on the basis of the material from the supervised interaction and that the supervised patient's material, and especially its encoded themes, consistently and with the sole exception of supervisory crises, should be the source of the supervisor's comments — however they are elaborated from that centre point.* Adherence to this principle not only ensures both the relative anonymity and relative neutrality of the supervisor, it also compels him or her to make use of the wisest processing system available in the supervisory situation — *the wisdom subsystem of the patient's deep unconscious system. Unconsciously, the patient is the teacher par excellence* (Langs, 1978, 1979, 1982).

The antidotes for abuses of neutrality and anonymity are easily stated, though difficult for many supervisors to adopt. Much of this resistance is based on deeply unconscious deviant-frame needs; supervisory misalliances in these areas are almost universal at present. Nevertheless, the securing of these aspects of the ideal frame begins with a supervisor's development of a concerned yet reserved attitude towards his or her supervisee. Supervision is not the arena for expressions of a supervisor's personal history or issues, nor is it the place for his or her *personal* opinions and advice. Interventions of that kind do a disservice to both parties to supervision and modify the role assignments that ideally each should accept as teacher and student.

COMMON FRAME MODIFICATIONS

As for the relative anonymity of the supervisor, the list of common frame violations is long and all too well rationalized. The issue is one of *relative* anonymity in that a small measure of inevitable self-revelation by a supervisor is inescapable and non-deviant. Thus, every mentor reveals something about himself or herself through his or her office setting and its appointments; way of speaking, working, dressing, and relating professionally; and ideas about the technique and theory of psychotherapy, even when they are strictly based on the material from the supervised interaction.

But most self-revelations extend beyond this inescapable and necessary minimum. For example, both anonymity and neutrality are modified whenever a supervisor speaks of his or her own professional training and teaching positions, and theoretical biases. Deviations arise too when the supervisee knows of or has heard clinical presentations by the supervisor and/or has read his or her papers and other writings. Beyond that, a supervisee may have had outside contact with a supervisor who may have been his or her teacher, advisor, co-worker, office-mate — and a host of other possibilities. Any type of prior or current (and anticipated in the future) professional contact between a supervisor and supervisee outside their supervisory relationship violates the ground rule that states that all of their contacts are made for the purpose of supervision in the supervisor's private office. The rule of relative anonymity also is violated in that some degree of self-revelation is inevitable under these circumstances.

A supervisor's relative anonymity also is modified significantly through all types of social contacts between a supervisor and supervisee — again past, present, and future. They may occur at institute functions, private parties, clubs, social situations, and the like — and all are frame deviant in powerful ways. Any situation in which the roles of the two parties to supervision shift from the professional domain to the social realm creates an inherently self-contradictory, deeply confusing, and crazy-making unconscious experience — and often leads to disruptions in conscious-system functioning. Consistently, the unconscious experience is one of seduction, incest, violent pursuit, loss of boundaries, and the like.

There is more still with respect to violations of relative anonymity. This aspect of the frame is altered whenever a supervisor makes personal comments of any kind — from self-revelations to opinions not based on the supervisory material. Here, too, the range runs from professional to personal/social allusions. However, any reference to a patient or other supervisee seen by the supervisor involves a frame violation of the other situation as well as the current one with the supervisee — even though such references are part of the basic teaching approach of many supervisors. Comments about other therapists and analysts, including a supervisee's current and former teachers, are also not infrequently and inappropriately made by supervisors.

Beyond these frame-modifying professional self-revelations lies a wide range of frame-deviant personal allusions by a supervisor to his or her life outside the professional sphere. They include references to family members and to incidents that concern them, social contacts and events, and personal opinions about anything in the outside world — from politics to books or movies, or whatever.

Supervision is a serious and delicate pursuit that involves the highly sensitive and easily disturbed conscious system of the emotion-processing mind of the supervisee. His or her second unconscious system takes in every unnoticed and often traumatic nuance of every adaptation-evoking stimulus from the supervisor, no matter how seemingly minor to the conscious system. And the supervisee's responses are not only communicative; they also involve behaviours with vast consequences in his or her professional endeavours and personal life. No longer can it defensively be argued that the secured frame asks too much of the supervisor. It cannot be stressed enough that the lax management of the supervisory frame damages all three parties to a supervision.

In principle, then, it is clear that the supervisor should teach as closely as possible from the material of the supervised session and should avoid and suppress all human but hurtful inclinations to engage in side comments and personal revelations. Doing therapy is an unnatural pursuit in that the therapist must curtail and manage all kinds of harmful conscious-system tendencies; doing supervision asks for more of this sacrifice in a situation where dropping one's guard is accepted practice.

Two cases in point

After Ms. Dyer had had to cancel two supervisory hours
with her supervisee, Ms. Cross, the supervisor explained
that she had married and had been on her honeymoon.
Ms. Cross responded with congratulations and consciously
was elated that her usually stand-offish supervisor had
shared some personal news with her. She then told a story
about her parents' marriage, recalling an incident in which
her mother had become very upset one night and revealed
to the patient that Ms. Cross' father had had a mistress for
many years. It was the kind of news Ms. Cross wished her
mother had kept to herself; it made it very difficult for her
to be with her father or to think well of her mother for
allowing the affair to go on for so many years. "It really
isn't the place of children to be party to their parents'
secrets", she concluded.

This *marginally related story* from Ms. Cross encodes her
unconscious perception of the illicit quality of her supervisor's
well-meaning self-revelation. Despite all good intentions, it is a
modification of the relative anonymity of the supervisor, and,
while consciously welcomed by her student, the unconscious
experience was very different. The deep unconscious response
saw the intervention as sharing an inappropriate sexual secret
(notice the frame break embedded in the secret which is about
an extramarital affair), and the deep wisdom subsystem fashioned an adaptive *model of rectification* — parents/supervisors
should not reveal their secrets to their children/supervisees.

Unfortunately, this entire unconscious experience went unrecognized by both the supervisor and supervisee who were
working on the basis of the standard model of supervision. The
following week Ms. Cross brought to supervision a disturbing
session in which she had made several self-revelations
of her own to the patient for whom she was receiving supervisory help. As we have seen so often now, unprocessed and
unrectified frame alterations by supervisors beget the acting
out via frame deviations by the unwittingly victimized supervisee.

* * *

By way of contrast, Mrs. Carter, a social worker, was in supervision with Dr. Ryan, a male psychologist. When Mrs. Carter, who was white (as was her supervisor), first presented a black female patient, she asked her supervisor if he had had any experience treating black people. When Dr. Ryan indicated that he thought that they should work from the material of the session that his supervisee was about to present, Mrs. Carter asked if, by any chance, he felt a special compassion with them and whether he had known many black people. She needed answers to these questions so she could be certain that she would be helped in working with this patient.

Dr. Ryan suggested that these questions were coming from some kind of inner pressure within Mrs. Carter and that its sources might be clarified if they could look at the material from the most recent session with the patient. While he did not discuss it with his supervisee, Dr. Ryan, who was working with the communicative model of supervision, had recognized that his student was trying to have him violate the rule of relative anonymity. He knew that his response should be, first, gently to maintain the secured frame by not answering his student's questions, and, second, to help the student discover the source of her frame-deviant pressures in the material of the session to be supervised.

Mrs. Carter responded by turning to her notes, but then looked away from them to remark that she was having a strange experience in that she suddenly remembered a black nanny who had taken care of her when she was a pre-school child. With all the fuss over seeing a black woman patient, she hadn't thought of her nanny, Louise, for many years, but now she could picture her again. Louise was a kind yet firm woman who was playful and yet able to set limits so things never got out of hand. She was a very loving soul; it would be wonderful if she were still alive so Mrs. Carter could see her again, but she had probably long since died.

The process notes contained a major frame deviation —
Mrs. Carter had inadvertently scheduled two clients at the
same time, and one of them was her black patient. Once
her delayed session was held, powerful stories of
persecution and harm had flooded the patient's mind, and
the supervisee had gone into system overload. She had
been overwhelmed by the material and unable to deal with
it; the altered frame and her feelings of conscious guilt
(and her unconscious guilt as well) had disturbed her
conscious functioning.

Mrs. Carter's conscious system had attempted to adapt to
these disturbances by having her supervisor modify an aspect
of the frame of the supervision — if he, her mentor, was a frame
breaker, then her own frame breaking wouldn't have been so
awful after all. Indeed, even this seemingly small frame alteration would have inappropriately sanctioned Mrs. Carter's own
frame break and momentarily relieved her of her sense of guilt.
This is a maladaptive effort at *cure through unconscious sanction* (Langs, 1985), and it occurs often in both psychotherapy
and its supervision. It is a maladaptive solution through misalliance and error that is far more commonly succumbed to by
therapists and supervisors than realized. It is the source of
many repetitive and overlooked frame modifications — and
their adverse consequences.

Dr. Ryan's holding the frame in a secured state evoked an
unconscious perception of a kind, loving caretaker who knew
when and how to set appropriate limits — much of the picture
was encoded in the story of Louise. Notice too the subsequent
indication of secured-frame death anxiety in the doubts about
whether Louise was still alive. This allusion encodes Mrs. Carter's concerns about surviving in a secured frame, what with her
guilt and such. Nevertheless, she had experienced an opportunity to introject a supervisor capable of holding the frame
against pressures to deviate. This episode served her well in
rectifying her own frames as a therapist and in working with
her black patient on the after-effects of her scheduling error
(which, for Mrs. Carter, had been an unconscious maladaptive
reaction to a serious illness in her mother).

RELATIVE NEUTRALITY AND ANONYMITY:
THE SUPERVISEE

The *patient* in psychotherapy is obliged to say whatever comes to mind, without censorship. In the two standard models of supervision, this complete openness is not required of the *supervisee*, who instead is asked essentially to recapture faithfully the sequential events of the session under supervision and to ask questions as need be. In addition, he or she is asked to listen with an open, receptive, yet reasonably discerning and critical mind, and to respond to the supervisor's interventions in a rational, inquisitive manner. Thus, the *supervisee's relative neutrality* involves both his or her presentation of clinical material and appropriate queries to the supervisor, and a proper attitude as a learner. These constraints on what a supervisee ideally is supposed to communicate sets the frame for his or her relative neutrality and anonymity (see also chapter eleven).

To paint the broader ground-rule picture first, in a manner similar to the supervisor, the ideal frame asks a supervisee to maintain a fundamentally secured frame for his or her supervision. While the primary responsibility for managing the frame falls to the supervisor, the student also has some responsibility in this regard. Overall, he or she should be mindful of the optimal frame and should find the means of deeply appreciating its value and the damage that he or she will suffer though frame modifications. This attitude requires that the supervisee resolve his or her pathological deviant-frame needs and secured-frame anxieties and be adept at trigger decoding — the only means of truly appreciating the ramifications of rules, frames, and boundaries. In all, a supervisee should try to safeguard the most ideal frame possible for his or her supervision — the frame should not be taken for granted or ignored.

The supervisee should adhere to all of the fixed-frame ground rules — that is, attend the supervisory sessions as scheduled and pay the fee in good time. He or she should strive for total privacy and confidentiality for the supervisory experience and therefore should not discuss the supervised case or the supervisory work with others. The sole acceptable exception to this rule is that a supervisee who is in his or her own psychotherapy is obliged to communicate without constraint to his or her therapist. To do so is, however, a modification of the supervisory frame — and complications do follow.

The ground rules of supervision call for the presentation of the process-note case material as the supervisee's central obligation. In this sense, then, all extraneous comments (perhaps with the exception of brief theoretical comments and allusions to the professional literature) are frame deviations by the supervisee — who, as can be seen, has his or her share in keeping to and maintaining the secured frame.

The patient is mandated to make full disclosure — to engage in maximal self-revelation; there is no relative anonymity for the psychotherapy patient. *There is however a requirement for the relative anonymity of the supervisee*; defining the boundaries of revelation by supervisees is an important and relatively unexamined task. The clearest aspects of this boundary relate to the private and social life of the supervisee, which has no place in the supervisory situation and should not be inquired about by the supervisor nor spontaneously revealed by the supervisee — unless a combined supervision and therapy is arranged (see chapters eleven and fourteen).

What then of the supervisee's professional life and world? In principle, the student should be supervised in light of his or her work with a given patient; all other information should be precluded from the supervisory interaction because it involves some measure of frame alteration. Case material always includes allusions to the setting of the therapy and other pertinent professional information, but the supervisor does not need to know anything beyond that. Such revelations invade the supervisee's right to privacy with respect to his or her professional life — and this includes the supervisee's training, theoretical preferences, clinical experience, patient load, and other such matters.

In principle, in situations that are ambiguous frame-wise, it is best to opt for the most frame-secured alternative. The final word on the supervisee ideally should come from his or her presented sessions. This material offers two sources for a supervisor's assessment of the supervisee. The first is the expected evaluation that a supervisor makes based on how well the student conforms to and uses the instructor's model of psychotherapy and its techniques — how much the supervisee seems to be learning about doing psychotherapy. This evaluation is made, though with different criteria, in both standard models of supervision — classically analytic, and communicative.

The second resource — and actually it is much richer and more incisive — comes from trigger decoding the *supervised patient's* narratives for their encoded perceptions and assessments of the interventions of the supervisee. Here, the supervisor benefits from the patient's role *unconsciously* as supervisor — and healer — to the supervisee (Searles, 1975; Langs, 1975, 1978, 1979, 1982). These trigger-decoded messages should be the primary basis for both teaching and evaluating a supervisee.

In this context, it is well to be reminded that the standard models of supervision, including the present communicative version, are not configured to carry out therapeutic efforts on behalf of the supervisee. This is a major limitation of all such models which focus on the presentation of the case material and have no viable means of allowing for the kinds of material that would facilitate therapeutic interventions by the supervisor. Indeed, the ground rules of these forms of supervision preclude free associations or self-revelations by the supervisee. This creates a somewhat vexing boundary for supervision, one that curtails the extent to which it can be successful — even when the supervisee is in his or her own personal therapy outside the supervision. Recognizing the constraints of the standard supervisory situation is part of a realistic perspective on the educational powers of a supervisory experience —and their limitations (Langs, in press a).

THE FRAMES OF PSYCHOTHERAPY
AND SUPERVISION

There are both similarities and differences between the frames of psychotherapy and of supervision — and they apply to the overall situation and to the requisites of both supervisor and supervisee. Both psychotherapy and supervision require optimally secured frames, and these are established in both situations in the first session — much of it through a therapist's or supervisor's delineation of the ground rules without much in the way of derivative or encoded material from the patient or supervisee. However, in principle, from there on the therapist will secure the frame almost exclusively at the behest of the patient's derivatives, whereas a supervisor often has no choice but to do so consciously and unilaterally when a frame problem is recognized.

At times of supervisory crisis, especially when the deviant framework of a supervision is playing a role, it may be necessary, however, for a supervisor to enlist narrative material from a supervisee in order to discover an overlooked frame-alteration or a much-needed frame-securing intervention and interpretation (see chapter twelve). At times a spontaneous coincidental story from a supervisee will, if properly trigger-decoded, direct a supervisor to an unnoticed frame deviation and reveal how it should be corrected. Deeply unconscious secured-frame needs are universals, and they exist in every situation in which an individual finds himself or herself — psychotherapy and its supervision included.

Specifically, the need for a stable, well-secured fixed frame is comparable for both situations, as are the requisites of total privacy and confidentiality — rules that clearly apply to supervisors as well as supervisees, and should apply as well to therapists and patients in psychotherapy. The relative anonymity of a supervisor is similar to that asked of a therapist. However, there is no relative anonymity for the therapy patient, who must agree to full disclosure without constraint, while the supervisee ideally maintains considerable anonymity regarding his or her professional and personal lives.

As for role requirements, the supervisor's interventions are similar to those of a therapist, although they are different in detail. The therapist is committed to frame-securing interventions as dictated by a patient's derivative material and to adaptation-oriented, interactional interpretations of the patient's themes in light of their triggers. These interventions are used to explain the unconscious basis for the prevailing patient-indicators (signs of emotional dysfunctions and frame deviations/resistances), and cure eventuates through both sound holding and this mixture of active interventions — frame-securing and interpretive.

The supervisor is also obliged to make interventions that resemble adaptational/interactional interpretations, but educating a supervisee requires other comments of a type not made by a psychotherapist. Thus, in teaching the supervisee sound interventional skills, the supervisor has two approaches. The first involves *critiquing or criticizing the interventions made by the student* — a form of confrontation that resembles many interventions made by standard-model, manifest-content psychotherapists, but not made by those working from the communicative model. The second method of teaching involves the supervisor's introduction of interventions of his or her own creation — *proposed or model interventions*, if you will. These efforts involve recommendations to the supervisee that are both frame-securing and interpretative — and, as we saw in chapter three, they require the same kind of *encoded validation* from the supervised patient as do the supervisee's efforts. It is well to be clear as to the similarities and differences between the frames of these two vital situations.

THE OVERALL FRAME OF SUPERVISION

To conclude this chapter, I summarize the essential ground rules of supervision in their secured-frame, optimal form.

1. A definitive fixed frame — a one-to-one relationship; a single, private setting; a set time for the supervisory sessions, which are of a fixed duration and frequency; and a single, fixed fee with the supervisee's responsibility for the time set aside for him or her and the supervisor's commitment to be present for all supervisory hours except for planned vacations and dire emergencies.

2. Total privacy and confidentiality, enforced by both parties to the supervision.

3. The relative anonymity and relative neutrality of both the supervisor and supervisee, including a supervisee's selec-

tion of an entirely or relatively frame-wise uncontaminated supervisor.

4. The offer of sequential process-note case material by the supervisee, and responses from the supervisor confined to managing and securing the frame of the supervision and teaching on the basis of the case material.

5. Clear role definitions for both the supervisor and the supervisee, and organizing the work of supervision around the explicit cognitive goal of teaching the supervisee the proper techniques of psychotherapy and the theory that stands behind such efforts.

6. Confinement of contact between the supervisor and supervisee to the supervisory sessions.

7. A group of additional usually unstated ground rules, such as the absence of physical contact between the supervisor and supervisee, refraining from any type of gift-giving or referrals by either party to the other, and the creation of an atmosphere of a questioning pursuit of knowledge, openness, honesty, and integrity on both sides of the dyad.

These ground rules clearly ask a lot of both supervisors and supervisees. It is easy to raise conscious-system protests against their restrictive qualities. However, these tenets give far more than they take away. They are the essential foundation for effective teaching and learning — and for growth and maturation on all sides. Anything less is compromised and harmful. Given that supervision often is done at the dawning of the career of a psychotherapist, the traumatic scars left by a frame-deviant supervision will probably be with the supervisee for the rest of his or her life — professional and private. We must insist, then, on the best possible conditions for this remarkable experience.

The process of supervision

We have established the framework for a sound and secured supervisory situation. It is time now to look at what transpires within that frame and to develop some *unconsciously validated* principles for the presentation of the supervisee and the interventions of the supervisor. Here too the communicative approach has shown that there are definitive precepts that configure supervision in a relatively optimal manner.

We have already seen that there are two levels of communication going on between the supervisor and supervisee. One is *conscious* and related to the defined task of the supervision, which is the education of the supervisee with stress on the validated techniques of psychotherapy. The other is generally *unconscious* and is related to the interaction between the supervisor and the supervisee, and especially the former's management of the framework of the supervision.

We have seen too that during interludes in which the supervisory frame is altered or secured, the communications of the supervisee are likely to shift from the single-message/ manifest-contents and implications mode of communication needed for the cognitive supervisory work to the double-message/encoded-contents mode of communication. The latter mode of expression is activated in the presence of frame impingements and is needed to work over the immediate supervisory interaction when its frame and the process of supervision are disturbed and the situation needs to be restored to a stable, optimal secured-frame state.

These considerations imply that a well-structured supervisory situation facilitates the supervisory teaching/learning process without notable interference from disturbing evoked deep perceptions and processes, and the communications and behaviours to which they lead. Thus, a stable, secured frame is optimal for teaching and learning and allows for a concentration of efforts on the manifest supervisory work (all the while inherently allowing unconsciously for a strong positive supervisory introject).

Frame alterations modify the nature of a supervisor's and supervisee's communications because the emotion-processing mind is compelled to adapt communicatively to the stressful aspects of the frame impingement. Even when a supervisor is not keyed into deep encoded meaning, disguised messages are generated by the disturbed supervisee, and they will exert negative effects on both parties to the supervision. In all, then, optimal supervision requires a stable secured frame.

We will proceed now on the basis of the assumption of an ideal, stable, and secured frame for a supervisory experience. The first question we will try to answer is this: *What are the validated guidelines for both a supervisor and a supervisee for carrying out an effective supervisory session?* The principles that we will develop pertain to all of the existing models of supervision, although they are not in common practice in the standard model — which therefore needs to be implemented according to the lines that will be developed in this chapter. With this in mind, let us turn now to the essential precepts of supervisory presentation and practice.

THE BASIC PROCESS OF SUPERVISION

With respect to the overall supervisory process, we will begin at the beginning with the supervisee and his or her preparation and presentation of the material for supervision. In this regard, we can state several guiding principles:

1. No notes should be made during the session that a supervisee will present to his or her supervisor — to do so violates the frame of the therapy.

2. The supervisee should write process notes immediately or very soon after finishing the session that will be supervised.

3. The notes should be written as an attempt to capture *strictly in sequence* the transactions of the entire session. They are, then, written in the order that the events and communications unfolded, and the attempt is made to reproduce the sequential-interactional transactions of the hour. It is to be expected that the results of these efforts will be incomplete and that they will have errors and voids. Nevertheless, teaching and learning how to do psychotherapy can be carried out effectively on the basis of this kind of material (see below).

Turning now to the supervision itself:

4. Each supervisory session should begin with and be based on the written process-note case material. The supervisor should *not* see the relevant notes in advance of the meeting with the supervisee. Supervision is an interactional-interpersonal learning experience that should be allowed to unfold spontaneously and without prior knowledge on the part of the supervisor. This precept assures the supervisor that he or she will experience the session in a manner similar to how the supervisee experienced it and allows for a *predictive approach* to doing supervision.

5. The case material should be presented in sequence, and all events should be described in the temporal order in which they occurred. This approach is, as noted, essential for predictive teaching by the supervisor and for the use of tests

of encoded or unconscious validation using the material from the supervised patient as the primary means of assessing the interventions of the supervisor.

6. All of the supervisor's teaching should unfold from the case material.

7. There are firm and sound criteria for the timing of a supervisor's interventions (see chapter ten). Supervision is therefore a highly disciplined art and is also part of the domain or clinical science of psychoanalysis (Langs, 1992e; Langs & Badalamenti, 1992).

8. The exquisitely honed *wisdom subsystem* of the adapting second unconscious system of a psychotherapy patient has a template — a remarkable aspect of its deep intelligence — that enables the system to know quite clearly when a patient has generated sufficient material for a therapist to intervene. This capacity, which is not available to the conscious system, is reflected in the encoded narratives of a patient who has experienced a therapist's missed opportunity to speak — usually via a failed interpretation or an overlooked chance to secure the frame. At such interludes, encoded narratives concerning missed opportunities, the inability to hear or understand, and similar themes emerge with utmost consistency.

In this context let us recall again that doing supervision in the light of encoded and decoded derivatives from a supervised patient's deep unconscious system taps into a system of the emotion-processing mind that embodies a degree of unconscious knowledge and adaptive capabilities that is not available on the conscious level — in the emotional realm, deep intelligence far exceeds conscious intelligence. This implies, first, that supervision conducted in the light of decoded derivatives is far more incisive than one that uses manifest contents and their implications alone; second, that a patient can, as suggested earlier, unconsciously supervise his or her therapist and the therapist's supervisor as well. Of course, in order to benefit from these remarkable unconscious efforts, the listener must *trigger-decode* the patient's narrative material in light of the prevailing adaptation-evoking interventions of the patient's therapist (and his or her supervisor) and thereby draw upon the wisdom of the deep unconscious system.

Unconscious validation of supervisory interventions is sought primarily from the subsequent material from the supervised patient. However, there is a secondary form of encoded validation that comes unconsciously from the supervisee himself or herself through marginally related stories or side comments that in some way have disguised validating elements. For example, a supervisee may, following a supervisor's intervention, think of someone who is perceptive or brilliant, or supportive or wise, thereby encoding the accuracy and helpfulness of the supervisor's comment — a form of interpersonal validation.

9. Neither the supervisee nor the supervisor should accept a supervisor's evaluations and proposed interventions without *encoded validation* in the material from the supervised patient.

10. In a given supervisory hour, the supervisory work should cover at least one full session. A once-weekly case is ideal for psychotherapy supervision. For twice-weekly patients, one session should briefly be summarized and the other presented in full. The selection of which session to concentrate on is left to the supervisee, although the supervisor may choose to focus his or her teaching efforts on either session depending on the key teaching points that emerge from the presentation.

11. The session to be supervised should be a current one — ideally, the last session that the supervisee has had with the patient under study.

12. The supervisee should feel free to ask questions at any point in a supervisory session. These queries may refer to the supervisor's comments or to the material of the session, including the supervisee's own silences and interventions. In responding to a supervisor's interventions, a degree of respectful scepticism is called for in the supervisee — a kind of sincere "show me" attitude. On the one hand, the

supervisee who simply accepts everything a supervisor says — usually because it is non-threatening or complimentary to the supervisee — should recognize his or her lack of critical thinking and bring these capabilities to bear on the supervisor's efforts. On the other hand, the overly sceptical and doubtful supervisee who consciously objects to almost all of his or her supervisor's recommendations and assessments should step back and examine the basic structure of the supervision and the fundamental nature of the instructor's teachings — there may well be serious problems in these areas. But, in addition, the supervisee should search himself or herself for unreasonable prejudices against the supervisor's efforts and should especially reconsider his or her position *whenever encoded validation from the supervised patient materializes* — the supervisee is likely to be in error in these cases.

The danger of submitting to the authority of, and of over-idealizing, the supervisor are so great that every possible precaution should be taken by both supervisor and supervisee to safeguard against blind and obeisant acceptance of a supervisor's pronouncements to a point where defensiveness, false beliefs and theories, and unsound techniques prevail without check. Encoded validation is the key preventative measure.

As for the supervisee's questions, the supervisor is best advised to *answer these queries on the basis of the case material.* Any question that lends itself to this principle should not be answered immediately or directly, but should await the material needed from the patient to provide an encoded, informed answer. Thus, *the supervised patient's unconscious communications are as much as possible the teaching instrument of the supervisor.* Occasionally, a question can be responded to on a theoretical basis, although both parties to supervision should understand that the validity of such answers cannot, as a rule, be determined. This kind of conscious-system response is especially vulnerable to unnoticed error and bias; it should be used infrequently and understood for its uncertainties.

13. Given the two basic systems of the mind — conscious and deeply unconscious — supervision should be conducted with the deep unconscious system as the ultimate arbitrator of the truth value of statements made by both the supervisor and the supervisee (for the latter, those he or she makes during either a therapy session or its supervision). In principle, conscious-system discussions should be kept to a minimum and derivative-based discussions favoured as much as possible.

14. When a supervisor is convinced that a supervisee has intervened in valid fashion, he or she should state that opinion and discuss the reasons for the positive assessment. However, the validity of the intervention must then be confirmed by the subsequent material from the patient lest a supervisory misalliance develop on the basis of shared misbeliefs in the form of invalid favourable evaluations of the supervisee's work. Without the use of encoded confirmation, there is no way to discover these shared blind spots.

15. As the supervisory hour draws to a close, the supervisor should summarize the main teaching points of the session and answer any final questions from the supervisee. In addition, the supervisor should attempt to anticipate the next session that the student will have with the patient and prepare the supervisee for likely issues — especially secured-frame moments and unresolved deviant-frame issues and erroneous or even valid interventions. Prediction is the tool of supervision until the very end of the work.

CLARIFYING THE PRECEPTS
OF SUPERVISION

Let us now take a closer look at these basic principles. I will begin with the supervisee's presentation because it is the fountainhead and power source of the entire supervisory experience. In explicating these basic principles, I again will discuss some of the more common departures from established basic tenets.

Process-note case material

The supervisory process should, as noted, begin with the presentation of process-note case material by the supervisee. The supervisor should not have an advance look at the material, nor should he or she have a copy of the notes — the supervisee should have the only copy of the material, and it should be destroyed after the supervisory hour.

Supervision is a living process that must unfold within a carefully defined frame and set of guidelines, but in natural fashion. The policy of the supervisee presenting from notes written after the session is the main exception to this unencumbered unfolding. It is a necessary compromise because experience has shown that the memory of a supervisee is a treacherous and unreliable cognitive function when it is in the throes of presenting to a supervisor. Without realizing it, the immediate situation and its adaptive tensions tend to create an endless series of distortions, repressions, denial, and other kinds of errors and lapses that render the spontaneously recalled material relatively unteachable. In addition, without process notes, a supervisee will often respond to a supervisor's teachings by reshaping the session at hand — consciously or unconsciously — in keeping with the supervisor's interventions. On the other hand, writing up a session immediately after it has been held, and doing so in private, creates conditions that favour the most accurate recall possible of a given therapy hour.

This brings up the often-raised question as to whether supervision can be done effectively from post-session process notes rather than from notes written or outlined during the on-going therapy hour — or from taperecorded sessions. A related issue is the question of whether recording sessions for purposes of supervision — or for any other reason except quantitative research — is appropriate in any way, or is such an extremely damaging violation of the ideal frame that inevitably it causes far more harm than any possible good.

The answer to these important questions begins with the finding that, without a doubt, *the techniques and theory of psychotherapy can be taught to a supervisee from post-session process notes alone*. The argument that important material is omitted from any recall of a session begins with a true statement — it is of course impossible to recollect a therapy hour fully, and dynamically motivated omissions and additions are certain to occur. The question, then, is whether a recalled session is sufficiently faithful to the *critical events* of that hour to be a secure basis for supervisory work.

Supervisees will, of course, have varying abilities to remember therapy sessions and to represent faithfully the essential happenings in their written notes. A supervisor should pay attention to the quality and length of these notes. If they are very long — perhaps three or four written pages for a forty-five- or fifty-minute session — they are probably acceptable. But if they are too brief, the supervisee must be asked to remember sessions more fully and to make future material more complete. In addition, the notes should not be in summary form, but should reflect an attempt to recapture in some detail the precise sequential communications from the supervisee and his or her patient — written as if to produce a condensed version of the actual happenings of the therapy hour.

In this regard, any inclination by a supervisee to forego written supervisory notes is a *supervisory resistance* and must be overruled. In self-processing supervision (chapter fourteen), it is usually possible to determine the unconscious and interactional basis for this resistance. In the standard models this is seldom feasible — though if the issue persists and interferes with the supervisory work, it may prove necessary to obtain encoded narratives from the supervisee in order to access his or her deep unconscious experiences of the supervision and its frame as they relate to this obstacle.

There are many reasons to believe that post-session process notes can be a sound basis for supervisory teaching and learning. Perhaps the least recognized support for this contention lies with the clinical evidence that strongly indicates that a major *unconscious* motive that guides the supervisee's *selection* of the material that he or she records after a session involves his or her conscious but especially *unconscious guilt* and an unwitting need to *confess errors and frame breaks* rather than to conceal them. The supervisor can therefore be assured that the vital interactional dynamics between the supervisee and his or her patient are very likely to be etched into the material that is written down after a session.

There are as well many supplementary arguments in favour of this approach. Recording therapy sessions is a blatant violation of the frame of the psychotherapy — and secondarily of the supervision, which becomes a party to the frame break. As such, it is an inherently destructive practice whose sanction by a supervisor will unconsciously be experienced by a supervisee as encouragement to engage in many other unneeded and harmful frame alterations. Unconsciously, this practice undermines the quality and integrity of the supervision and creates a destructive image of the supervisor that inevitably is introjected and exploited by the supervisee — to the detriment of both himself or herself and his or her patients.

While many patients will agree to having their sessions recorded for supervision or other purposes, careful attention to their *encoded narrative material* reveals that the recording is seen as invasive, a way of introducing an interfering third party, and a violation of the patient's rights to privacy and confidentiality. The recording of a session is also unconsciously viewed as a damaging, seductive act of fusion and incorporation that causes great harm to the patient — and to the therapist as well.

Exploration shows that many of the patients who agree to have their sessions recorded are motivated unconsciously by needs to be punished for their real and imagined misdeeds — pressures from their deep unconscious fear/guilt subsystems. In their seeming permanency, recordings unconsciously deny destruction and death — and separation (the patient is "forever" merged with the therapist). Recording is also accepted in order to have the opportunity, unconsciously, to view the therapist who makes such a request as mad and exploitative, thereby lessening the patient's own sense of guilt, madness, and hurtfulness. This entails a kind of *cure through nefarious comparison* (Langs, 1985), in that the unconsciously perceived psychopathology of the therapist who records sessions allows the patient to feel healthier, saner, and less harmful than his or her revered healer — an unconscious source of much emotional relief.

Along different lines, it is all but impossible to supervise a recorded session. There is too much material, and too much chaos and uncertainty, to allow for proper teaching in a supervisory hour. Having the supervisor read the transcript before-hand is a frame violation that interferes with the supervisory process — and the transcriber is a third party who violates the privacy and confidentiality of the therapy and supervision. Oddly enough, effective supervision relies on a supervisee's conscious and unconscious filtering of the material of the therapy hour as he or she prepares a presentation — the un-conscious selection and reshaping actually enhances the teaching efforts.

Driven by unconscious needs to confess, a supervisee will offer a sweep of a supervised session that is almost certain to reveal the essential issues of the hour. Initially, the supervisee lacks principles with which to organize the happenings of a session, and the notes may be somewhat difficult to prepare in sequence. But in time, as the supervisee's understanding of the deeper, unconscious structure of therapy sessions expands, he or she will develop ways of organizing the sequential material and effectively recalling the session. Recollection is further facilitated as a supervisee comes to comprehend the central role played by frame-related interventions and issues and how the frame organizes the patient's encoded material. The bottom line is that supervisory work based on process-note case material written soon after a psychotherapy session is a viable and effective basis for educating the supervisee.

The need for sequential reporting

The dictum that the supervisee should present the process-note material in the sequence in which the material unfolded has a number of important ramifications. Just as the patient has the inviolable right to begin each therapy session, the supervisee has the comparable right to start the supervisory hour with the case material that he or she has prepared — usually the most recent transactions of the therapy.

With an ongoing case, the supervisee should *not* remind the supervisor of the previous hour's material or of prior supervi-sory comments. By simply offering the fresh case material, the supervisee enables the supervisor to begin each supervisory session with a relatively open and unbiased mind — at least in part (see below). This rule resembles Bion's (1967) sage advice to therapists to begin each therapy session without desire, memory, or understanding. This approach is an attempt to safeguard against fixed biases and misconceptions and allows for a fresh beginning for each supervisory session — previous assessments recede into the background. The tendency among supervisors (and supervisees) to adopt fixed ideas, formulations and views of a patient and his or her therapy is so great that everything possible should be done to create room for new ideas and reconceptualizations.

However, this rule of unprejudiced and memory-less beginnings applies to only half of the mind of the supervisor. With the other half of his or her mind, it is equally essential that he or she quickly recapture the triggers and themes of the prior session as the supervisory presentation unfolds. The fresh material should begin to stimulate the recall of the recent frame issues and the responsive material from the patient, as well as the most recent interventions of the supervisee — his or her errors or sound interventions. *A mixture of knowing and not knowing* is the ideal approach for the supervisor — and the supervisee.

After exchanging greetings, then, the supervisee sits in his or her chair, takes out the process-note case material from a suitable briefcase, which is used for the sake of privacy, and begins to present the hour to be supervised — from beginning to end. *The supervisor always listens at first*, although he or she may be called on by the material to intervene relatively early on. In general, the teaching should be interactive, with questions and probes rather than the immediate offer of ideas, formulations, or proposals by the supervisor.

As much as possible, the supervisee should be encouraged to think autonomously and to base his or her ideas and formulations on the material of the session under study. The supervisee should actively join with the supervisor in formulating the material of the therapy hour — both the patient's communications and the supervisee's interventions. This kind of interactive teaching in which the supervisee is pressed to think relatively independently is an essential part of ideal supervisory work.

A case in point

Dr. Boyd was a psychologist in a psychotherapy training
programme; he was in supervision with a woman
psychotherapist, Dr. Dewey. It was the institute's policy to
work from videotaped sessions, so Dr. Boyd was
instructed to obtain written permission from his first case,
Ms. Norman, to record her sessions. Obediently, Dr. Boyd
asked his patient in her initial session at the institute's
clinic for her permission to record their sessions with the
video camera in the office in which he was seeing her. He
indicated that he wanted to do so in order to study her
material more carefully after each hour. Ms. Norman
laughed and said that she had expected something like
that, sure, it was fine. She signed the release, and Dr.
Boyd then asked her how he could help her. (The correct
opening query is, *"With what may I be of help?"*)

Ms. Norman remarked that it was difficult for her to talk,
and she fell silent for a long while. She then said that she
might as well come right out with it, she was an alcoholic
and couldn't get her drinking under control. She went on
to speak mainly of her childhood and of her father, who
was a violent man and who often beat her mother and his
daughter — the patient.

Ms. Norman said she never felt safe — he would barge into
her bedroom drunk and out of his mind and start beating
on her as she slept. It was a nightmare. Once he tried to
get her to go to bed with one of his friends — to make her
into a prostitute. It was all so crazy; she refused to do it
and ran away. Her mother never did anything about any of
it, she just looked away; she should not have been so blind
and should have done something to change the situation.
And her father should have known how much damage he
was doing and gotten himself under control. She couldn't
say anything to him without getting beaten still harder. It
ruined her life.

When the tape of this segment of the patient's session was
played in supervision, working from the standard model of

supervision (recording sessions is unthinkable in the communicative model), Dr. Dewey focused on the patient's psychopathology. She expressed her impression that this would be a difficult case because of the patient's early abuse, her lack of a constructive figure with whom to identify, and her poor impulse control and her evident paranoid trends. Nothing was said for the moment about technique or the effects of recording the sessions.

In commenting, we may note that the main trigger for the patient in this opening segment of material is, of course, the videotaping of her session by the therapist. What the conscious mind accepts in the way of a frame modification with a laugh and a word, the second unconscious system protests against vehemently and extensively. This outrage is expressed through Ms. Norman's encoded stories — the therapist's recording of her sessions unconsciously made him in reality quite like her abusive father, and, worse still, one dare not speak out to such men lest the abuse intensify.

The trigger-decoded themes reveal a personally selective and valid unconscious experience of the recording of the session by the therapist as a senselessly invasive and violent act directed against Ms. Norman, and as a way of prostituting her as well. The plea for rectification is encoded in her plaintive comment that her mother should not have been blind to the abuse and should have done something to change what was happening, and that her father also should have known the damage he was doing — damage which now unwittingly was being repeated in her therapy. The father's offer of the patient sexually to a friend specifically encodes the supervisor's instructions to the supervisee to record the patient's sessions — a misuse of the patient that is truly and unconsciously tinged with affront, prostitution, and incestuous sexuality. Strange indeed is a supervisory situation and psychotherapy that repeats in such a highly traumatic form the past pathogenic actions of a patient's parents in the name of curing her of her "neurosis".

Primarily, it was this patient's *unconscious guilt* — for her own and her parents' (and now, her therapist's) acts of seduction and violence against others — that impelled Ms. Norman to accept conditions of therapy that unconsciously would punish, prostitute, and harm her. In response, she might well suffer a severe symptomatic regression, or, at great cost, relief might materialize in some sectors of her life through her unconscious realization that her therapist was more insane than she was (another *cure through nefarious comparison*; Langs, 1985). It also seems likely that the unconscious realization that her therapist and his supervisor were as abusive and mad as her parents would enable her to forgive her parents for their trans-gressions — after all, this merely is the way adults and people in authority and with power behave.

Suffice it to add that none of this was interpreted or rectified in the therapy situation. Ms. Norman began the next session by reporting a nightmare in which a group of people were on a rampage. They broke into her bedroom and threatened to kill her. Somewhere their leader was hovering above them, watch-ing everything that was going on. Kill her slowly, his voice whispered, at which point she awoke in terror.

In the supervision, the dream prompted Dr. Dewey to recommend a confrontative, reality-testing approach with this patient — a recommendation that was not explored for indica-tions of validation. Dr. Boyd was afraid that his patient was psychotic and asked a series of questions about arranging for medication. In discussing this issue, Dr. Dewey recommended consultation with the clinic psychiatrist.

To comment further, systems theory tells us that patients and therapists create P/T systems that operate under a given set of conditions. Ms. Norman would communicate and behave very differently under secured-frame conditions as compared to her regressive response to the frame deviations that she had accepted in having her sessions recorded in a training-centre clinic. Secured frames are ego-enhancing, whereas altered frames promote emotional dysfunctions. And again we see that one frame deviation begets another — the recordings lead to the introduction of a new third party to the therapy in the form of the consulting psychiatrist. These vicious deviant-frame cycles often end tragically.

Ms. Norman's unconscious perception of the recording of her hours is quite clear — it is a way of being observed under great threat and, psychologically, an act of murder. The supervisor appears to be portrayed as the hovering figure instructing the others to kill the patient — another remarkably accurate encoded perception of an unconscious but real implication of Dr. Dewey's instructions to Dr. Boyd to record the sessions. This setting is in truth quite psychotic; the patient introjects its madness, and, unconsciously, her own psychotic core is activated and expressed in her dream.

> To offer one last fragment, later in this second session Ms.
> Norman talked about wanting to stop drinking. The
> problem was that she has a boyfriend who also drinks and
> keeps plying her with booze. One night she became
> frightened of him and developed a feeling that he wanted
> to harm or get rid of her. She was scared enough to get out
> of his apartment; she refused to answer the telephone
> when he called her at her girlfriend's house.

The effects of this kind of overwhelming frame modification — recording a patient's sessions — spill over from dreams and narratives into reality and behaviour, thereby affecting the life of the victimized patient. As I have indicated, there is no just need for recording sessions for supervisory purposes. In addition, the harm done to the patient — and supervisee (and supervisor) — is immeasurable. Granted Ms. Norman's sensitivities in this area, clinical study has nonetheless shown comparable reactions in all types of patients. Much the same, although on a smaller scale, occurs when a supervisee takes notes during sessions. Once we key in on the emotion-processing mind as an adaptive organ, and recognize its *unconscious* processing of emotionally charged triggers within psychotherapy, our understanding of the devastating effects of frame modifications will, I suspect, compel us to abandon these strikingly harmful practices.

CHAPTER NINE

The supervisor:
basic issues

We have to this point considered a variety of principles that are available to guide the work of a supervisor of psychotherapy. In the present and following chapter I integrate these scattered ideas into a comprehensive statement of basic precepts that configure the supervisory work and experience into an optimal situation for the teaching and learning of the proper techniques of psychotherapy. I begin by touching on several background issues that have a bearing on offering effective, unmarred supervision. In the next chapter, I offer a set of definitive precepts that can be used to help a supervisor to navigate the treacherous seas of supervision — the conscious system stands ever-ready to sabotage this potentially fine process.

SOME INTRODUCTORY CONCEPTS

Let us recall that our fundamental approach has been to embrace the proposition that to be considered valid, a supervisory intervention must be confirmed through encoded material from

141

the patient (in the standard models, encoded confirmation from the supervisee is secondary). This means that there are criteria of sound and unsound supervisory criticisms and proposals, and that, in general, each class of interventions will have distinctive effects on the supervisee and on the therapy that is being supervised. Both the management of the supervisory frame and a set of validated techniques of teaching are required for an ideal supervisory experience. We will now explore how this goal is best fulfilled — and the nature of the inevitable obstacles that stand in the way of its achievement.

We may begin with a reminder that the supervisor's primary responsibility to the supervisee is to define the criteria for valid and effective therapeutic interventions — to teach the supervisee the techniques of psychotherapy. Thus, *issues of formulating and intervening should be at the forefront of the supervisory work*, and discussions of theory, the psychopathology of the patient, and similar topics should spin out from the concentration on the treatment approach. Many supervisors avoid issues of technique, or they present opinions on these matters that are indefinite and highly tentative. The correct approach is far more specific and concentrated on issues of technique.

There is a common belief — and it is based entirely on defensive conscious-system listening and thinking — that there are no absolutes in psychotherapy. Much of therapy practice is left to the intuitions of the supervisee, and it is considered good teaching to present different options and allow the supervisee to choose from them — after all, it is argued, it is his or her patient. This way of thinking arises because the standard model of supervision has not been able to develop generally accepted criteria of correct/validated interventions. As a result, opinions can vary and the number of possible options are nearly infinite. In general, the conscious system is an inherently ambiguous realm which is clouded by an assortment of vagaries and a lack of a clear means of discovering and confirming definitive principles.

In contrast, supervisors who use the standard communicative model of supervision find that the second unconscious system is far more definitive than its conscious counterpart.

Trigger decoding moves supervision from the uncertain realm of the conscious system into the remarkably definitive (and reliable) world of the deep unconscious experience and processing — and into an incisive strategy for teaching efforts that are anchored, of course, in the search for encoded validation. The work of a supervisor should be disciplined and structured, even as it is intuitive and sensitive to the needs of the supervisee — and his or her supervised patient (see below).

THE MOTIVES OF THE SUPERVISOR

Let us now ask: *What motivates the psychotherapy supervisor? What are the goals and satisfactions that lead therapists to do such work?*

To answer, the primary motivations of the average supervisor appear to involve the satisfactions of being an effective teacher and bringing sound ideas of technique and theory to a supervisee; enhancing one's income by earning a suitable fee where this is the case; and having an opportunity to relate to and favourably influence the career of a neophyte or education-seeking psychotherapist. Secondarily, supervisors generally are interested in ensuring the best possible therapy for the supervised patient.

Still another secondary motive stems from the expectation that any supervisor who does effective supervisory work and is open-minded is certain to learn and grow from these endeavours — the more effective the supervisor, the more extensive his or her own education. As we would expect, little fresh insight comes from the direct and conscious statements of either the supervised patient or the supervisee. Most of this knowledge stems instead from their encoded messages and from the supervisee's errors and, even more so, the supervisor's own eventually recognized mistakes (his or her non-validated interventions) — and the supervised patient's responses to them.

Beyond these healthy and appropriate satisfactions, most supervisors will seek out a number of additional gratifications that are more self-serving and inappropriate than in the best interests of the supervisory work. Among these open or hidden agendas may be something as simple and human as a supervisor's wish to be especially well thought of by the supervisee and to curry favour with him or her. Often, however, this includes the hope for or efforts to obtain referrals from the supervised student — an extremely common frame modification that is harmful unconsciously for all concerned, including the supervised patient whose needs momentarily are subjugated to those of the supervisor. In principle, any departure from the ideal frame will have an adverse effect not only on the supervisor and the supervisee, but on the supervised patient as well.

For example, deviant motives of this kind may prompt a supervisor consciously or unconsciously to avoid or soften much-needed criticisms of the work of a supervisee to the detriment of his or her education and the progress of the supervised therapy. The conscious system of a supervisee will be unconsciously motivated to seize on any subsidiary motive of this kind to justify his or her own errors and frame alterations, and, overall, there will be a diminution in the extent to which the supervisory work focuses on the vital images from the supervised patient's second unconscious system and its telling contents and processes. The supervisor's pathological needs tend to meet a responsive set of comparable needs in the supervisee, resulting in major supervisory misalliances — for example, a supervisor's wishes for referrals join with the supervisee's needs to curry favour with his or her teacher.

A supervisor may also have a vested interest in a particular theory of therapy or treatment modality, one that creates blind spots, inflexibility, and needs to pressure the supervisee to work in a particular manner. It is essential that the supervisor or supervisee have the means of distinguishing these unwarranted biases from *the absolutely necessary and unconsciously validated constraints that are needed to define sound psychotherapy.* The latter, which are reflected in the fundamentals of listening and intervening, can spawn a variety of sound and fresh modalities of therapy and modes of supervision based on unconsciously validated theoretical constructs and practices — the communicative approach may well be but one such possibility.

In addition to these errant motives, there is a wide range of potential needs and issues within a supervisor that can interfere with sound supervision. This includes all forms of supervisory countertransferences such as needs to be overly beneficent, to control or manipulate the supervisee for personal gain, to adopt an uncalled-for authoritarian or seductive position, or to express unresolved sadistic needs through unnecessarily — that is, invalidly — criticizing or attacking the supervisee and his or her work with the supervised patient.

There also may be a variety of "neurotic" anxieties aroused in the supervisor in the course of doing supervision. These may stem from the conditions of the supervision: for example, the context of a training program places the supervisor in a vulnerable position vis-à-vis the overseeing committees of the institute. More basically, a supervisor may have difficulty managing the issues evoked by a secured or modified frame in the supervised therapy or the supervisory situation itself. Or the supervisor's anxieties may be evoked by attributes of the supervisee — for example, an especially attractive or unattractive supervisee who arouses personal and inappropriate reactions in the mentor. And, finally, the problem may lie with the supervised patient — for example, a feature of the supervised patient that arouses untoward conscious and unconscious issues for the teacher.

There may in addition be any number of secondary relationships and third-party contaminants that complicate the supervisory situation. A supervisor may know patients being seen by the supervisee, or be acquainted with his or her fellow students, colleagues, personal therapist, and other teachers, as well as the supervisee's family and friends. Some of these people may be allies or enemies of the supervisor, and the contamination inevitably will influence his or her work with the supervisee. Biases, inappropriate attitudes, blind spots, over-indulgence, or excessive harshness may disturb the supervisor's work with the supervisee. Situations of competition — between teachers of the same supervisee or among the supervisees seeing a particular supervisor — also may materialize. All such contacts are not only frame-deviant, they are the source of many conscious and unconscious needs and motives that do damage to the supervisory work.

A supervisor should be on the alert for sources of deviant motives, and he or she should secure the frame of a given supervisory situation by reducing contaminations to an absolute minimum. He or she must maintain a never-ending vigilance for activated secured-frame anxieties and deviant-frame needs — they are perpetually active and at issue. In addition, these errant needs should be self-processed for unconscious sources and effects, and kept in check as much as possible so that their enactment is precluded or quickly rectified if a lapse does occur. Maintaining a secured frame and curtailing these all-too human, but inappropriate, needs requires the continual self-processing of the supervisor.

> To offer a brief illustration, Dr. George (a supervising male psychologist) mentioned to his supervisee, Dr. Archer (also a male psychologist) that he had some open time for referrals. The student soon interrupted his planned presentation to mention that he had a bisexual friend whom he might be able to refer to his supervisor, but he warned Dr. George that the friend actually had seduced two previous therapists — one a man, the other a woman. If the friend called him, Dr. George had better take care that he does not become his third victim.

The emotion-processing mind is a miraculous invention of evolution. At the very moment that this supervisee consciously is complying with his supervisor's frame-deviant request and entering into an unconscious collusive misalliance with his mentor, he is encoding his unconscious perceptions of the seductiveness to which he is falling prey. It is the supervisee who is the victim here and, indirectly, the supervised patient. Indeed, in the therapy session that followed this unrectified and uninterpreted frame-altering interaction, Dr. Archer changed an hour for his patient and was flooded with images of incestuous seduction — unconsciously, he had found a way to act out a version of the frame break that he had shared with his supervisor who had implicitly sanctioned adaptation via frame alterations. Once more, a frame break in supervision led to a frame break in the supervised therapy.

THE COMPETING NEEDS OF A SUPERVISEE
AND THE SUPERVISED PATIENT

We have identified two basic conscious goals to supervision:
first, the education of the supervisee with respect to the
techniques and theory of psychotherapy, and, second, the
achievement of the best possible therapy for the supervised
patient. Often, these goals are consonant with each other, in
that the teaching offered to the supervisee leads to more effective work with his or her patient. However, there also are times
when the needs of a supervised patient and of his or her
supervised therapist appear to be in conflict. For example, a
supervisor might not want to confront a supervisee on a particular clinical issue with the supervised patient because he or
she believes that it would be far more disturbing than helpful to
the supervisee at the moment. There are indeed principles of
tact and dosage in doing supervision, and it is important not to
create system overload in the supervisee lest he or she feel
more assaulted than enlightened. Yet holding back a much-
needed comment is a disservice to the patient, whose therapy
will suffer because of uncorrected errors by the supervisee.

This brings up the question of whose needs should have
primacy in supervision — those of the supervisee or those of the
supervised patient? That is, can a supervisee be spared a
teaching point because it may well be too much for him or her
to handle at a given moment, or must the point be made —
however gently and firmly — because the supervised patient
will suffer from its omission?

Translated into practical terms, the need to teach not infrequently means that, at times, a supervisor will be obliged to
decode a supervised patient's material for some very painful
unconscious perceptions of the supervisee (and often of the
supervisor himself or herself as well). The reason for doing this
work does not lie with the sadism of the supervisor, but with a
constructive need to confront and deal with these disturbing
perceptions in order to set the supervisee on the right track.
The student will often feel narcissistically wounded and at-
tacked by these translations and may be quite unprepared to
deal with their ramifications. But the key question is whether

the hurts suffered in this manner justify sparing the supervisee the confrontation; a related issue is whether avoiding the indicated supervisory intervention and the patient's legitimately jaundiced view of his or her therapist actually harms both the supervisee and the patient. After all, the problem lies not only with a cognitive omission and failure to teach as needed, but also with an unconscious introject within the supervisee of a supervisor who backs away from unconscious meaning — clearly a disservice to the student.

It appears, then, that a supervisor's greater commitment is to the supervised patient, and that in most instances working with the supervisee on the patient's hurtful yet accurate encoded perceptions simultaneously fulfills the supervisor's commitment to both the supervisee and the supervised patient. Indeed, the supervisee cannot be spared these realizations, without which there would be no cognitive basis for, or motivation to, change from harmful to helpful techniques and interventions.

The supervisor should set the stage for this kind of intervention by offering a perspective on the nature of unconscious communication. While this will not, of course, totally reassure the student, it does provide a framework for the kind of painful unconscious perceptions of the supervisee on which teaching from the communicative model of supervision is based. Nevertheless, it must also be understood that teaching of this kind is not a license for the sadism of the teacher or the masochism of the supervisee. Nor should the supervisee back away from this kind of supervision because he or she finds the patient's decoded images painful to endure. At issue are validated supervisory interventions and, beyond them, the making of an effective, non-hurtful psychotherapist — there is no other way for this to happen.

In all, then, a supervisee is obliged to understand that teaching from a patient's encoded perceptions is not a matter of unnecessary attack, but one of proper teaching technique. The second unconscious system does not pull its punches, and supervisees who want to learn to do effective psychotherapy cannot be spared these blows. However, this type of intervention by a supervisor must be well grounded in the material from the patient, clearly indicated by the therapy situation, not invoked gratuitously, and eventually confirmed by the material from the supervised patient.

These are delicate issues, and a supervisee's reasonable understanding of the central problem enables the supervisory work to move forward as it should. A clear path must be negotiated between the Scylla of a sadomasochistic misalliance between supervisor and supervisee and the Charybdis of allowing a supervisee's hurtful interventions go unexplored and uncorrected. As noted, the failure to confront and modify such practices is a failure of supervision — it allows the unconscious (and often conscious) guilt of the supervisee to fester and causes a measure of dysfunction in his or her work and life.

For the supervisee, these ideas imply that he or she must enter supervision with, or quickly develop, a tough skin. Doing therapy in a manner that provides access to the deep unconscious system of the emotion-processing mind borders on the impossible and is all too often a painful experience for the conscious system of the psychotherapist. The essential design of the conscious system precludes access to deep unconscious contents and silently creates a host of obstacles to the development of trigger-decoded insights because the process brings into awareness contents and meanings that are intolerable to behold — here, in terms of the patient's unconscious view of the supervisee.

This means that, basically, the evolved design of the human mind works against the stated first goal of supervision, namely, to help the supervisee become an effective psychotherapist. It is in the nature of both supervisor and supervisee to do otherwise. Surprisingly, then, neither party to supervision is deeply inclined to ensure effective psychotherapy for the supervised patient — the human mind needs a great deal of training and perseverance to do so. As a result, sound supervision is a difficult and disturbing undertaking for all concerned. To ease the way, let us turn now to some basic precepts of doing supervision.

CHAPTER TEN

The supervisor:
basic precepts of supervision

The communicative approach has generated a series of *unconsciously validated* principles for the methods, timing, and style of intervening by a supervisor. There is no doubt that adhering to these tenets promotes a strong supervisory experience, while departures from these guidelines will always cause some harm to each member of the S/S/P system and interfere with the education of the supervisee. I will list and discuss each of these basic precepts.

1. *The supervisor is obligated to afford the supervisee the privilege of speaking first and should allow the case material to unfold before commenting*

Supervision involves reactive teaching; it should not be developed around the unilateral and arbitrary, typically self-serving, comments of the supervisor. Just as the patient orchestrates the interventions of his or her psychotherapist, the supervisee and the supervised patient similarly dictate the interventions of the supervisor.

2. *A supervisor should attend to the unfolding material from a session with two foci: first, the material from the patient, which should be formulated along adaptational-interactional lines in terms of triggers and encoded themes; second, the silences and active interventions of the supervisee, which should be considered for their implications and validity*

The supervisor must work from a well-established, basic model of the mind and of the therapeutic interaction and should base his or her comments on an assessment of the moment-to-moment transactions of a given session. The communicative approach has proven to be the most valid among the models available at present with which to ensure the success of these efforts.

In principle, the supervisor attends to the material from the supervised patient in order to determine whether the patient has communicated the necessary material for intervention — *frame-securing efforts and trigger-decoded interpretations.* There is a definitive *recipe for intervening* in that the communication of certain constellations of material calls for an intervention by a therapist — as it does also for a supervisor.

There are three components to the communicative expressions from patients. The first consists of *self-indicators,* and these are indications of the patient's resistances (mostly in the form of frame breaks) and symptoms; the second consists of *adaptation-evoking triggers,* and these are constituted as the interventions of the therapist, primarily in regard to the management of the ground rules or framework of the therapy; and the third is the *narrative–thematic pool,* which is made up of encoded, storied images that convey the patient's unconscious perceptions of the implications of the active, repressed triggers — the interventions of the supervisee — to which the patient is unconsciously adapting. When each of these three elements of expression is available in the material from a patient, an intervention is called for — although in some situations all that is needed are well-represented triggers and a strong thematic pool (see below).

3. *The essential issues in listening and formulating the material from a supervised patient lie with the representations of the triggers and the availability of powerful encoded themes*

Triggers may be alluded to *manifestly* — for example, the patient may mention that the therapist was late to the last session or that he or she had increased the fee. Alternatively, triggers may be conveyed in *encoded form along with a general allusion to therapy* — a so-called *non-specific bridge to therapy*. The latter element is a means of indicating that the narrative images are connected latently with the therapist or therapy. For example, a reference to a teacher's lateness may encode a therapist's lateness to a session, but in order for the therapist to intervene there must also be some non-specific allusion to the therapy or therapist — for example, a comment from the patient that the office is stuffy or that therapy seems stuck.

In order for a therapist to intervene, *there must be a clear representation of the repressed adaptation-evoking trigger* — which is, as a rule, a prior frame-related intervention of the therapist. This requisite is fulfilled if the patient directly mentions something contemporaneously frame-related that the therapist said or did, or alludes in encoded fashion to an image that can easily be seen to represent or describe thematically the frame-connected trigger and adds a bridge to therapy. Once this part of the recipe for intervening has been filled, the search shifts to the *thematic pool*.

Stories of all kinds, from dreams to fantasies, carry encoded themes that need to be lifted from their manifest contexts and brought into approximation — *linked or transposed* — to the active, repressed triggers for a given session. A usable *derivative network or thematic pool* should have one or more *powerful themes* so that the linking and the deep insight it conveys is of major consequence emotionally. Powerful themes are those of overt sexuality, violence, harm, injury, illness, death, dishonesty, incidents that are unlikely to have happened in reality, important genetic figures and incidents, and references to ground rules, frames, and boundaries.

The emergence of one or more strong themes is enough to fill the thematic part of the recipe for intervening — although the presence of several such themes is ideal. Nevertheless, themes that link to triggers so as to convey valid encoded perceptions of the implications of that trigger are sufficient cause to interpret the material on hand and, if the derivatives so direct, to secure the frame as well.

Self-indicators are the targets for intervening. The linking of triggers to themes should illuminate the unconscious meanings of a patient's active frame alterations and other resistances and/or his or her symptoms — they are always significantly triggered in part by the unconscious meanings of an intervention by the therapist (a systemic concept of great validity). Thus, *therapist-created triggers evoke both encoded material and a patient's symptoms and resistances — the trigger connects to both types of phenomena.*

There are, however, caveats to this aspect of the recipe for intervening. Whenever a therapist has modified the frame of a therapy, there may be no evident self-indicators. Under these conditions, the therapist's frame break is the primary dysfunctional behaviour of the P/T system, and it should be the main target for understanding by linking triggers to themes. Thus, the derivative material will decode around the frame-deviant intervention of the therapist, and there is no need to wait for a self-indicator before the therapist intervenes.

The recipe for intervening is filled, then, whenever a patient offers a workable representation of an active trigger — a prior frame-related intervention by the therapist, or an effort at understanding that was either valid or not — and also communicates a set of strong responsive encoded themes or derivatives. Self-indicators — expressions of the patient's psychopathology — may or may not be present depending on whether the therapist has secured the frame (self-indicators will then be present) or modified it (self-indicators are likely to be absent). In essence, this recipe orchestrates the supervisory teaching.

4. *The guiding principle for intervening in psycho-*
    therapy — and in supervision — is that the therapist or
    supervisor remains silent until the recipe for
    intervening has been filled, at which point he or she
    intervenes on the basis of the material on hand from a
    given session

A sound intervention is built entirely with the material from the patient — his or her representation of the triggers and the available thematic pool. Depending on the material, the comment will involve a frame-securing effort and/or an adaptational, trigger-decoded interpretation.

The structure of the ideal intervention is quite consistent. It is a logical, adaptively framed *cause* (the evocative trigger) and *effect* (the encoded images and the self-indicators) statement. In general, it begins with the stimulus or trigger and links its implications to the encoded thematic material. The statement is configured as the patient's personally selected but valid encoded perceptions of the therapist in light of the implications of his or her recent (frame-related) interventions.

A representative intervention sounds much like this:

"I [the therapist] did this or that [the trigger], which you have alluded to directly or indirectly in that or this way [identifying the representation of the stimulus in the patient's material], and you perceived the trigger to mean such and such, which is reflected in this and that theme in your story about whatever [linking triggers to themes] — and this accounts for such and such symptom, frame deviation, or other resistance [explaining the unconscious basis of the self-indicator in terms of the trigger-decoded images]. Your themes also indicate that I should secure this or that ground rule [utilizing the patient's model of rectification]."

The supervisor works with the template of this model intervention in mind and teaches it to the supervisee via the material of each supervised session.

5. *An important technical principle states that only the material from the ongoing session is used in a therapist's or supervisor's interventions*

It is the patient who creates the therapist's interventions — and those of the supervisor as well. The second unconscious system and its wisdom subsystem has the ability quite unconsciously to provide a therapist or his or her supervisor with all of the elements required for an intervention when one is needed. And because that system is primarily focused on the immediate interaction, only the associations in that particular session are relevant to deep unconscious system functioning.

6. *In this light, there are four distinctive situations that may occur in a given supervisory hour*

They are:

a. The supervisee is silent, and the supervisor's assessment is that the silence is appropriate and valid — that is, the patient has not filled the recipe for intervening.

b. The supervisee is silent, and the supervisor evaluates the silence as inappropriate because an intervention has been missed — that is, the patient has filled the recipe for intervening.

c. The supervisee has intervened, and the supervisor assesses the effort as correct and likely to obtain encoded validation from the patient — that is, the patient has filled the recipe for intervening and the supervisee has properly interpreted the patient's material or used it to secure an aspect of the therapy frame.

d. The supervisee has intervened, and the supervisor believes that he or she has been in error — that is, either the recipe for intervening had not been filled by the patient or the supervisee did not properly structure his or her comment.

A supervisor is mandated to intervene if his or her supervisee has been silent for a long time in a session, if an inappropriate silence (i.e. missed intervention) is detected, or if the supervisee has intervened actively. In addition, the supervisor should, when a supervisee is in error, make a specific recommendation as to the intervention that the supervisee should have made. Because the communicative approach provides specific criteria for intervening and for the nature of what should be said to the patient, the supervisor can speak incisively about each of these four types of efforts by his or her supervisee.

The supervisor's comment should predict the patient's response to the supervisee's effort (whether silence or active comment) and should include, when indicated, the supervisor's proposed alternative intervention. The validity of both the supervisee's and the supervisor's comments are then checked out in the material from the patient that follows the point at which the supervisor interrupted the supervisee's presentation to teach.

Let us consider now the nature of a supervisor's intervention under each of the four conditions listed above.

    a. *The supervisee is silent, and the supervisor's assessment is that the silence is appropriate and valid — recipe for intervening is unfilled.*

Silence by a therapist is of two kinds: first, *appropriate silence* that occurs when the recipe for intervening has not as yet been fulfilled; second, *inappropriate silence* — the silence of a missed intervention, which occurs when the recipe for intervening has been fulfilled by the patient and the supervisee fails to interpret and/or secure the frame as directed by the patient's encoded derivatives.

Each form of silence is responded to by a patient with a distinctive set of encoded images. *Appropriate silence is unconsciously validated* through allusions to people who are wise listeners, patient, and otherwise well-functioning and helpful. On the other hand, *inappropriate silence* is not confirmed; it is reacted to with encoded themes of neglect and missed opportunities and the like.

If the supervisee has been silent for much of a session, then the teacher can make one of two assessments. This evaluation is based entirely on whether the patient has fulfilled the recipe for intervening. In the first instance, the supervisor decides that there is no clear representation of a repressed trigger and/or that there are no meaningful and strong derivative themes. This implies that no intervention could have been made by the supervisee and that the patient's second unconscious system understands that this is the case. Therefore the patient's derivatives will confirm the silence in the latter part of a session because it is the correct intervention at the moment.

The supervisor who is convinced that a supervisee's continuing silence is valid should pause about half-way into the presented session to have the supervisee join him or her in assessing the material from the patient to that point in the hour. On that basis, the silence is then evaluated. Since we are considering a therapist-silence when the recipe for intervening has not been fulfilled, the supervisor and supervisee can be expected to agree on the elements that are missing for an adaptational/interactional intervention. In this way, the supervisor will affirm the supervisee's silence and then predict encoded validation via images of attentive and well-functioning figures. If such images appear later in the session, the therapist's and supervisor's formulations are both confirmed — each for its own reasons. But if encoded validation does *not* ensue, then the supervisor must reassess the material from the patient and search for a missing, active trigger in order to discover the basis for an evidently missed intervention. The supervisee must join with his or her mentor in this pursuit, and if the supervisor does not engage in such a search, the supervisee should call for it.

b.   *The supervisee is silent, and the supervisor's evaluation is that the silence is inappropriate because an intervention has been missed — the recipe for intervening had been filled.*

This is the second possibility when a supervisee is silent for an extended period in a session. In this instance, the supervisee's and supervisor's assessment of the patient's material differ — the former, through his or her silence in the session, reveals a belief that there was no basis on which to intervene, but the latter disagrees and argues that the principles of listening and formulating indicate that there has been a *missed intervention*.

Here, the supervisor has two tasks: first, to work interactively with the supervisee to help him or her to recognize that an intervention was feasible and to define what it should have been; second, to make *two predictions* — the non-validation of the supervisee's silence and the encoded validation of the newly proposed intervention by the supervisor.

The teaching under these circumstances begins with helping the supervisee see that he or she should have intervened. This means that the patient's material contained a well-represented, active trigger and strong encoded themes that link to that trigger. The most common source of a supervisee's failure to intervene correctly involves missing a clear (direct or encoded) representation of an adaptation-evoking trigger (again, one that usually is frame-related). Once the trigger is established, connecting the encoded themes to the trigger as encoded perceptions of the therapist in light of the interventional stimulus is usually rather straightforward.

As for the supervisor's predictions, the first is, of course, that the therapist's silence will not be validated by the patient's imagery and themes. Thus, negative themes related to not being understood or to people *not* being there for the patient are expected to emerge. In addition, even though it never was offered to the patient, the supervisor's proposed "correct" intervention — and, in this case, an intervention must be developed — should obtain encoded confirmation in the subsequent material from the patient.

As noted, this validation transpires because the formulated intervention simply expresses in direct words the unconscious processing of an active trigger by the deep unconscious system of the supervised patient. The patient cannot consciously make his or her own interpretations; all he or she can do is provide the therapist with a portrayal of the trigger and make available the responsive encoded themes — linking and trigger decoding must be done by the therapist. As a result, a correctly formulated intervention by a supervisor will find a correspondence with the patient's encoded material — and validation therefore will be in evidence.

As is true in principle of all of a supervisor's interventions, *failure to obtain encoded confirmation calls for reformulation* — it must be taken as an indication of supervisory error. As a rule, the problem here also lies with a misidentification of the most powerful trigger. Once that repressed stimulus is found, the thematic threads should connect nicely with its implications. Incidentally, the material from the patient offers many valuable clues to missing adaptation-evoking triggers — the patient is processing the meanings of the repressed trigger in his or her second unconscious system and conveying the results through his or her encoded stories.

> c. *The supervisee has intervened, and the supervisor assesses the effort as correct and likely to obtain encoded validation from the patient — the recipe for intervening was filled and properly interpreted and/or used to secure an aspect of the therapy frame.*

Here, the supervisor believes that the supervisee has linked an active trigger represented in the patient's material with the proper thematic threads from the patient's encoded narratives — and has done so in terms of activated and valid unconscious perceptions of the implications of the repressed trigger. The appraised soundness of this type of intervention should be discussed with the supervisee — including a congratulatory compliment for work well done — and encoded validation predicted. The subsequent material should, of course, unconsciously confirm the supervisee's effort either interpersonally or cognitively — or both. As always, a failure to obtain derivative validation calls for reformulation — beginning with a search for triggers that have been overlooked. In this case, both the supervisee and supervisor have been in error, so they must avoid a defensive supervisory misalliance in which they convince themselves that they are correct in their assessment of the material and the encoded images wrong — a possibility that almost never exists in reality. Both the supervisor and the supervisee must learn to trust and believe in the meanings and implications of encoded images and their themes. Human beings are far more honest and trustworthy when they communicate unconsciously as compared to consciously and directly.

d. *The supervisee has intervened, and the supervisor be-lieves that he or she has been in error — either the recipe for intervening had not been filled or the supervisee did not properly structure his or her comment.*

In this difficult situation, the supervisee has intervened, but, in the opinion of the supervisor, he or she has done so without properly using communicative principles. The forms that the error may take are almost limitless, and *each particular errone-ous intervention places into the patient a destructive set of disturbing implications and meanings.* It is essential that the supervisor help the supervisee sort out all of these complex inputs.

The teaching here is complicated. First, the supervisor should help the supervisee to realize the error that he or she has made. This involves two aspects of the intervention — the failure to adhere soundly to the adaptive model of the commu-nicative approach (the cognitive error), and the conscious and especially *unconscious meanings expressed to the patient through the intervention* (the nature of the patient's introject). The first problem is established by reviewing the material from the patient and enabling the supervisee to recognize that an error has been made. On this basis, the first supervisory pre-diction is that the supervisee's comment will not be confirmed and that the expected themes will centre around images of error and being misunderstood and the like.

The second step is to formulate with the supervisee the nature of the meanings imparted though the erroneous com-ment. Identifying the crucial properties of an errant interven-tion will anticipate the patient's unconscious perceptions of the supervisee's mistake and allow for the second prediction — *the nature of the patient's unconscious response to the implications of the supervisee's error.*

In this regard, anticipation is greatly aided by realizing that for the second unconscious system the two areas of greatest importance are *ground rules/frame and level of addressed meaning.* A third issue is whether a supervisee, as a strongly invested healer, has intervened correctly or incorrectly in the previous session. In formulating expected responses to a supervisee's error, stressing the attributes of his or her intervention along these three dimensions will facilitate the development of a correct set of expectations.

Any intervention that modifies a frame or fails to secure the frame when the patient's encoded material speaks for such a measure will be experienced unconsciously as a failure of the therapist to maintain a secured frame — and the patient's encoded narratives will address that issue. Themes reflecting the meanings of a particular frame modification will abound — loss of boundaries, corruption, forms of merger, fears of death and entrapment, seduction and violence — depending on the nature of the frame break. The supervisor can be quite precise, once he or she understands the prevailing trigger, about how the patient's response was missed by the supervisee and what the latter substituted for the correct stimulus.

Similarly, any failure by a therapist to trigger-decode the patient's material — and usually this means that the therapist was working on a manifest-content/implications level of meaning — will be perceived unconsciously as a flight from encoded meaning and perceptions. The themes will reflect the deep unconscious system's processing of the implications of the therapist's flight from the world of deep unconscious experience. The responsive images commonly involve ignorance, dread of knowledge, fears of the unknown or of the deep, and such.

In addition, any likely psychodynamic meaning inherent to the error — for example, the seductiveness or hostility of the supervisee's comment, the ways in which he or she intervened in order to avoid a patient's sexual or violent images, or indications of severe death anxiety in the therapist — will be detected by the patient's second unconscious system and reflected in his or her encoded narratives. Sound supervision requires a grasp of the remarkable capacities of the deep unconscious system of the emotion-processing mind — and freely using the patient's encoded reflections of the workings of his or her second unconscious system as the chief resource in supervisory teaching.

The third and final step in the teaching process here lies with determining with the supervisee the proper formulation of the patient's material and the intervention that should have been made to the patient. This leads to the third prediction: namely, that this new comment will obtain encoded validation in the material that follows. Thus, a correct assessment of the key trigger-decoded meanings in the patient's material will find encoded support in the continuing session because the revised formulation touches on the unconscious triggers and issues that the patient actually continues to work over in the session.

* * *

A few additional principles are worthy of note. Supervisory work is always cast in the framework of an active, ever-present, spiralling conscious and unconscious interaction between patient and therapist. While the conscious system often is deflected from a focus on this ongoing interaction, the deep unconscious system is always centred on this interplay and its implications and ramifications. The patient's encoded material, therefore, is always a reflection of unconscious efforts to adapt to the silences and comments of the therapist. It is this adaptive interaction that makes a predictive approach to supervision feasible. It is the supervisor's job to bring into the realm of conscious experience the operations of the patient's second unconscious system.

In listening to the patient's material, a supervisor should monitor the themes in the narrative images. In general, positive themes suggest that the supervisee is handling the session well. On the other hand, negative themes suggest that the supervisee has either made an erroneous intervention or is engaged in a silence that constitutes a missed intervention. The specific threads in the themes will direct the supervisor to the nature of the error — for example, themes of frame violations speak for frame modifications by the supervisee; themes of deafness suggest a missed intervention; themes of exposure hint at the presence of a third party to the therapy; and so on. These same themes should be taken, secondarily, to allude as well to the supervisor's efforts in the prior supervisory session, which are transmitted to the patient via the supervisee's fresh interventions in the new session. *The material from a patient in supervision should be continually monitored for his or her un-*

conscious perception and assessment of the supervisor and his or her teachings.

* * *

In psychotherapy there are specific indications that an intervention by the therapist is called for — essentially it is marked by the patient fulfilling the recipe for intervening. In much the same way, there are specific indications that a supervisory intervention should be made. Of course, a supervisor may elect to comment on any aspect of the case material as the presentation moves along — the patient's way of communicating, a frame allusion, something about the patient's psychopathology, a minor point of technique, and whatever. But there are, in addition to these spontaneous remarks, definitive moments when a supervisor should in principle engage in teaching efforts. The timing of these interventions follows from our discussion of the possible situations with which a supervisor may be faced in regard to the work of the supervisee.

To list the indications of a need for a supervisory comment, the following are the basic rules. *The supervisor should intervene whenever*:

a. *The supervisee has intervened.* Here, the teaching will be shaped, as noted, by the supervisor's assessment of the validity and nature of the supervisee's comment.

b. *When the supervisee has been silent and the material has taken on definitive unconscious meaning.* This implies that the patient has fulfilled the recipe for intervening so that active triggers and responsive encoded themes are available for intervening — and that the supervisee should have spoken around this time in the session. In this connection, there are two types of sessions. First, those in which the trigger is alluded to early on and the supervisor simply waits for a string of encoded themes to follow — and, once they appear, the supervisory teaching is begun. Second, those in which the powerful themes come first and the supervisor waits for a clear direct or encoded representation of the trigger — upon which he or she begins to teach. Other predictions are made depending on how the supervisee handled the session from that point on.

c. *When the supervisee has been silent and between one-half and two-thirds of the session has passed without the patient fulfilling the recipe for intervening.* Here, the supervisor will interrupt the supervisee to discuss the case material in order to affirm the supervisee's silence and to identify the missing elements of the recipe for intervening that are missing from the supervised patient's material. In addition, there should be a discussion of the source of this type of communicative resistance (i.e. the failure to fulfil the recipe) — including the interventions of the therapist that have triggered the flatness of the material. These triggers may, on rare occasions, be frame-securing in nature; more typically, they involve a frame deviation that has led momentarily to a shut-down of derivative material. Other possibilities include an acute, realistic crisis that has activated the coping skills of the conscious system and caused a temporary shut-down of the processing mechanisms of the deep unconscious system and, along different lines, the presence of a stable frame without an acute impingement so that the patient is, for the moment, lying fallow and does not need to express encoded meaning. The prediction here is, of course, that encoded validation of the supervisee's silence is in the offing.

d. *The emergence of a major symptom or resistance in the supervised patient.* Whenever a strong self-indicator materializes in the course of a session, it behoves the supervisor to speak up and explore with the supervisee the unconscious sources of the dysfunction and to determine what material is available — and what is lacking and therefore needed — to deal interpretively and frame-wise with the problem. This is especially necessary when the continuation of the therapy is threatened or when a patient is proposing a frame alteration or acting in deviant fashion.

e. *After a patient has free-associated for a while following an intervention by the supervisee or a proposed interven-*

tion of the supervisor. Comments at this point are needed because there has been a *prediction* of validation or its lack, and the material must be discussed in light of this issue. The *validating process* must receive continual discussion and elaboration as a supervisory hour unfolds.

f.   *Whenever a frame issue arises in respect to the supervisory situation.* The last cause for a supervisory intervention pertains to the supervisory relationship and interaction itself. In the standard models of supervision there is, as a rule, no call for comment about the supervision unless a problem materializes. The issue may involve a dissatisfaction with the supervisory work on the part of either party to the supervision or it may involve the ground rules of the supervisory situation. In principle, working over such issues will require some encoded narrative material from the supervisee — which he or she, surprisingly enough, virtually always unwittingly supplies (see chapters chapter twelve and fourteen).

* * *

In summary, the key principles of supervision follow from this discussion. First, the supervisory frame should be as secured as possible. Within that context, the supervisor should keep the supervisory work with the supervised sessions centred on frames and encoded meaning. The stress in teaching should be on issues of technique, and the other elements that enter the picture should be attached to issues of formulating and intervening. Trigger decoding and encoded validation are at the heart of sound psychotherapy and are essential to sound supervision as well. The supervisory work is primarily based on the supervisee's process-note case material and is constrained to the ideas and recommendations that unfold from that central source.

Ultimately, the work of the supervisor draws its best efforts from the *unconscious wisdom of the supervised patient* (Langs, 1978). In its simplest form, it can be said that an effective supervisor simply has learned to decode and anticipate a supervised patient's unconscious, encoded supervisory efforts on behalf of his or her therapist — the supervisee — and the supervisor as well.

A clinical vignette

We can now give substance to these principles by examining several sessions in the private supervision of Dr. Sands by Dr. Sommers — both were women psychiatrists — concerning the psychotherapy of Mr. Stanley. The frame of this supervision was quite secure, so we will concentrate on the material of the supervised sessions.

The therapy took place once weekly in Dr. Sands' private office. The referral had been from a professional source, and the frame of the treatment had been well secured. Three months into the therapy, the patient asked if he could have a reduction in his fee — which was 125 dollars per session — because he was under financial pressure. Dr. Sands said that she would not answer the question immediately, but would wait to see what emerged as they went along.

As presented in supervision through process notes written after the hour, the patient began the next session by ruminating about his boss, who was hard to read — "you never knew where he stood on an issue." The patient then described in great detail an argument he had had with the boss over some merchandise a customer had ordered that hadn't been shipped in timely fashion. Next, the patient spent a good deal of time analysing his boss' character structure — the man was obsessive to a fault. The patient added that he and his boss had gone back and forth over who was to blame for the delay and, after much discussion, they had decided that the head of the shipping department was at fault.

At this point, realizing that about two-thirds of the session was over, Dr. Sommers, who was using the communicative model of supervision as her base, asked the supervisee to pause and formulate the material. Dr. Sands said she

could not see any representation of a significant trigger
and added that the themes seemed flat to her. Dr.
Sommers agreed with this evaluation and asked what the
supervisee thought might be the source of this
communicative resistance — the failure to fill the recipe for
intervening. Dr. Sands was uncertain as to the answer and
Dr. Sommers asked a series of questions that led the
supervisee to suggest that in all likelihood it was her most
recent frame-related trigger — her comment that she would
not as yet respond to the patient's request for a reduced
fee. Dr. Sommers suggested that the patient's vagueness
might reflect something in her supervisee's answer to her
patient that suggested that she might reduce the fee and
yet might not.

Dr. Sands now remembered that in fact she had responded
to the request in a non-neutral way by saying that a fee
reduction was possible, but that she needed time to think
about it. Dr. Sommers then indicated that when a patient
requests a frame modification, the responsive intervention
should be made in a clearly neutral fashion without any
suggestion of an inclination to modify the frame. It may well
have been this frame-related uncertainty that had
produced the uncertainty in, and the uncertain qualities of,
the material of this session. "In any case", the supervisor
added, "for the moment they could expect validation of the
supervisee's silence in the session because it did appear
that no intervention was possible or called for."

In the session, the patient went on to say that it was nice
that his boss had listened to him for a change. Dr. Sands
looked up from her notes and suggested that the image
validated her silent listening and Dr. Sommers agreed.
With that, the supervisory hour (which contained other
discussions that are not pertinent here) ended.

Dr. Sands' presentation of the next session began with her
reporting that her patient had begun by complaining that
he had had a difficult week. Uncharacteristically, he had
been involved in a fight with the comptroller of their
company — and it wasn't even his battle. It seems that the

comptroller had recommended a series of pay reductions for the office staff. Even though his salary would not be affected, Mr. Stanley had argued furiously for not cutting costs that way. Too many people would be hurt, and it was a way of exploiting their vulnerable positions — on and on he had raged against the proposal. Maybe waiting to hear about the therapist's decision regarding his fee had set him off — he had no way of knowing.

Mr. Stanley had had a dream in which his sister, who had died of meningitis, came into his bedroom and tried to get him to follow her somewhere — she was tempting him with all kinds of gifts if only he would come along. It was like she was trying to lure him to join her in death. He had never gotten over her loss; to this day he believes that the doctors had committed malpractice and had screwed up her medications and killed her.

At this point in the supervisory hour, Dr. Sommers elected to intervene. Her criterion was that the patient had filled the recipe for intervening — he had alluded directly to the frame-related trigger (the anticipated decision of the therapist regarding reducing his fee) and had produced several clear bridging themes (e.g. the money issue at work) and a model of rectification that spoke for maintaining the secured frame (don't reduce anyone's pay). There were also some very powerful encoded themes that embodied the patient's personally selected unconscious perceptions of the therapist in light of the *anticipated trigger*— the possibility that Dr. Sands would reduce Mr. Stanley's fee. Unconsciously, the expected intervention was seen by the patient as an inappropriate pay cut, as Dr. Sands allowing herself to be exploited, and as an act that could cause the demise of the therapist or the therapy — a fatal error.

I will not detail here the teaching through which this supervisor engaged her supervisee in order to elicit these realizations. The two of them agreed that the supervisee should have intervened around this time in the session and, much to her delight, Dr. Sands said that she had.

The comment she had made did, as formulated, touch on the trigger of an expected decrease in the patient's fee and the encoded perceptions outlined above (though the supervisee did omit the allusion to actually killing the patient psychologically — the doctor's murder of the sister).

In all, the intervention was met with high praise by Dr. Sommers, who then added the few missing thematic elements that the supervisee had failed to include in her comment. She also stressed and praised the fact that Dr. Sands definitively secured the frame by indicating that unconsciously the patient had made clear that there should be no reduction in her pay — that it would be unfair to her and exploitative. Dr. Sommers indicated that encoded validation most definitely should follow this kind of frame-securing interpretive effort, after which some expression of secured-frame anxiety could also be expected to emerge.

Dr. Sands went on with the session. The patient had paused after she had made her extended comment and said that it all made sense, but he really was in financial straits — he'd have to see how things worked out. Mr. Stanley thought next of an earlier incident with the controller. The patient had gone to him for some personal financial advice regarding a real-estate investment he was thinking of making. The controller had warned him not to get involved with a real-estate deal, he didn't trust the property market at the time. It turned out that the man was visionary because the real-estate market had collapsed soon after the deal was consummated and Mr. Stanley would have lost his entire investment. His mother was good at handling money, but his father never had a penny. The patient hoped he'd never be like him.

Dr. Sands then intervened and pointed out that these images seemed to suggest that holding the fee as it is was a wise decision which would avoid a possible disaster, and that the patient saw her much like his mother — wise in handling money — and unlike his father. In response, Mr.

Stanley fell silent for a moment, and then said that Dr. Sands' office seemed stuffy today, maybe she could open the door — no, he was only kidding.

In supervision, this responsive material was discussed for the signs of *interpersonal validation* (the allusion to the wise controller) and for its measure of additional cognitive validation (the genetic links to the parents). Discussion also brought out that secured-frame anxiety did indeed materialize in the reference the patient made to the stuffy (entrapping?) office and his wish for the door to be opened — a clear expression of a wish to modify the frame and gain relief from the newly experienced entrapping claustrum. The fact that the patient expressed these anxieties in a humorous way spoke for a favourable adaptation to these conflicts. The benefits of sound supervision based on the communicative model are reaped by each member of the extended S/S/P system.

SOME ADDITIONAL PERSPECTIVES FOR SUPERVISORS

There are many unresolved problems inherent in today's approaches to doing supervision. Perhaps the greatest threat to effective supervisory work lies with the fact that a supervisor must do his or her work using the highly defensive conscious system. As a result, there are endless pressures to modify the framework of the supervision itself and to sanction frame alterations in the supervised therapy. There is as well a universal dread of deep unconscious meaning that must be counteracted to allow for sound readings of the encoded communications from supervised patients and the interventions of their therapist/supervisees.

The inclination and temptation to use the supervisory situation to express and gratify a supervisor's inappropriate or pathological needs is enormous. Given that every expression of countertransference in a psychotherapy expresses such tendencies, we can appreciate that this danger is all the greater in supervision. Who among us is not needy, searching for someone — anyone — to hear us out, especially at times of stress and distress? It asks a great deal of a supervisor to refrain from introducing such needs into his or her work with a supervisee — but not doing so is his or her commitment to both the supervisee and the supervised patient.

The main safeguard against error and misalliance in supervision is, of course, the use of trigger decoding and the insistence on encoded validation for all interventions in the supervisory field. The opportunities for straying from the assigned path of the supervisory process are great and the path itself is quite narrow. But, nevertheless, it is a path that leads to the most effective and least costly adaptations and modes of symptom resolution known to humankind.

THE COINCIDENTAL EDUCATION
OF THE SUPERVISOR

A well-established maxim of psychotherapy supervision states that *the supervisor must learn and grow through his or her teaching experience.* This growth is by no means simply an intellectual happening, nor does it come mainly from seeing new things in a supervised patient's material or a supervisee's interventions, or in their interaction. True growth is a personal event and comes primarily as a coincidental effect of the supervisory process, which is, of course, devoted mainly to the education of the supervisee as a psychotherapist.

Most of this learning is, painfully, the consequence of *supervisory errors*, which are, as is true with countertransference expressions in doing psychotherapy, absolutely inevitable (Langs, 1980). The problem does not lie with their occurrence, but with their *recognition*. To learn and benefit from a mistake requires consciously realizing that the error has been committed. In supervision, this can be accomplished in two ways: first, by accepting as mistaken all supervisory interventions that do not obtain encoded validation from the material of the supervised patient. In that case, the problem is usually that the supervisor has used the wrong trigger in integrating the derivative themes; thus, the search should be initiated for the correct trigger, one that better organizes the patient's encoded material.

The second means of identifying supervisory countertransferences and errors is by allowing any sense of discomfort, extreme fantasy or affect, or feeling that things are amiss to be a signal of possible error. The search for these problems may take the form just described, but, in addition, the supervisor is well advised to engage in self-processing in order to discover the deep unconscious nature and sources of his or her failing (Langs, 1992f, 1993a).

Recognizing errors and pursuing their roots and rectification are a most compelling and moving means of generating deep inner change and growth in a supervisor. These efforts are made *privately*, and the supervisee should not be burdened with these pursuits except as they materialize openly in the course of the supervisory work — as when a supervisor attempts to reformulate the supervised patient's material in light of the non-validation of his or her thinking by utilizing the encoded recommendations of the supervised patient. Learning in the course of the sound conduct of a supervision is a *sine qua non* for those who strive to teach effective psychotherapy.

CHAPTER ELEVEN

The supervisee:
responsibilities and entitlements

V irtually everything covered so far in this book can be recruited by a supervisee for his or her own edification and perspectives on sound supervision. The means through which a supervisee can monitor his or her own efforts to learn and do psychotherapy and assess the work of his or her supervisor have also been made available. In this chapter, however, I focus quite specifically on the supervisee in order to bring his or her essential issues before us for discussion and illumination. I will, in the main, develop two areas of importance to the supervisee: first, his or her responsibilities to the supervisor, the supervisory process and the supervisory frame, and the means by which he or she can specifically evaluate his or her own participation in the supervisory process (*self-assessment*); second, the means by which the supervisee can evaluate the supervisor with whom he or she is working (*the assessment of the supervisor*) — and the choices that are available to the student, depending on the nature of that appraisal.

175

A SUPERVISEE'S BASIC ATTITUDE

It is not uncommon to find supervisees who are quite naive regarding their contribution to the supervisory process. While managing the supervision is, as we saw, the primary responsibility of the supervisor, the supervisee also has a large share of accountability as well. The supervisee's role begins with his or her basic or general attitude towards the supervision and the supervisor. Ideally, we would expect a strong sense of commitment to the setting, schedule, and other aspects of the fixed frame, along with a true sense of openness to the supervisor's teaching. Nevertheless, there should also be a capacity to evaluate independently what is offered and to keep a sharp ear open for the test of encoded validation in response to a supervisor's appraisal of the supervisee's work and his or her proposed alternative interventions.

A supervisee should also be prepared to ask questions geared towards his or her enlightenment and to speak up when he or she feels a sense of disagreement with the position adopted by the supervisor. A supervisee may formulate or intervene in a way that may or may not be supported by the supervisor, but whatever the match-up, it is essential that the student accept *the encoded material from the supervised patient* as the ultimate voice that speaks to the validity of his or her own work. Encoded narratives must also be the arbitrator of every assessment of the supervisor's efforts and of every disagreement between the two parties to the teaching situation. In all, a supervisee should operate within supervision with a deep respect for unconscious communication and the second unconscious system whose encoded messages — perceptions, adaptations, viewpoints, interpretations, models of frame-securing rectifications, and the like — embody the greatest wisdom available within and to the S/S/P system.

SUPERVISION UNDER THE AUSPICES OF TRAINING PROGRAMS

Special problems arise for the supervisee who is being seen under the auspices of a training program. The ideal attitude under these conditions is difficult to define. For one thing, the deviant frame of these supervisory situations inevitably interferes with the teaching and learning, and with the overall integrity of the supervisory experience. Secondary motives are introduced on both sides of the desk — the supervisor is under scrutiny even though the evaluative focus primarily is on the supervisee.

Often, the underlying issues are quite serious, such as the supervisee's opportunity to continue in the training program — and, at times, as a psychotherapist. There is also the concern about being thought of as a good therapist, and about the expectations of teaching opportunities at the institute and of current or later referrals. Although a referral from a supervisor is frame-deviant, it nonetheless touches on the supervisee's livelihood and it takes a great deal of conviction for a supervisee to accept the idea that, unconsciously, referrals from their mentors have harmful consequences — which they do always.

Concern also exists in the supervisee regarding who is informed about his or her supervised therapeutic work and how the supervision will affect his or her status at the institute. The picture of the supervisor is distinctly mixed — there is a sense of his or her power, authority, expertise (hopefully), and position as someone who has a strong say in the fate of the student. Thus, respect and admiration (when present) is inescapably mixed with helplessness, fear, and dread — and depression as well, especially after a difficult teaching experience. These emotions certainly are not the attributes of an ideal support system and frame for efficient learning.

How, then, should the supervisee approach supervision in a training situation? First, he or she must trust himself or herself to be capable of learning how to do effective psychotherapy and be quite prepared to learn from mistakes in particular. It is unimaginable to think of a good supervisor without seeing him or her as a compassionate teacher who expects the supervisee to make errors of commission and omission. Both supervisor and supervisee should expect that the supervisory experience will unfold with the student's ignorance gradually transforming itself into the skills of an effective psychotherapist — all's well that ends well.

The training situation asks the supervisee to trust both himself or herself and the supervisor, and to recognize and accept the inevitable pains of learning — especially when it comes to psychotherapy and takes place in, of all settings, an evaluative training program. And while the hurts cut deeply, the discovery that in truth a particular supervisee is not designed mentally and emotionally to be a psychotherapist is more a painful gift than insensitive harm — as long as the evaluation is well founded. Of course, any supervisory situation in which this possibility arises is in crisis and must be handled in special ways — perhaps through a change in the supervisor or turning to self-processing supervision (see chapter fourteen).

In any case, the supervisee has the right and obligation to himself or herself, and even to the supervisor, to evaluate the work of his or her mentor in order to be sure that the supervisory frame is otherwise well secured and that the teaching is valid and sound. Being in a training situation should not imply extremes of passivity and the absence of autonomous judgements and appraisals. A supervisee should stand strong yet listen with respect — and rightfully ask for encoded validation of what he or she is being taught.

THE RESPONSIBILITIES OF THE SUPERVISEE

Let us turn now to the primary obligations of a supervisee to the supervisory process and frame. *To state these as responsibilities, the supervisee should:*

1. Ensure an optimally secured frame for the supervision

As is true of the supervisor, the supervisee should be committed to as secure a frame as possible for his or her supervisory experience. This implies three possibilities:

  a. *The supervisee accepts an ideal frame when it is proposed by the supervisor, and agrees also with the secured-frame aspects of an altered frame.*

This precept indicates that a supervisee does not request a frame modification from a supervisor who is offering a secured frame, nor does he or she ask for additional frame deviations from a supervisor who is structuring the supervisory work with departures from the ideal ground rules. It is virtually certain that a supervisee will unwittingly request further frame modifications from a supervisor who has not offered the best conditions possible for the supervision — frame deviations beget frame deviations. But even when a supervisor is not especially mindful of the supervisory frame, the supervisee should be clear on its status — and do what he or she can to keep the frame as secured as possible.

b.   *The supervisee makes active efforts to have the supervisory frame secured when a supervisor has proposed or is working within a modified frame.*

The supervisee must, even when a supervisor does not do so, actively seek the most ideal frame possible for his or her learning experience. Both secured-frame anxieties and pathological deviant-frame needs must be combated so that the supervisee can bring up frame problems with the supervisor. Those teachers who work from the communicative model of supervision are likely to be open to and understand the frame issues that his or her supervisee brings up — it is likely that the deviant situation is one of inadvertent oversight.

On the other hand, a supervisor who works from the standard psychoanalytic model of supervision is unlikely to appreciate the extensive ramifications of the ground rules of supervision. He or she will rationalize existing deviations and oppose their exploration and rectification. The student who rightly is convinced that he or she is being harmed by the frame alterations of a supervisory situation, and that his or her opportunities to learn are suffering, will recognize that this mismatch speaks for a supervisory crisis (see chapter twelve) — at times, the problem suggests the need to find a new supervisor, unless the present one vows to change his or her basic attitude towards the communicative approach and its validated precepts.

c.   *The supervisee engages in frame-securing activities in response to a modified frame that has been created by his or her supervisor.*

A supervisee is free and should be inclined to correct a fee that is too low or to ask that his or her supervisor not change the time of the supervisory hour. He or she can explain a decision *not* to provide material from the supervision to a supervisor so that he or she can publish it in a paper or book. Or a student can ask for regular supervisory sessions with a clearly defined time for the work. There are many details of the ground rules of supervision to which an alert supervisee can attend.

In general, this means that a supervisee should comply with and adhere to a fixed frame that is as secured as possible without altering the frame himself or herself. Thus, a supervisee should attend all scheduled supervisory sessions except for reasons of severe illness or emergency, pay a reasonable and fair fee to the supervisor, accept a consistent time and place for the supervision, and the like. This adherence to an ideal frame extends to the other ground rules of the supervision as well. The supervisee maintains his or her relative anonymity and neutrality, as well as the privacy and confidentiality of the supervision (see chapters six and seven). In addition, he or she accepts and tries to ensure adherence to these constraints by the supervisor.

To fulfil these obligations a supervisee must have a grasp of the adaptive design of the emotion-processing mind and, especially, its deep unconscious system. He or she needs to be committed to an adaptive-interactional way of listening and formulating both the material from the patient and his or her own interventions, and he or she also should be adept at trigger decoding. The supervisee will also need a deep understanding of the influence of ground rules and frames on his or her functioning — in both therapy and supervision. The development and maintenance of a secured frame for a supervisory experience asks a lot of the supervisee — as it does of the supervisor — but it is well rewarded.

Maintaining a secured supervisory space may at times require that the supervisee express encoded narrative material when an acute frame issue is at hand. Supervisees tend to do this spontaneously because frame breaks and frame-securing moments psycho-biologically evoke a human need to respond unconsciously and derivatively to such situations. The main tasks are for the supervisee to recognize the nature of his or her communications and needs, and to help the supervisor to appreciate the existence of an active frame-related trigger within the supervisory situation — usually constituted by some frame-related intervention that he or she has carried out or is planning to make. However, if the teacher fails to trigger-decode a student's narrative material in light of activated frame-related triggers, the supervisee should strive to do so (see chapter fourteen).

2. *Adhere to the rules governing the process of the supervision*

Supervisees, as is true of many supervisors, consciously have lax and unclear views of the structure of the supervisory situation. There is, then, a universal temptation to veer off from the assigned roles and tasks of supervision in an effort to satisfy a wide range of pathological needs for gratification and defence. The conscious wish for personal advice, to engage in uncalled-for self-revelations, a chance to talk about peers and other mentors or to discuss whatever other extraneous issues come to mind, all motivate the supervisee to depart from his or her assigned role — which is to offer honestly crafted and sufficiently detailed process-note case material written immediately or soon after sessions and to learn the techniques of psychotherapy from the supervisor on that basis.

Beneath all of the rationalizations used to excuse these departures from the ideal frame, there are deeply unconscious needs to sabotage the supervision or to recruit it for ill gain. Commonly invoked excuses include the argument that not modifying the frame makes supervision cold, rigid, unfeeling, mechanical, and such. Yet all of these conscious-system justifications reflect a fateful failure to appreciate the second unconscious system and the unconscious forces unleashed by frame alterations of that kind.

Some supervisees feel inhibited with regard to asking questions of, or challenging, their supervisors' teachings and ideas. This is, as noted, especially problematic when the supervision involves formal training. Nevertheless, a supervisee's questioning attitude is an essential part of the supervisory process and should be sustained in a fair and decent manner. The supervisee's responsibilities in supervision shift from active (presenting case material) to receptive (listening attentively to the supervisor's comments) back to active (asking questions and commenting as needed).

The supervisory situation should be treated with the same kind of commitment and respect that the supervisee has for the therapeutic situation in which he or she works. Failures to adhere to these requisites speak for major supervisory impediments and for *resistances* in the supervisee that must be resolved if effective learning is to occur. Still, the supervisee should be quite clear that even though he or she must take primary responsibility for these resistances, their roots are always interactional in nature.

In pursuing the sources of these usually frame-breaking obstacles — for example, not doing process notes, missing supervisory sessions, *blindly* opposing supervisory advice, and such — it is essential to discover the triggers from the supervisor that have precipitated their use by the supervisee. As always, then, the exploration of an intractable resistance in a supervisee begins with a scrutiny of the frame-related triggers reflected in the supervisor's management of the ground rules of the supervision. From there, the exploration fans out to take into account the personal inclinations of the supervisee and other qualities in the supervisor — for example, the tone of his or her approach, signs of latent or overt hostility and/or seductiveness, impatience, proneness to non-validated suggestions, and so forth. In general, discussions of difficult issues of this kind are seldom resolved via conscious-system give-and-take exploration. Often, the success of efforts to resolve a supervisee's resistances depends on a shift to self-processing supervision — or on the private self-processing of the student and/or teacher.

3. *Keep in check the wish to satisfy inappropriate needs in the supervision*

It is a given that a supervisee wishes to please and find favour with his or her supervisor. This is a natural motive, but it may lead to unnatural and pathological behaviours such as blind submissiveness to the supervisor's interventions, the use of non-validated techniques favoured by the supervisor but harmful to the patient and supervisee himself or herself, the acceptance of unneeded frame deviations created by the teacher, or efforts to have contacts with the supervisor outside the supervision. All of these frame alterations extract a costly price from everyone in the S/S/P system — they should be curtailed to the greatest extent possible.

It is evident, then, that both supervisee and supervisor must maintain an unswerving devotion and commitment to the primary goals of their work together. This is a principle that is easily violated not only because of a multitude of conscious-system distractions and needs, but also because of the afore-mentioned unconscious needs in both parties to supervision to move the process into frame-deviant territories and away from its ideal course.

4. *Maintain an open mind with respect to the teachings of the supervisor and insist on encoded validation of all supervisory formulations of the material and all proposed interventions*

These maxims, which have been alluded to earlier, deserve special emphasis here. Many supervisees select a supervisor because the latter has an investment in a particular approach to psychotherapy — classically Freudian, Jungian, Kleinian, etc. This creates a great danger of harmful supervisory mis-alliances in which shared blind-spots and errors are quite prevalent. The hidden motive of the supervisee is to maintain a fixed view of psychotherapy and of psychopathology that often is replete with error. Little viable knowledge or genuine growth will eventuate under these circumstances.

On the other hand, a supervisee may enter into supervision with a supervisor whose theoretical preferences are unknown to or different from those of the supervisee. This may lead to a supervisory crisis in which the supervisee adopts an en-trenched position, in opposition to the supervisor's teachings (see chapter twelve). When the issue is one of competing theories, neither of them grounded in an independent means of validation, there is little hope of a satisfying resolution. All too often it becomes a matter of a supervisee's capitulation and submission to the supervisor or his or her rebellion — neither is a decent solution.

There is, as far as I know, only one clear way out of these dilemmas—namely, the use of encoded validation from the material from the supervised patient as the means by which a supervisor's work is judged and evaluated. Unconscious confirmation is an independent entity which does, of course, rely on the good judgement and sense of the decoder. Nevertheless, any number of theories of the emotion-processing mind and its dysfunctions, and of the psychotherapeutic process, may evolve from the implementation of this standard. The communicative approach is the only known theory to arise in this way, but others may well follow. Still, it is a theory that is testable — within whatever human limits apply — and it offers the supervisee a yardstick for measuring both his or her own work and that of the supervisor.

This guiding principle serves another critical function: it protects all concerned from the natural tendency of the conscious system — conscious thinking and functioning — to move away from the centrality of deep unconscious experience and into the risky conscious-system realm. This means that the supervisory process is always under motivational pressure to veer off from this vital centre point; the requirement of encoded validation is the magnet that brings the process back onto course.

For a supervisee, this guideline serves to counteract the behavioural effects of the universal fear of deep unconscious meaning and the secured frames to which they relate. These distracting forces are supplemented as a rule by the individual dysfunctional needs of a given supervisee, many of them quite unconscious. Yet all such needs promote pathological searches for a supervisor's collusive sanction of the supervisee's erroneous interventions, and subtly or grossly encourage inappropriate recommendations of technique by the teacher. Perhaps the most common form of present-day misalliance between supervisor and supervisee involves the offer of unprincipled suggestions by the former and their uncritical acceptance by the latter — all of it without a search for unconscious validation in the material on hand from the supervised patient.

The *conscious system* is so set on erroneous forms of therapy that it cannot be relied on to provide any sound means of assessing the validity of a supervisee's wishes or a supervisor's interventions. Direct agreement by a supervisee with a formulation of his or her supervisor is often the result of an unconscious pathological need and neurotically prejudiced judgement, rather than a reflection of a sound appraisal. *For reasons of both defence and basic design, the conscious system is so committed in the emotional domain to non-validated modes of formulating and doing therapy that it is to be mistrusted and not used by a supervisee as the instrument of evaluation of a supervisor's work.*

The only viable and definitive assessment of supervisory interventions stems from an *unconscious* appraisal rather than one that is conscious — a principle that applies equally to both psychotherapy and its supervision. This implies that there are two potential sources for these evaluations — the unconscious communications from the supervised patient and the unconscious messages from the supervisee. In a straightforward supervisory situation, the former source of validation is primary and the latter is used in supplementary fashion. However, in the type of self-processing supervision to be described in chapter fourteen, both methods can be applied with great effectiveness.

The supervisee must develop an inner template of encoded validation from his or her patients and also consistently apply this criterion to all supervisory interventions. The supervisee is entitled to be assured that the criterion of disguised validation will be at the centre of all teaching efforts by the supervisor. Furthermore, the evaluation of the patient's material should be a fair one, and efforts should be made to safeguard against the supervisor's need to prove that he or she is correct in stating a formulation by stretching the reading of the disguised material to support his or her position. In practice, encoded validation is usually quite disarming and unexpectedly clear; there is no need to force one's reading of the derivative material. The supervisee, mindful of his or her own resistances and anxieties, nevertheless should be rationally satisfied with his or her supervisor's appraisal and should be able in some way to add to what has been proposed. As noted, an open-minded, please-prove-it-to-me, attitude seems best.

When a supervisee attempts to intervene according to the teachings of the supervisor, two considerations apply. First, the supervisee should check out his or her intervention to be certain that the advice has been well used — for example, communicatively, that a sound piece of trigger decoding has been carried out. Second, as we would expect, after intervening, the supervisee should also attend to the material from the patient for encoded validation. If confirmation appears, all is well in both the psychotherapy and the supervision. If it does not materialize, then either the recommendation of the supervisor was in error or the supervisee misapplied it.

Careful listening to and formulating of the ensuing material from the patient is the best way to discover the source of non-validation. As noted, the most common cause is the failure to intervene interactionally or the selection of the wrong trigger for linking with the encoded themes. Quite naturally, since it is an aspect of the supervisee's presentation in the supervisory session that follows these efforts, this problem will come up for discussion in the next supervisory session. In general, the supervisee can expect that the supervisor will be able to help him or her understand the basis for non-validation from the patient — and offer fresh recommendations as well.

Any objection by a supervisee to the principle of guidance via encoded material from the patient should be seen as a basic *resistance* to the need to structure psychotherapy and its supervision as pursuits of the second unconscious system and its powerful unconscious expressions. The invocation of mani-fest-content/surface-implications, conscious-system forms of therapy and supervision is a flight from secured frames and deep meaning and from that part of the emotion-processing mind that houses the power of emotional life. Conscious-system work may, defensively, bring a modicum of relief to the S/S/P system, but it is costly and flawed relief at best. It is far wiser to attempt to resolve these resistances and their unconscious sources than to succumb to them.

A SUPERVISEE'S NEED
FOR PERSONAL THERAPY

In raising the issue of emotional dysfunctions in supervisees, we are, of course, broaching the subject of how such difficulties can be recognized in supervision, how and when a supervisor should bring up the question of therapy for the supervisee, and with whom a supervisee should pursue his or her own personal psychotherapy. A supervisor will of course monitor a supervisee's work with the question of countertransferences and emotional difficulties in mind. If he or she believes that the emotional problems of a supervisee are interfering with his or her learning processes and doing effective psychotherapy, the supervisor will, as a rule, inquire as to whether the supervisee is in personal therapy — and whether the supervisee feels the need for treatment if he or she is not at the moment pursuing that option.

While a supervisor can recommend psychotherapy, the final decision belongs, of course, to the supervisee. Indeed, the student should be judged solely on the basis of his or her work with the supervised patient — the inquiry into the supervisee's status vis-à-vis personal therapy is, of course, a frame alteration (ideally, this is not something that the supervisee should reveal or discuss with his or her supervisor). In this regard, the supervisee himself or herself should also engage in self-monitoring in order to recognize the scope and effects of his or her own dysfunctions — and deal accordingly with the decision regarding personal treatment.

It can be safely stated that countertransference expressions are inevitable in doing psychotherapy, and that every error made by a supervisee has an element of psychopathology to it. Given that a supervisee's rate of error is often quite high, especially early in his or her therapy work, does this mean that there is a repeated call for personal therapy in everyone who becomes a supervisee? The answer is both yes and no. Yes, because doing psychotherapy is the kind of endeavour that brings out an individual's psychopathology — and there's plenty of it in all of us. No, because there must also be room for cognitive learning and for relatively benign mistakes. In principle, the issue of a supervisee's personal need for therapy need not come up unless there are repeated errors, a consistent inability to develop sound techniques, or an acute issue or major lapse that is so serious as to merit immediate attention — for example, a supervisee's extreme verbal assault of a patient, forgetting a patient's sessions, being openly seductive or strongly hating or loving a patient, and the like.

As noted, the decision as to whether to seek treatment belongs entirely to the supervisee. The supervisor may make a recommendation or even engage in a conscious-system discussion of this need with the supervisee, but the final decision is the supervisee's alone. When a supervisor and supervisee openly disagree in this regard — for example, when a teacher advocates therapy and the student does not — a supervisory crisis is likely to ensue. Several considerations then need to be brought forth. First, the supervisor must allow the supervisee a reasonable latitude for error. Second, the expressed difficulties of the supervisee are not simply the consequences of personal intrapsychic conflicts and his or her problem alone. They are manifestations of the supervised P/T system and the S/S system within the supervisory frame. The supervisor is therefore obligated to determine how much of the problem stems from the supervisee's interaction with the particular patient under study, but, even more so, how much comes from the supervisory situation itself — its framework and the nature of what the supervisor himself or herself is teaching. These are complex issues that call for self-processing and self-processing supervision for their resolution (see chapters twelve to fourteen).

The supervisee should not accept sole accountability for any difficulty experienced in his or her therapeutic work or supervision. Nevertheless, the dysfunction is his or hers. If rectifying frames and working through the interactional issues does not resolve the emotional difficulties and the ways in which they are interfering with the supervisee's work, then personal treatment or possibly self-processing supervision are indicated. To maintain a secured frame, *the supervisor should refrain from recommending a therapist to his or her student* — the supervisee should pursue that search outside the supervisory frame.

Finally, what are the issues and recourse *when a supervisee believes that his or her supervisor is repeatedly off the mark or is suffering from emotional difficulties?* Clearly, a supervisee should continually assess the education that he or she is receiving from a supervisor and should keep a wary eye open for a supervisor's dysfunctions — teachers are in no way immune from emotional difficulties that interfere with their supervisory work. As we have seen, the key guide is encoded validation from the supervised patient. Other impressions, which come from conscious-system assessments, are far less reliable and will need some kind of unconscious confirmation. Nevertheless, a confused, unhelpful, seductive, hostile, deprecatory, and otherwise nasty and unnecessarily hurtful supervisor will need to be confronted at some point in the work — and, at times, the supervision will need to be terminated by the supervisee. Because much of this falls into the domain of supervisory crises, we will considered these problems further in the next chapter.

TERMINATING SUPERVISION

The problem of ending supervision involves a host of issues that need clarification, much of it mainly from the vantage point of the supervisee. In principle, *we would expect supervision to be terminated when a supervisee has shown a relative mastery of the techniques of psychotherapy and is making interventions that are consistently obtaining encoded validation from his or her patients.*

One approach to termination begins when a supervisor recognizes that the supervisee has reached the primary goal of supervision, as reflected in his or her work with patients, and suggests that supervision end at some agreed-upon time. However, supervisors tend to be reluctant to let go of supervisees and are inclined to extend the teaching relationship beyond a fair point of termination. The problem is complicated by the difficulties that supervisees have in making self-assessments and in giving up their mentors, with whom they tend to form idealizing and clinging misalliances. Because of this, the supervisee should monitor his or her own work and be alert for the point at which he or she feels a sense of reasonable competency as a psychotherapist.

The identification of a sensible termination point is no easy matter, although the hope is that both supervisor and supervisee will decide at around the same time that the student has reached that end-point. Wise or unwise, in private supervision the termination decision belongs primarily to the supervisee — at most, the supervisor should serve as a guide by introducing this possibility when necessary and in helping the supervisee explore the basis for his or her own thoughts of ending supervision.

There are many complexities to this decision. For example, there are inherent obstacles to learning the communicative version of psychotherapy, and expectations of a supervisee cannot be too high and unrealistic — relative mastery is usually sufficient. This should, however, include a capacity in the supervisee to secure frames at the behest of patients' encoded directives — being able to interpret and manage deviant and secured frames is part of the essential goals of the learning experience. The appropriate end-point of a supervision is therefore not precisely definable, and the determination entails a measure of clinical-supervisor/supervisee judgement — along with the understanding that perfection is an ideal sought for but never fully achieved.

If a supervisor proposes termination to the supervisee, the latter's reaction can be either to agree with the proposal or to disagree and ask to continue their work together. In the first instance, a termination date is agreed upon and adhered to — there is little in the way of issue. The main principle is to *maintain the usual supervisory frame and structure to the very end of supervision — and afterwards as well.* It is important for a supervisor and supervisee not to succumb to the temptation to modify the frame of supervision because of the separation and death anxieties that are mobilized by the end of a supervisory experience.

All too often, the prospect of terminating the supervisory relationship prompts a variety of carefully but erroneously rationalized efforts to modify the supervisory frame. The frame modifications may be proposed or enacted primarily by either party to supervision, but the response of the other member of the dyad — supervisee or supervisor — should be to sustain the secured frame and not allow alterations to proceed. Unless the supervisory model is self-processing supervision, each party should then process the underlying issues on his or her own. However, should a supervisory crisis develop, some type of mutual exploration will be needed (see chapter twelve).

Both supervisor and supervisee should be alert to the effects of terminating the supervision on the work of the supervisee — especially with the supervised patient. Because so much of an individual's termination anxieties often remains unconscious, this generates strong *displaced effects* in the professional and private lives of both the supervisor and the supervisee. Frame alterations and missed interventions, and other inadvertent errors, are not uncommon at such times. They tend to draw the patient unduly close to, or to create excessive distance from, the supervisee and are used unconsciously to deny the real and underlying experiences of loss and death that occur with the end of a supervisory relationship. The termination of supervision is a powerful adaptation-evoking trigger that needs careful processing both through the supervisory material and on a personal–individual basis by both parties to supervision.

As noted, the supervisee has a responsibility to monitor his or her own progress as the student, and to recognize the transition to a point of doing effective therapeutic work. The danger of a supervisory misalliance in which the supervision is prematurely terminated because of an antagonism between supervisor and supervisee or extended beyond its necessary duration can be safeguarded only through frequent assessments of the status of the supervisee's clinical work — and being able to sense when enough is enough.

If a supervisee believes that he or she has reached the point of relative mastery of the techniques of psychotherapy, he or she should propose that the supervision end soon and explain the basis for this request. If the supervisor agrees, matters again move forward as planned, with supervision being terminated at the end of a future month or two, or at the time of a planned vacation by the supervisor. If the supervisor disagrees, he or she should explain the basis for wanting to continue the supervisory work, and the supervisee should attempt to ascertain if these objections to stopping supervision are valid. In addition to this general reappraisal, the work done by the supervisee in the weeks that follow should be carefully assessed for its effectiveness and possible failings. After a few weeks of observing, the issue of termination can then be reconsidered in light of these contemporary observations of the supervisee's work.

Finally, note must be made of the *forced termination* of supervision in a clinic or training program or for other reasons — for example, a supervisor or supervisee leaving the area, an extended or serious illness in either party, and so on. These terminations are highly traumatic for both supervisor and supervisee, and they activate strong unconscious anxieties and conflicts. The supervisee must safeguard his or her work with the supervised and other patients against the displaced effects of such a premature or forced termination — and he or she should undertake some form of self-processing to work through the unconscious issues that have been aroused by this traumatic trigger.

In principle, despite common practice, a supervisee in training, whose supervision is terminated because he or she has completed, or is compelled to leave, the program, should seek out a new supervisor rather than continue with the present teacher. On the one hand, the change in the conditions of the supervision to the private office of the supervisor — if such is the case — may move the supervision with the present supervisor towards a more secured frame. But on the other hand, the extended experience of a frame-deviant supervision, and the boundary and other problems inherent to this type of transfer, give a frame-altered cast to the continuing supervision that is best avoided. If supervision is, however, continued with the same supervisor, self-processing supervision appears to be the best framework for these extended efforts.

THE POST-TERMINATION PERIOD

Finally, let us consider the possible relationships that can develop between a supervisor and his or her supervisee once supervision is terminated. What are the ground rules for their behaviour and contacts at that juncture?

The specifics of the ideal post-supervision frame are difficult to determine because little solid data is available on which to base the assessment. Furthermore, the relentless human search for opportunities for deviant-frame gratification and defence has made the post-termination period an opportune time for ill-rationalized decisions to abandon the secured frame in favour of a wide range of frame-deviant interactions. Nevertheless, the basic principles of frame maintenance apply to this as they do to any other professional or life situation — secured frames serve emotional health and the sound functioning of both supervisor and supervisee, while frame deviations create trouble.

Ideally and without substantial question, *the ground rules of supervision call for no further contact of any kind between a former supervisor and supervisee.* The appropriate place for their meetings is that of the supervisor's professional office, and the appropriate purpose is the education of the supervisee. Once the supervisory experience is at an end, there is no need or reason for the two parties to supervision to meet again — indeed, to do so is to engage in a significant modification of the supervisory frame. The responsibility to maintain that frame and the nature of its secured condition does not change with termination, and neither the supervisor nor the supervisee should seize this opportunity to gain pathological deviant-frame satisfactions with harmful, unconsciously transmitted consequences for both parties.

Holding to the supervisory frame is the sole means through which the healthy secured-frame needs of both supervisor and supervisee are satisfied and reinforced. This type of secured-frame experience is vital to their effective work as therapists — and to their personal lives. In this regard, all protests against this dictum and all actions that violate this aspect of the secured frame — and they are plentiful — are, in important ways, efforts to justify frame modifications consciously in the face of strong secured-frame, death-related anxieties. The conscious system greatly prefers frame-altering solutions in coping with these termination, death-related, and other anxieties rather than holding to the secured frame and constructively working through the activated issues — conscious and unconscious. Both supervisor and supervisee should be forewarned against accepting conscious-system preferences in these situations — trigger decoding and accessing the wisdom of the deep unconscious system serves them far better.

Nature is nature, and a price is paid for all frame modifications — no matter how seemingly well-rationalized. A fair assessment of thoughts of post-supervision contact can be made only through personal self-processing and listening to one's own encoded derivatives as they are activated by the termination experience and by any specific movement towards holding the supervisory frame secured or modifying it. The deep unconscious system is always very clear about these choices — it never wavers from advocating frame-securing alternatives even as the conscious system waffles and compromises and proposes deviations again and again.

Trigger decoding alone can provide the necessary deep insights into these conflicts and issues, and, without exception, it will speak clearly for frame maintenance rather than frame alteration. This applies when the further contact is professional — for example, teaching in the same setting, working on papers or books together, doing other professional tasks together, and so on — or personal, as seen when there is post-termination social contact of any kind. Of course, the more removed the frame deviation is from the professional realm, the stronger the disturbing unconscious impact and effects.

Unconsciously, all such departures from the ideal frame are seen as incestuous, assaultive, invasive, seductive, and the like. Indeed, these frame-modifying practices play a large role in the perpetuation of shared psychopathology, errant interventions, abuse of patients, and the use of harmful frame alterations that characterize the practice of psychotherapy today — they are hurtful to both practitioners and their patients. They also make constructive change all but impossible for a field that is very much in need of such changes.

SELF-SUPERVISION
AND LATER SUPERVISORY EXPERIENCES

Two common issues arise once a given supervision has been terminated. The first is the shift from learning from a mentor to self-supervision, while the second arises whenever a terminated supervisee feels a need for further clinical enlightenment and training.

In principle, a psychotherapist continuously monitors his or her work with patients for countertransference expressions throughout his or her career. After a sound supervisory experience or two, a therapist is usually capable of sufficient self-observation (however limited this function may be) to pick up a need to work through a therapeutic error or frame-break, or a disturbing constellation of feelings or other reactions to a particular patient — and then to engage in personal self-processing to access the deepest roots of the difficulty. The necessary techniques for this type of self-healing have been presented elsewhere (Langs, 1993a) and will be outlined in chapter fourteen.

If the countertransference difficulties persist or there seems to be a fundamental problem in carrying out effective psychotherapy in general, both psychotherapy and additional supervision should be considered. Personal self-processing therapy or self-processing supervision are the best options under these circumstances. However, if the choice is simply to seek further supervision, it is best, as a rule, to find a new supervisor and to select someone who is relatively contamination-free frame-wise (see chapter five). As I have stressed, doing psychotherapy is an unnatural pursuit and will therefore always have its arduous side; the need for further supervisory and therapeutic help after a therapist feels secure in his or her work is not uncommon and is a humbling reminder of the compromised design of the emotion-processing psyche.

CONCLUDING COMMENTS

As is true in doing psychotherapy, the role of the supervisee in supervision is a mixed one. It is passive and accepting, open to learning on the one hand, yet, on the other, active, sceptical, questioning, and insistent on encoded evidence for all of a supervisor's pronouncements. Given that the supervisory relationship is tilted in favour of the expertise and power of the supervisor, the supervisee is hard-pressed to maintain a balanced position that is fair to both himself or herself and the supervisor. In all, the supervisee must protect himself or herself from a supervisor's failures as a teacher, and from a mentor's domination, arbitrariness, authoritarianism, and other damaging traits and behaviours. But, in addition, a student also must be on guard against the over-idealization of the supervisor and any tendency not to carry out a fair scrutiny and appraisal of the supervisor's efforts.

The potential for blind spots in a supervisee is enormous — he or she has a lot to be concerned with beyond presenting process-note case material. There are many pitfalls in being supervised, and many opportunities for a supervisee to behave in ways that are masochistic and hurtful to his or her development as a therapist. Being supervised is not an easy position to be in, and ultimately the now familiar two safeguards must be repeatedly invoked: first, the validation of the supervisor's proposals in the encoded material of the supervised patient; second, the use of personal self-processing to enable the supervisee's own deep unconscious wisdom to indicate his or her deep perceptions and evaluations of the supervisor's efforts — and of the supervisee's own conscious picture of the supervisory experience.

Standing up for his or her rights and the right to sound supervision is something a supervisee must at times do in a fair and validatable manner. Yet, at the same time, he or she also must avoid being arbitrary, biased, irrational, controlling, unfair, and the like. Being supervised is essential to the development of every psychotherapist, yet ensuring oneself a place in a fair and effective supervisory experience is a difficult endeavour. Making use of the *wisdom of the second unconscious system and its encoded derivatives* is by far the best means of ensuring that a supervisee will be well supervised in ways that will give him or her the foundation of a rewarding and effective future as a psychotherapist.

CHAPTER TWELVE

Supervisory crises

Although many supervisory experiences go reasonably well from beginning to end, it is in the nature of the process that moments of dissatisfaction are called forth on both sides of the desk. In the extreme, a supervisory crisis materializes, one that may be instigated by the supervisor or supervisee — or both. These crises jeopardize the continuation of the supervision or seriously impair the teaching and learning atmosphere. They may also raise serious questions about the competency of the supervisor and the skills and learning abilities of the supervisee and, in a training situation, call into question his or her status as a student. In all, then, we are dealing with critical moments of disequilibrium and disturbance within the supervisory situation, and they require prompt and concentrated attention.

Supervisory crises may arise as the result of a single acute dysfunctional behaviour by either party to the supervision — one that almost always has its precursors in previous lesser difficulties. Or they may arise as the culmination of chronic and insidious, but mounting problems that reach a breaking point. In addition, a crisis may arise primarily because of the supervisee's work with the supervised patient or be centred around issues that directly involve the supervisory couple—most crises will involve both of these arenas.

Supervisory crises have special importance for reasons that stand beyond their dangers to the parties to supervision and the supervised patient, who, without a doubt, always suffers from such interludes—the work of the supervisee cannot help but be affected regardless of the nature of the emergency. The additional problem is that these pressing predicaments are extremely difficult to deal with and resolve in the standard supervisory settings. After all, the supervisory situation is designed for the education of the supervisee via an exploration of his or her work with the supervised patient; it is not configured to examine the relationship between the supervisor and supervisee except in the most superficial and direct conscious-system manner.

Supervisory crises, however, involve the teacher and his or her student. They are not primarily about the clinical work of the supervisee, although that aspect may secondarily be at issue. These situations compel us to re-examine the resources available to resolve acute conflicts between the parties to supervision, and doing so reveals a great deal about the structure and process of supervision—and its limitations. We are confronted by the basic constraints of, and come upon a critical flaw in, the standard models of supervision—classical and communicative. Indeed, the essential configurations of today's supervisory settings and processes are called into serious question by these considerations.

SOME BASIC CAVEATS

Before we begin to explore the specific nature of these difficult situations and seek ways to find adaptive solutions to the problems they entail, four perspectives will help to orient us.

1. *In principle, all supervisory crises are interactional events with contributions from both supervisor and supervisee—no matter who seems most dysfunctional at the moment*

We must accept with all seriousness the concept that a supervisor and his or her supervisee are fundamentally a two-person, S/S, system and that all events within that system and its individual subsystems (the supervisor and the supervisee) have inputs from both parties to the system — and the frame that they have created for their transactions.

The supervisor who raises a major issue with his or her supervisee must be prepared to search for and discover his or her own accountability, however large or small — and to make it part of the discussion that ensues. Much the same applies, of course, to the supervisee when he or she is the prime mover in this kind of situation. The supervised patient must, in all such cases, be seen as a secondary factor, even though the case may well be part of the problem — the centre of these storms lies within the S/S system.

2. *In both standard models of supervision, the supervisor and supervisee are, by and large, limited to the manifest-content/conscious realm of communication and experience in attempting to explore and resolve these crises*

Supervision is not presently designed to access the unconscious experience of either the supervisor or the supervisee, although, of course, each can do so on their own. It is here that the framework and design of supervision becomes a critical issue.

As noted, supervision is structured so that only the supervised patient is afforded the opportunity to communicate the encoded narrative material that allows for access to the second unconscious system. The supervisor should, in principle, never offer spontaneous narratives, although lapses are common. Similarly, the supervisee should confine his or her comments to the material from the patient and to necessary questions and discussions of technique and theory — he or she also should not offer spontaneous narratives during a supervisory presentation. Indeed, to do so generates unconscious communications that are not, as a rule, trigger-decoded. As a result, both parties to supervision are exposed to unconscious meanings that are not brought into awareness; they therefore fester in their deep unconscious systems where they motivate many conscious behaviours with untoward effects.

3. *Encoded validation of all of a supervisor's or supervisee's impressions and interventions, whether the source of confirmation is the supervised patient or the supervisee (and, quite rarely, the supervisor), is the only means of providing order and reliable meaning to the disorder of all supervisory crises*

We will be discussing supervisory crises as they occur in both of the standard models of supervision. In the classical analytic model there are no clear means of validating an impression that one or the other party to supervision is dysfunctional or is causing serious problems. Conscious-system impressions are exceedingly unreliable, even when one makes use of a lexicon of supposedly clear signs of difficulty in either the supervisee or the supervisor — relatively obvious indications of counter-transference in the supervisee, and problems with the teaching methods and demeanour of the supervisor. These situations therefore typically revolve around issues of authority, power, determination, and conviction; there is no sound arbitrator of the truth of the situation. In the standard communicative model of supervision, encoded validation is an inherent and essential part of the process. The transfer of this safeguard to crisis situations is therefore somewhat easier to make than with the classical paradigms.

4. *To ensure fairness and a sound basis for discussions of crisis issues, encoded validation ultimately must be applied to the impression that a crisis exists, to who is dysfunctional at the moment, to the sources of the emergency situation, and to the dynamics of the underlying issues — in substance, to all formulations and interventions of both the supervisor and the supervisee*

This principle simply states that every aspect and formulation of a supervisory crisis should, to the greatest extent possible, be subjected to unconscious confirmation. This raises the problem of how to develop the narratives needed for such efforts at validation. The supervised patient, who usually is quite unaware of the specifics of a given crisis, can be relied on for only a small part of the much-needed validating material. Thus, another source of encoded derivatives must be made available in these situations, and, clearly, they must come primarily from the supervisee. If critical unconscious factors are to be addressed, the supervisee must provide the narrative material for this effort.

The need for unconscious confirmation cannot be stressed enough. This need arises because of the oft-mentioned fallibility of the conscious system in dealing with emotionally charged issues. Countless errors and injustices have been made because the working over of a supervisory crisis was confined to the manifest-content/implications conscious-system realm. The surface dissatisfactions of both a supervisor and a supervisee draw their power not only from direct experiences, but also from their reverberations in the deep unconscious realm.

Each party to therapy operates through both conscious and unconscious perception — and the latter must be respected for its power over the emotionally charged supervisory experience. Subjective impressions in either party to supervision are in general an insufficient basis for evaluating and settling a crisis situation. Conscious-system discussions are notorious for their inherently biased, arbitrary, and argumentative qualities, and for their inability to change the minds of the antagonists. The great wisdom of the second unconscious system should be brought into play so that the situation is dealt with in incisive fashion. For the moment, however, we will continue to concentrate on the more cognitive, conscious-system aspects of these difficult situations.

CRISES RAISED BY THE SUPERVISOR

What, then, can happen to convince a supervisor that a supervisee and his or her supervision is in a state of crisis? Once more, I will proceed systematically and offer a list of the major sources of crisis from the supervisor's vantage point.

1. *Failures by the supervisee to maintain his or her part of the framework necessary for effective supervision*

We begin, as we should, with the supervisory situation itself and, in particular, its ground rules. A supervisory crisis is signalled whenever a supervisee unilaterally modifies the ground rules, frames, and/or boundaries of the supervisory situation in a way that significantly interferes with the learning experience.

The problem can involve an acute break in the frame (e.g. a supervisee becoming personally involved with a member of his or her supervisor's family) or when a supervisee refuses to write process-note case material after the sessions with the supervised patient — a decision that makes proper teaching virtually impossible. Other possibilities include a supervisee's revelation of a disruptive personal secret (e.g. a powerful and unmodifiable sexual attraction to his or her supervisor) or of having knowledge of the supervisor that mars the supervisory atmosphere (e.g. a supervisee knows about an affair that his or her supervisor has had with a patient). As these examples suggest, violations of the frame by the supervisor are often part of the picture and problem, even though the focus is on the supervisee.

A supervisory emergency also arises when a supervisee is repeatedly late to supervision or misses more than a very rare supervisory hour. A decision by a supervisee to seek out a second opinion, no matter how democratic that may seem, is also a frame break of major proportions — and a sign of crisis. Finally, efforts by a supervisee to modify the ground rules of his or her relationship with the supervisor — for example, being overly hurtful or seductive, trying persistently to become involved socially, and such — are indicators of major difficulties. Indeed, repeated frame alterations of any kind by a supervisee, and many single flagrant violations of the frame of supervision, call for a shift into the crisis mode (see below).

While these crises are called forth by a frame-deviant behaviour or defiant attitude by a supervisee, the supervisor must nevertheless be mindful that a supervisee's behaviours do not arise in a vacuum, but are formed within a highly sensitive conscious and unconscious interaction with the supervisor. As we have seen, it is not uncommon for a supervisee's intractable frame alterations to arise in the context of frame alterations by the supervisor. In dealing with these acute problems, then, their sources in the S/S system—such as the supervisor's frame management of the supervisory situation and other behaviours—must be identified.

2. Serious issues in the learning attitude of the supervisee

Another source of crisis within the supervisory relationship involves the basic attitude of the supervisee towards his or her mentor. In general, the healthy scepticism of the supervisee must be balanced against an openness to learn from his or her teacher. Not surprisingly, there are two extremes to the kinds of problems that can arise in this regard. The more easily identified is, of course, the oppositional supervisee who refuses to accept and challenges much of what a supervisor says, including the latter's *unconsciously validated* assessments, critiques, and recommendations. As a result, no learning of significance can transpire, and the supervision is wasted. Rather than learning effective techniques and theories from the supervisor, the supervisee is locked into a personal belief system — often with the qualities of a fixed delusion — that remains unmodified despite all supervisory efforts, including the repeated offer of encoded validation in the material from the supervised patient. At some point, often early in supervision, when the fixity of this kind of blind and blanket repudiation of the supervisor's efforts becomes evident, the supervisor has no choice but to raise this problem directly with the supervisee so that it can be dealt with.

The main issue in defining this type of crisis lies with the supervisor's need to be quite certain that the supervisee's objections to his or her teachings are indeed quite arbitrary, insubstantial, and personally prejudiced. In the standard model of supervision, there is grave difficulty in establishing this sense of irrational opposition. Often, these situations come down to a supervisee's accepting a supervisor's teachings or moving on. There are no clear validating principles, so the supervisee either takes what is taught or opposes it. In this type of crisis, the supervisee is simply opposed to the supervisor's teachings — they do not fit his conscious and especially unconscious needs, and so he resists the mentor's efforts.

On the other hand, in the communicative model of supervision, in which *encoded validation* of the supervisor's pronouncements is a *sine qua non*, this type of crisis has a different configuration. The supervisor's efforts are supported by unconscious validation, and the supervisee's position is inherently more irrational, neurotic, and a reflection of deep anxieties connected with secured frames and trigger-decoded, unconscious meanings. The supervisee then finds surface rationalizations to justify a flight from communicative supervision without realizing his or her deeper motives.

In this situation, the supervisor's contribution to the crisis situation is largely his or her capacity to trigger-decode and to tolerate both unconscious meaning and secured frames — in both supervision and therapy. It is these healthy abilities that pose an extreme threat to the supervisee in crisis, largely because he or she is unable to cope with the underlying issues. Under these circumstances, the supervisory crises comes down to whether the supervisee will tolerate doing communicative psychotherapy or take flight into less demanding and more frame-deviant and uninsightful forms of therapy.

The other, far more insidious learning problem arises when a supervisee is too compliant, so that validation of the supervisor's comments is not sought and everything the mentor says is accepted on blind faith. Here, too, despite appearances, there is no genuine and effective learning — only empty acquiescence. Given the usual narcissism of the supervisor, this type of crisis is often missed; nevertheless, at some point the supervisor may come to recognize this malignant resistance for what it is and realize that he or she is faced with a supervisory crisis. Here, too, the issue must be joined.

3. *A supervisee's behaviours, interventions, and ways of working with his or her patients call into serious question his or her qualifications as a psychotherapist*

Shifting now to crises that arise by virtue of serious problems in a supervisee's work with the supervised patient: a supervisor may see a supervision in crisis when a supervisee behaves unethically (e.g. overcharges a patient, engages in dishonest billing practices, seduces or abuses a patient, etc.); intervenes in openly harmful ways (e.g. is verbally assaultive and/or seductive, far too self-revealing, overactive without adequate controls); repeatedly fails to make proper and much-needed interventions; or otherwise reveals traits, attitudes, and behaviours that indicate that the supervisee may well be unable to make use of sound principles of therapy. The conviction that a supervisee is being more harmful than helpful to his or her patients broadly defines this type of crisis. At some point, as these problems mount or when the supervisee does something quite outrageous, concerns of this kind must be explored with the supervisee — and resolved.

4. *Any other difficulty in the supervisee that arouses grave concern within the supervisor*

There is a wide range of problems that cannot be catalogued easily that nonetheless reach emergency proportions. For example, the supervisee may be under attack at his or her job or involved in a family crisis in ways that interfere with his or her doing sound psychotherapy or jeopardize the supervision. Or a supervisee may not have a patient to present, or may become so anxious or depressed as to show impairments of functioning in the therapy and/or supervision — a problem that again raises the question of the role that personal therapy plays in supervisory crises (see below). The supervisee may suffer a loss of income or reconsider his or her present finances so as to be convinced that he or she cannot afford to continue the supervision. In addition, the supervisee may fall ill emotionally or physically, or both, thereby creating a crisis of termination for the supervision.

Given that there are so many possible disruptive behaviours, issues, and interventions that a supervisee may engage in, the possibilities of acute problems are limitless. The key principle here is that *a supervisor must at all times be alert for the development of a crisis situation and should give such happenings priority over all other concerns in the supervision — no effective teaching can be done until the urgent issues are resolved.*

CRISES RAISED BY SUPERVISEES

Let us turn now to the other side of the teaching situation. Among the most common reasons that a supervisee comes to believe that his or her supervision is in a state of crisis, the following are especially pertinent.

1. *Failures by the supervisor to maintain his or her part of the necessary framework for effective supervision*

As is true of the supervisee, crises in supervision occur when a supervisor repeatedly modifies the supervisory frame, or does so on a single occasion, in a way that has a devastating effect on the supervisee and supervisory work. Many frame modifications can make learning all but impossible for the supervisee. This may arise, for example, when a supervisor is frequently late to, or absent from, the supervisory hour, keeps changing the time of the appointment, makes seductive or aggressive overtures, or has physical contact with the supervisee in any but the most inadvertent and innocuous way. As a result of these behaviours, the situation is deprived of the effective, neutral holding environment that is needed to support the supervisee as he or she learns. In addition, the supervisor's actions are traumatic and anti-therapeutic — they burden the supervisee with pathological introjective identifications and be-lie the supervisor's words and render them ineffective and harmful to the supervisee. Maintaining a relatively secured frame is the foundation for sound supervisory work and for establishing a relationship in which crises are unlikely to occur. Failing to do so is a sure path to a crisis situation.

Other possible frame modifications include efforts by a supervisor to become socially involved with a supervisee, re-quests for personal or professional favours and/or referrals or for collaboration of any kind, and indications of dishonesty or corruption. Personal self-revelations by a supervisor to a supervisee or the leakage of transactions of the supervision to third parties by a supervisor (with the unfortunate and ques-tionable exception of reports to education committees at training institutes, even when done with the full knowledge and consent of the supervisee) are also serious breaches of the supervisory frame and call for confrontation and exploration.

A supervisee should be on the alert for these types of lapses and for all other modifications of the ideal frame by a supervi-sor (see chapters four to seven). If they are serious or repetitive, he or she should bring them up directly with the mentor. *There is no viable supervisory setting in which the possibility of con-fronting a supervisor who has evidently or possibly created a supervisory crisis is precluded.* Indeed, the refusal of a supervi-sor (or supervisee) to allow a crisis situation to be explored and discussed is itself a grave danger to the supervisory process.

2. Serious issues in the teaching methods and attitudes of the supervisor

A supervisor who fails to allow for unconscious validation of his or her interventions through the process-note case material of the supervised patient sooner or later should be called into question by the supervisee. Much the same applies if a supervi-sor demeans the supervisee, appears to be either overly silent or overly active in teaching, autocratic and insistent on silent acceptance and obedience, repeatedly uncertain as to what should be done with the supervised patient, frequently in error as measured by the material from the patient that follows the supervisor's formulations, ready to deny a share of responsibility for the course of the supervised psychotherapy, or otherwise chronically unsatisfactory as a teacher. In sum, any indication of ineffectual teaching or openly hurtful attitudes towards a supervisee should, if they are not brought under control, prompt a supervisee to confront his or her supervisor with the relevant issues.

3. *A supervisor's behaviours, interventions, and ways of working with the supervisee and his or her own patients (if revealed) call into serious question his or her qualifications as a teacher and psychotherapist*

A supervisor who in any way reveals himself or herself as dishonest, corruptible, a violator of rules, frames, and boundaries, and otherwise untrustworthy and/or unprofessional should be confronted and the issues examined openly in the supervisory hour.

4. *Any other difficulty in the supervisor that arouses grave concern within the supervisee*

With supervisors, too, there are any number of problems that may arise as supervisory emergencies that are not easily placed into a single group. Acute or extended illness, emotional decompensation, signs of personal conflict with the supervisee — these are examples of the kinds of generally repetitive and sometimes acute problems that may be cause for grave concern in a supervisee.

In all, then, a supervisee must concentrate on learning his or her trade and the theory behind it but must, in addition, quietly monitor the status and qualities of his or her supervisor's work. It takes courage and strength to be critical of a supervisor, but if a supervisee is patient and fair, takes the time to confirm via self-processing his or her impressions of the supervisor several times over, is prepared to recognize his or her own contributions to the problem (S/S system considerations), and is able to see his or her supervisor, hopefully, as a well-meaning human being, however flawed, then these issues can be negotiated with due concern and openness on both sides.

DEALING WITH SUPERVISORY CRISES

I have already argued that the standard supervisory situations are not configured to allow for the deep exploration and management of supervisory crises. Nevertheless, initially a supervisor working on the basis of these models should deal with these issues by using *conscious-system resources* buttressed by his or her knowledge of the architecture of the emotion-processing mind. Supervision is an emotionally charged situation that deals with another strongly charged situation in the form of the supervised therapy. As a result, unconscious motives and forces play a significant role in the supervisor's teaching and the supervisee's learning — and in their crises as well. The failure to deal with these unconscious forces is therefore remiss and in some way belies the supervision itself, where the unconscious aspects of both the patient's dysfunctions and the therapeutic interaction must be afforded serious and prime consideration. Without a clear means of discovering and working through the unconscious forces behind a supervisory crisis, the problem often either goes unresolved or is settled in a weak and tentative manner that is likely to break down. In some instances, however, direct confrontation is able to stimulate the necessary changes in the supervisee or supervisor — even though the deeper issues remain untouched or are resolved through personal therapy or self-processing.

In terms of the attitudes of the supervisor and supervisee, there are two types of supervisory crises: the first are matters of *consensus* between the supervisor and supervisee, while the second are matters of *debate*. Thus, some urgent supervisory issues arise because there is a serious problem that both supervisor and supervisee acknowledge, and the resolution will require some kind of change in one or both parties. For example, if a supervisee is missing many supervisory sessions, this behaviour is self-evident and must be rectified if the supervision is to be effective. Change may then transpire either through conscious-system discussion and direct efforts by the supervisee to attend the hours, or, failing that, it may require introducing the supervisee's encoded narrative material into the supervisory hour and using trigger decoding, however restricted, to reach deeper insights as to the unconscious emotional sources of the problem — as they operate in both parties to the supervision.

In the more debatable crises, the accused party usually is meeting his or her role requirements and holding to the frame of the supervision — *the issue is one of impressions rather than incontrovertible frame-deviant behaviours*. Here, there is a confrontation with a seeming major difficulty in the supervisee's or supervisor's work or teaching, but there is no consensus as to the existence of the purported problem. Still, the very introduction of a debatable issue speaks for tensions that are probably of crisis proportions.

For example, a supervisee may feel that a supervisor is being overly harsh or seductive, and the supervisor may not agree with this assessment of his or her behaviours and comments. Or a supervisor may be very critical of the work of a supervisee and argue that his or her interventions are in error and harmful, and the student may feel that his or her mentor's appraisal is off the mark. In these instances, there is little likelihood of true resolution, and almost always it becomes necessary to access the student's second unconscious system to unearth the underlying issues and point to how they may be resolved. The deep unconscious system is likely to emit encoded messages that, when properly trigger-decoded, will offer a rather unbiased and accurate picture of the situation and the contributions of each party. Often, strong underlying anxieties in either the supervisor or the supervisee, or both, are playing a significant part in these disputes.

Let us turn now to the basic precepts for dealing with supervisory crises. They are:

1. *Both the supervisor and the supervisee must be open to the introduction of supervisory crises by either party to a supervision without rancour or punitive consequences; an acceptance of serious confrontation must prevail on both sides*

A generally unstated ground rule of supervision allows for the introduction by either member of the dyad of any notable matter of concern, whether it is of lesser or of emergency proportions. Simply put, a supervisor must accept a criticism or issue raised by his or her supervisee truly without undue defensiveness and with a willingness to face and discuss all such problems. Because this is an ideal attitude that is difficult to adopt, the supervisor must be on the alert, when these distressing predicaments are raised by a supervisee, to maintain his or her sense of fairness and relative neutrality — especially when the supervisor is convinced, hopefully based on solid evidence, that the supervisee actually has no reason for his or her complaint.

Wounded narcissistically and sometimes professionally, the supervisor may be inclined, consciously or unconsciously, to react with blind denial or to exact revenge and vengeance on the supervisee who "dares" to raise such questions. Nevertheless, these issues must be joined; failure to allow for such efforts eventually creates a different type of crisis — the intractability of the supervisor — that is likely to lead to the termination of the supervision. Both supervisor and supervisee are obligated to bring up and explore together any problem that appears to be disturbing the supervisory process.

While often anxious and depressed when these issues are raised by his or her supervisor, a supervisee must be able to withstand the trauma and use the experience to learn and grow. Even when the problem identified by the supervisor seems questionable or non-existent to the supervisee, there should be a receptivity that allows for a constructive search for and discussion of the supposed difficulty.

For the supervisor, raising major issues with a supervisee must be well timed and handled sensitively, yet without unnecessary delay. It is to be remembered that the therapy of the supervised patient must be preserved and allowed the best opportunity for a favourable outcome. Sparing a supervisee a confrontation not only harms the supervised patient, but is also a disservice to the supervisee whose opportunities for learning and favourable development are delayed or precluded — at least until the issues that are disturbing the supervisory process are raised and resolved. With all due fairness and consideration for the feelings and needs of a supervisee, if there is a major obstacle to his or her learning how to do effective psychotherapy, the supervisor must confront and explore the problem with due haste.

Matters are, as a rule, considerably more difficult when the supervisee is the prime mover and he or she introduces a major complaint about the supervisor. Given the power-base and narcissism of many supervisors, this kind of confrontation is often experienced, without due thought, as an unfounded assault, and the supervisee is made to suffer in one way or another — through gross or subtle counterattacks by the supervisor, a bad report, tension in the supervisory relationship, and similar kinds of conscious or unconscious countermeasures. These responses are, of course, not only quite unfair to the supervisee, but are also frank expressions of a supervisor's countertransferences — further indications of crisis. The proper attitude should be one of patient listening, an exploration of the basis for the complaint, and efforts directed towards their resolution (see below).

Even more difficult to recognize are what are termed *crises of supervisory misalliances*, in which the supervision is foundering but neither party recognizes that a crisis is at hand. Both supervisor and supervisee should maintain vigilance for this kind of insidious dysfunctional situation. Common signs of an unrecognized problem are major lapses in the work of the supervisee, repeated failures to obtain encoded validation for a supervisor's and/or supervisee's interventions, the continual existence of tension and discordance in the supervisory relationship, marked therapeutic failures in the work of the supervisee, and similar signs of unsettled problems in learning and doing sound therapeutic work. An ability to recognize when things are amiss is crucial to identifying this more subtle type of supervisory misalliance.

2. *Once brought up, a supervisory crisis must take precedence over other matters and should be dealt with in the supervisory session at hand*

Whoever the prime mover is in alerting the supervisory couple to a crisis in their midst, the situation must be attended to at once. The matter should occupy as little supervisory time as possible so that sufficient time is reserved for the case material, which is the primary target of the supervisory session. However, if the crisis is severe and relatively intractable, it may prove necessary to use a full supervisory hour — or more if needed — to deal with the problem. Indeed, major issues that are interfering grossly with the learning process must be resolved before supervision can be helpful to the supervisee. Furthermore, the stalemated or overly resistant supervisee cannot benefit from supervision until the obstacles to learning are modified or removed. Clearly, then, these problems should be moved to the top of a supervisory agenda when they materialize.

3. *There are major differences in how a problem raised about a supervisee is handled, as compared to those that pertain to the supervisor*

a. *Complaints about the supervisor.*

The following principles apply to how a supervisor should respond when a supervisee raises a serious issue with respect to his or her teachings, attitudes, methods, and frame-management efforts:

(1) *The supervisor should listen carefully to the complaint.*

He or she should ask about the basis for the grievance and for specific instances in which the problem arose. The supervisor's attitude should be calm, receptive, patient, open to recognizing errors or unwarranted behaviours, non-punitive, and reasonably responsive.

> (2) *Initially, the complaint must be addressed on its own terms — manifestly, without the aid of encoded expressions.*

Given the structure of the standard models of supervision, the first recourse in a supervisory crisis must fall to the conscious systems of supervisor and supervisee. These direct efforts to resolve the crisis may be successful — for example, a supervisor may recognize a previously overlooked failing or problem and make efforts to modify the difficulty. Nevertheless, as discussed earlier, conscious-system dialogues, no matter how well-meaning, are notorious for their unreliability and for the fixity of the respective positions adopted by the two parties to the interchange. Relying on conscious-system discussions of supervisory crises greatly increases the risk of not being able to resolve the problems in question. As a result, all too often the crisis leads to an interruption of the supervision or a tense truce that allows the supervision to continue with little settled. If matters are not going well, finding the means to access the supervisee's deep unconscious system and its wisdom is called for (see below).

> (3) *The supervisor should take seriously any complaint from a supervisee and treat it as valid until proven otherwise.*

Proceeding for the moment in terms of conscious-system efforts, it is well for a supervisor to handle all criticisms directed against him or her as valid conscious perceptions until there is incontrovertible evidence that the situation is otherwise — that is, a matter of misperception and a reflection of the supervisee's anxieties. This calls for a search for signs that the supervisee's concerns are well founded, and this self-exploration should include a search for similar complaints from other supervisees. In addition, entirely on his or her own, the supervisor can engage in self-processing in order to confirm or refute the existence of the difficulty and, if the problem does exist, to use the process as a means of arriving at its deeper sources and insightfully resolving the crisis.

(4) *If the supervisor agrees with the supervisee that there is a problem, he or she should acknowledge it and discuss its manifestations and ramifications in the supervision — without becoming personally self-revealing.*

The supervisor should affirm a supervisory countertransference problem to his or her supervisee and indicate a genuine resolve to rectify the situation, including all frame alterations that can be secured. For example, undue latenesses or absences should cease or a hostile attitude should be brought under control. In discussing the nature and sources of the problem, the supervisee's contribution to the difficulty, if any, should be mentioned — though not in a way that makes him or her overly responsible for the supervisor's problem. The supervisee should also be reassured that the supervisor will, on his or own, explore the unconscious sources of the problem in an effort to see to it that it is firmly dealt with and resolved.

(5) *If the supervisor, after considerable self-scrutiny and self-exploration, cannot find a basis for the supervisee's complaint, he or she must honestly indicate that this is the case.*

Under these conditions, the supervisor is shifting the primary problem back to the supervisee in the form of his or her misperception of the mentor. However, the supervisor should remain open to self-discovery and must also, in keeping with systemic principles, find a contribution on his or her side even when the main difficulty lies with the student. This means that the supervisor is obliged to discover the *kernel of truth* in the student's concerns and to acknowledge it in the discussion that ensues.

In this instance, the dialogue will centre on the reasons why each party believes as he or she does, and efforts should be directed at correcting misconceptions and misunderstandings. Some kind of resolution or peace must be made if the supervision is to continue and be effective. As a rule, each side will have to give a little and get a little so that both parties are satisfied. Serious errors and breaches of the frame must be rectified, however, while more elusive complaints —

allusions to *impression triggers* — call for acknowledging the truths that they contain and for explaining why the rest seem unfounded.

> (6) *If a supervisory crisis proves to be intractable — that is, a supervisor's problem cannot be modified or resolved — then arrangements should be made to terminate the supervision.*

The decision to terminate a supervision because of an unresolved crisis should be extremely rare in a given supervisor's work with supervisees, but it can happen with any supervisor no matter how competent he or she may be. If at all possible, the irresolvable issues should be identified and discussed so that both parties have some sense of why they could not create a meeting of the minds.

Among the causes of the demise of a supervisory relationship because of an irresolvable problem mainly in the supervisor, the first possibility is that the supervisor has failed profoundly to recognize a legitimate complaint and to see his or her own failings. In this case, given that supervisee is right and the teaching is marred by an unacknowledged problem in the supervisor, termination is a wise move.

On the other hand, an unresolvable crisis may arise because unconsciously the supervisee cannot bear the sound teachings of the supervisor and has conjured up one or another unconsciously driven complaint to justify terminating their work together. In the communicative model of supervision, a supervisor attempts to enable the supervisee to make a profound shift from deviant to secured frames, and from the first to the second unconscious system domain — moves that are sources of deep dread for everyone. For reasons of early and later trauma, irresolvable types of psychopathology, current unbearable life circumstances including illness in oneself or close others, and much more, there are supervisees (and supervisors) who simply cannot tolerate working with the communicative approach.

The conscious system almost never acknowledges the underlying secured-frame anxieties and dread of deep unconscious meaning from which these supervisees suffer. In almost all cases, the student can only make up a conscious-system rationalization to justify flight from the supervision — he or she will find and raise any number of spurious issues to justify this decision. At this point we come upon the limitations of conscious-system efforts to resolve a supervisory crisis — the conscious system functions primarily as a puppet and unknowing spokesperson for the deep unconscious fear/guilt system, the source of almost all of our neurotic and mini-psychotic, deeply irrational behaviours. A manifest-content/implications discussion simply cannot get beneath the rationalizations of the supervisee's conscious system and reach into the deeper roots of the issues at hand.

Nevertheless, supervisees, who often somehow know or sense that they are actually leaving a constructive supervisory experience, should rest easy in understanding that supervisory work modelled on the communicative approach has simply caused them conscious-system overload. The architecture of their emotion-processing minds interacting with their personal histories has more or less sealed their fates. Only rarely can something be done to modify these vulnerabilities, and doing so requires communicative self-processing — a subject we soon address in chapter fourteen. However, the likelihood of this happening is exceedingly small because a supervisee who is terrified unconsciously of secured frames and deep unconscious meaning will seldom risk getting involved in a form of therapy or of therapy combined with supervision — self-processing supervision — that enables these issues to materialize. A supervisee should be encouraged to develop the realistic perspective that everyone has some degree of limitation in their ability to do dynamic psychotherapy — this too is a consequence of the design of the emotion-processing mind.

Similar considerations apply to supervisors: if their work has been carried out with all due tact and sensitivity, and has obtained encoded validation in most instances, they can rest well, knowing that they have done the best they could. Every supervisor must face the fact that there is no paradigm and model of therapy that everyone can tolerate and learn. The issue of the best possible therapy for psychotherapy patients is secondary here, although always a background concern; the overriding interest is in the best possible supervision for the supervisee. We are what we are, even as we strive to be better.

Despite these perspectives, a conscientious supervisee will feel badly when a supervision is terminated early, and a supervisor will feel a sense of failure and hurt. Yet the way it is, is the way it is — supervisors must surrender their fantasies of omnipotence before beginning their supervisory practices. And supervisees must be realistic about how much they can be taught and about the limiting factors that exist within themselves, their supervisors, and their supervisory situations.

If termination is agreed upon, the supervisee should find his or her own new supervisor. It is unwise for a supervisor to meddle with that decision — for example, to make a referral. Indeed, the choice of supervisor reveals a great deal about the supervisee, and he or she should be allowed to chart his or her own course. It may be frustrating to realize that supervisees often select the most dysfunctional and pathological supervisor whom they can consciously rationalize and tolerate, but here, too, human nature is simply expressing its overwhelming needs.

The dread of secured frames and deep meaning is so great, and the fear of personal death and needs for punishment so extreme, that aberrant choices of supervisors are exceedingly common. Supervisors who will support and sanction errant and hurtful interventions and who will give license to the pathology and inappropriate defences of a supervisee, however consciously or unconsciously it is done, are in great demand by supervisees. There are as yet no clear safeguards against the supervisory misalliances that unfold under these circumstances, and they are seldom recognized for what they are.

In supervisory situations that take place under the aegis of a training program, a supervisee's complaints against a supervisor tend to raise ominous issues. A supervisee should, of course, have a clear avenue through which to voice such complaints, beginning with the supervisor himself or herself. And there should be no penalty whatsoever when a supervisee casts doubts over the quality of the teaching and supervisory frame that he or she is receiving. Still, these are delicate matters that need to be orchestrated very carefully lest harm come to both the supervisor and the supervisee under these circumstances. Indeed, one can readily sense how this kind of contaminated frame complicates the supervisory experience and generates

undue anxiety in both members of the supervisory dyad —
especially at times of crisis.

b. *Complaints about the supervisee.*

The principles and limitations for dealing with seemingly fixed
and serious problems in a supervisee are rather similar to
those discussed for the complaints about the supervisor. The
stress must be on clear documentation of the problem (verbally, of course) and openness of discussion. The supervisee
must strive to find the means of recognizing properly identified
difficulties and of acknowledging legitimate complaints; he or
she must also be committed to finding the means to modify
these problems.

Rare indeed should be the situation in which a supervisor
states a problem and the supervisee disagrees with its existence or importance. If this is the case, however, the matter
calls for full discussion and the best resolution possible.
If a supervisor nevertheless believes that a supervisee is
unteachable, supervision should be terminated and, again, the
supervisee should be allowed to find his or her own new supervisor.

(1) *The question of therapy for a supervisee.*

Many problems related to a supervisor's complaints about a
supervisee relate to the issue of personal psychotherapy for
the student. On his or her side, a supervisor with a recurrent
or seemingly intractable teaching problem should consider
personal therapy of some kind — especially self-processing
therapy, which is exceedingly helpful with these kinds of difficulties. However, this decision is a private matter for the
supervisor, and it should not be discussed with the student —
it should simply be acted upon.

The situation is different with the supervisee. Chronic problems cannot as a rule be truly and lastingly modified without
therapeutic help. It is therefore the responsibility of the supervisor to bring up the need for personal therapy with a student
who seems to be in trouble — or in crisis. This is best done
through leading questions and by allowing the supervisee to
find his or her own need for treatment and own motivations to
pursue it.

To preserve the supervisory frame and to avoid what often are unforeseen complications that can derail the supervisory work, as noted, the supervisor should *not* make the referral to a therapist for the troubled supervisee. In the standard models of supervision, the therapy issue should be kept separate from the supervision — the supervisee should be allowed to find his or her own way. In general, a supervisor's preferences for a particular type of therapist are well known to the supervisee. While the model in question may or may not be valid, the choice of a therapist who works in ways that are incompatible with those of the supervisor is an ominous sign of deep resistance against the supervision and portends the likely development of future crises.

In principle, then, when supervisory crises arise in the standard models of supervision, they should be dealt with manifestly and via conscious-system efforts — no matter how limited they may be. Both supervisor and supervisee should be encouraged to accept the criticisms offered by their opposite party and to seek out the unconscious sources of these difficulties on their own. If the situation nonetheless proves to be intractable, a shift to self-processing supervision or to the use of its methods is called for — temporarily or permanently (see chapter fourteen).

Situations in crisis

Dr. Herbert was in standard model supervision with Dr. Moore in the context of a psychotherapy training program. Both supervisor and supervisee were women, as was the supervised patient, Ms. Garber, who had entered therapy after making a suicidal gesture when her boyfriend left her.

Dr. Herbert was familiar with the communicative approach and tried to use the standard of encoded validation in assessing the work of her supervisor. However, without exception, encoded validation did not materialize when Dr. Moore made a formulation or advised an intervention, or when Dr. Herbert intervened as best she could in keeping with her supervisor's recommendations.

The supervisee would, on rare occasion after a disappointment with her work with the patient, who seemed stalemated in the therapy, mention to her supervisor the lack of encoded validation of her comments and the way the therapy seemed stuck. Dr. Moore's typical response was that Ms. Garber was a very resistant borderline patient with poor impulse control and little insight, and that encoded validation was not an effective sign of good supervision.

Matters drifted along until one supervisory hour in which Dr. Herbert presented a session that seemed especially confusing to Dr. Moore. The case material had indicated that Dr. Herbert had become ill the previous week and, on the day of the patient's session, had called her patient at home to cancel her session. Because the situation was urgent, and because she did not have the patient's work telephone number and decided not to ask for it, Dr. Herbert had left a message for Ms. Garber with her mother, with whom the patient lived.

The following session, which was presented in the supervisory session that we are now considering, the patient's narratives were about robbers breaking into her aunt's house, a time when the patient was chased by a man with a knife, and a weird moment on the day after the missed session, when the patient mistakenly found that she had gone into the Men's rather than the Ladies' Room at work. Symptomatically, the patient had been in a panic state for the entire week and had become suicidal again; she was convinced that her ex-husband was stalking her apartment and intended to harm her in some way. She was thinking of leaving the city and felt disorganized and uncertain about what to do.

Dr. Herbert had been very anxious in the patient's session and had lost all sense of the communicative approach. The supervisee had reassured her patient that no one was after her, even though Dr. Herbert had no basis for that statement. She also had told the patient that things would settle down, adding that maybe the cancelled session had created a void that had upset her. In response Ms. Garber said that at the moment she felt more anxious than ever and that she couldn't think straight.

Dr. Moore saw this episode as a "borderline regression" and suggested that Dr. Herbert increase the patient's sessions from once to twice weekly. In that same supervisory hour, Dr. Moore asked her supervisee to change the time of the supervision because she had been appointed director of the training program's clinic; they agreed upon a new time.

In the following supervisory session, Dr. Herbert reported that she herself had had an anxiety attack after dreaming that someone had dynamited a concrete floor on which she was standing. She began to fall and was certain that she was going to die, when she awoke in terror.

As for her patient, Dr. Herbert had proposed the increase in the frequency of the sessions, and the patient had refused at first, but then acquiesced. Her main narrative then centred on an incident that had occurred to a girlfriend at work. She had been mugged on the street and her purse had been taken from her. Not finished, the thief had followed her home and broken into her apartment and held her captive for hours. He had tried to rape her, but she had managed to flee before he could penetrate her.

Neither this material nor the supervisee's own earlier dream were trigger-decoded by either the supervisor or the supervisee. The patient called after her session to terminate the therapy. Dr. Herbert felt that her supervisor had failed to be helpful and, to support her position, she pointed to the repeated lack of encoded validation of her efforts. Dr. Moore rejected this argument outright and accused her supervisee of being unable to work with borderline patients.

Seeing that they were going in circles, and mindful of her dream, which she was convinced was her unconscious perception of the insecure frame of the supervision and the supervisor's lack of support (there were additional encoded associations that seemed to confirm this idea),

Dr. Herbert said that she thought that the time had come for her to talk with the supervision committee about a change in supervisor. Not only was encoded validation lacking, but both the supervision and the supervised therapy were in shambles. Unfortunately, Dr. Moore became enraged — there are few constraints on conscious-system supervisors — and accused her supervisee of being paranoid and irrational and projecting her own pathology into her. However, the supervision committee was not as jaundiced in their view of Dr. Herbert, and they agreed to reassign her to a new teacher.

This vignette illustrates the kind of spiralling crisis that is not uncommon when a standard-model supervisory experience begins to deteriorate. The failure to use trigger decoding and the confinement of the work to manifest contents and their implications generates a supervisory situation that is arbitrary and easily victimized by a supervisor's countertransferences and derivative deafness. If there are active frame issues in either the supervision or the supervised therapy — or both as was the case here — resistance, regression, acting out, and other dysfunctional behaviours and symptoms are inevitable in both the supervisee and his or her supervised patient, and the supervisor as well.

Conscious-system efforts are frame-insensitive and unconsciously inclined towards frame alterations; furthermore, there is no sense of adaptation-oriented encoded communication. As a result, the frame breaks may well get out of hand, and both the supervised therapy and the supervision itself can fall apart. There were in this supervisory situation abundant derivatives available from both the supervisee and her patient to allow for very effective efforts at trigger-decoded interpretation and frame securing. Failing that, anger, confrontation, lack of true understanding, and action-discharge prevailed.

The supervisee appears to have been justified in claiming that her supervisor's efforts were not being confirmed unconsciously and were failing her as well. The primary source of crisis here was the insensitivity of this supervisor to encoded material and frame issues. But notice how the supervisor's failings were introjected by the supervisee who herself failed to trigger-decode her patient's strong encoded response to her absence and especially to the invasive telephone call and message to a third party that she had made — supervisees are deeply influenced by their supervisors' frame deviations and unconscious communications.

The absence of a secured supervisory frame impaired the holding qualities of the supervisory situation, and the supervisor's non-validated interventions compounded the problem. Together, they made learning all but impossible (of course, there was almost nothing meaningful for the supervisee to learn), and the supervisee's conscious functioning deteriorated. Soon everyone was in crisis — the supervisor, the supervisee, and the supervised patient. With little hope of frame rectification and almost no attention to encoded derivatives, the supervised patient terminated her therapy — a decision triggered by one last invasive frame alteration by her ill-advised therapist.

Indeed, when a therapist is frame-insensitive, destructive errors of this kind are inescapable. At the very moment that the patient is reeling from unconscious perceptions triggered by her therapist's telephone call and message to her mother, a deviation fraught with qualities of seduction and pursuit, the supervisor has the therapist propose another frame alteration with similar qualities. Once the therapist had failed to hear the patient's encoded response to this increasingly deviant situation, the patient had virtually no other recourse but to terminate her therapy before she was further assaulted by her therapist.

Similar anxieties and concerns prompted Dr. Herbert to terminate her supervision with Dr. Moore. Had the supervisor been able to trigger-decode her supervisee's derivative material, and had she been able similarly to decode the images from Ms. Garber, there would have been a great deal of deep insight available for all concerned. Failing that, and unable to appreciate the traumatic qualities of her own frame modification — the change in the time of the supervision — the supervisor had projectively identified (dumped) so much frame deviation, denial of unconscious meaning, and deep anxieties into her supervisee that she too was in a state of overload and had no recourse but to flee the supervision. Sad to say, Dr.

Moore's continued assault on her supervisee when she elected to try to end the supervision only aggravated this difficult situation further.

Only trigger decoding within both the supervision and supervised therapy could have saved the day. But this again speaks for the principles delineated in this chapter for dealing with supervisory crises. Experiences of the kind described here, with hurt for all three members of the S/S/P system, can be prevented through the adoption of sound supervisory principles — especially at times of crisis. As part of this model, when conscious-system exchanges fail to resolve an emergency situation, the use of a supervisee's encoded material seems advisable.

CONCLUDING COMMENTS

In all, then, in the standard model of supervision, supervisory crises take precedence over other work, require honesty on all sides, call for open and candid exploration, and should be resolved before returning to the clinical work with the supervised patient. It is, however, only the experienced communicative therapist, who is familiar with the adaptive functioning of the two systems of the emotion-processing mind — conscious and deeply unconscious — who can appreciate how constrained and restricted conscious-system efforts are in dealing with these problems.

I have already cast a shadow over the standard models of supervision, and we turn now to an exploration of the gravity of their unnoticed flaws — and they are considerable. This discussion will lead us to a possible solution to the dilemmas created by the constraints of these standard models of supervision.

CHAPTER THIRTEEN

Taking issue with
the standard models
of supervision

I t behoves us now to consider what appear to be the main problems with the standard models of supervision. We were faced with a limitation of supervision when we discovered that supervisory crises can be dealt with only on a manifest-content/implications level and in the realm of the rather unreliable conscious system. We realized that this all but eliminated the use of deep unconscious intelligence and that it cut off all access to the deeply unconscious motives that empower the supervisory experience as well its crises. We saw, too, that it may be possible to modify the standard models of supervision at times of crisis to develop encoded images from a supervisee. But is this modification of those models sufficient to render them complete, or do these basic models of supervision require changing?

To pursue this question, in this chapter I define more incisively the problems with the standard models that we have been touching on and show clearly that they reflect significant flaws in these paradigms. As we will see, there are indications that these limitations do appear to call for major changes in the basic structure of the supervision of dynamic psychotherapies and psychoanalysis. Indeed, once the problem is defined, in chapter fourteen we turn to one possible solution.

THE ADAPTATIONS
OF THE EMOTION-PROCESSING MIND

To introduce the relevant issues, I first summarize some of the key features of the emotion-processing mind (see also chapter two).

1. The emotion-processing mind is comprised of two distinctive systems — a conscious system with its own superficial unconscious subsystem, and a deep or second unconscious system with both a remarkable deep wisdom subsystem and equally compelling, dysfunction-motivating fear/guilt system. The conscious system is essentially unreliable in the emotional domain. The second unconscious system is, on the other hand, quite reliable and wise in this regard. Both effective psychotherapy and effective supervision must, therefore, have a means of accessing the processes and insights of this deep unconscious system.

2. As we have seen, the conscious mind has the capacity to address and scrutinize past, present, or future events and interactions. However, the design of the second unconscious system is such that it is always primarily focused on its immediate stimuli (triggers) and interactions. Allusions to the past or future are, then, part of efforts to adapt unconsciously to the adaptation-evoking impingements of the immediate moment.

3. While the conscious system is frame-insensitive and inclined towards frame alterations, the second unconscious system is highly frame-sensitive and inclined towards frame-securing efforts.

4. The conscious system experiences the world globally, whereas the second unconscious system experiences the world in terms of specific impingements and their precise implications and meanings.

5. The conscious system is insensitive to whether the meanings that are being expressed by a patient and addressed by a therapist are restricted to the surface of messages or extend from the manifest into the trigger-encoded and trigger-decoded realm. However, the level of expressed and addressed meaning is a prime issue for the deep unconscious system.

6. The power of emotional life is sustained and affected by the second unconscious system far more than by its conscious-system counterpart. By and large, the conscious system is the great rationalizer for behaviours and choices motivated by deep unconscious needs unknown to the conscious mind.

7. The only known means of accessing deep unconscious processes and adaptive wisdom is through trigger decoding — the linking of encoded narrative themes to their adaptation-evoking triggers in an immediate relationship and interaction.

While there are other distinguishing features of the two systems of the emotion-processing mind, these seven will enable us to define the issues we now need to address.

SUPERVISION
IN LIGHT OF THE EVOLVED DESIGN
OF THE HUMAN PSYCHE

What does this outline tell us about the supervisory process and experience? To begin to answer, there are many principles of supervision that I have presented in this book that were developed in light of these insights into the basic design of the emotion-processing mind. For example, virtually all of the precepts related to establishing and maintaining the supervisory frame have been fashioned with these realizations in mind. These insights also guided the delineation of the supervisory process and the unconsciously validating methodology spelt out in earlier chapters.

There is, however, a more fundamental issue raised by our understanding of the evolved architecture of the human psyche. Given that the power of emotional life — and of both therapy and supervision — lies with the *deep unconscious system*, how can supervision hope to be deeply effective or consistent in its teachings if the adaptations and messages from that system are *excluded from* the supervisory process and experience even though they are a major force in the supervisory interaction and a prime aspect of the techniques being taught to the supervisee? How can a supervisor stress the key role of deep unconscious experience while excluding it from consideration as it powerfully and unconsciously influences the supervisory situation in which these ideas are being taught?

In the standard communicative model of supervision, these deep processes are dealt with in working over the presented case material. But while this approach provides an important opportunity to explore and deal with the frame and power of the supervised therapy, it does not touch on the immediate interaction between the supervisor and supervisee. Nevertheless, the second unconscious systems of both parties to the supervision are actively processing that very interaction. At each moment in supervision, the greatest and deepest power lies in an unconscious domain that goes untouched by the standard models of supervision. Today's supervisory efforts are *conscious-system efforts* even when they address the deeply unconscious interaction between a supervisee and his or her supervised patient. *The realm of communication and meaning that is being deeply and unconsciously experienced and cathected by both supervisor and supervisee goes unnoticed and unexplored.*

The deep power of the supervisory experience is all but ignored and wasted in the standard models. This avoidance of deep meaning undermines the supervisor's efforts to help the supervisee to work effectively in the realm of this second world of experience in his or her efforts as a psychotherapist. There may, of course, be a measure of cognitive learning so that a supervisee grasps the rudiments of adaptation-oriented listening, trigger decoding, and interactional, frame-related intervening. But all the while, the behaviour and focus of the supervision belies this emphasis and need, and any existing additional unconscious impediments to learning are entirely ignored.

Contradictory messages from the conscious and deep unconscious systems tend to drive people crazy. This kind of pressure certainly interferes with learning and compromises all efforts to work therapeutically within secured frames and with deeply encoded meanings. The situation, in essence, is unwise, hurtful, and untenable.

In sum, then, we can see that while a supervisor and supervisee are focused consciously on events outside their immediate interaction, their respective deep unconscious systems are entirely concentrated on their own immediate interplay and the three dimensions that primarily concern and are processed by the deep unconscious system — frame, level of meaning, and help or harm.

While it is true that conscious-system learning can transpire under these conditions, there are two important caveats to this statement. First, conscious-system learning is deeply affected by the three factors that unconsciously are monitored and processed by the deep unconscious system. If these factors are awry, they undermine the learning experience and can unconsciously foster dysfunctional responses in the supervisee — responses whose deep roots are entirely missed because they are not considered in the supervisory work.

Second, supervision that ignores deep unconscious experience belies the basic principles of psychoanalysis and psychoanalytically oriented therapies which give credence and overriding importance to the (deep) unconscious domain. To try to teach about and deal with the unconscious interaction between the supervisee and his or her patient, while at the same time ignoring a compelling immediate interaction between the supervisee and supervisor, is self-contradictory and therefore undermines the entire supervisory process.

We must conclude, then, that supervision that is conducted in a way that excludes the deep unconscious experience of the participants is flawed, incomplete, ineffective, and harmful in that a major source of experience and learning, however unconscious, is excluded from the work. The situation is something like taking care of a small brush-fire ten miles away from your home when an entire forest is aflame in your own backyard.

A case example

Mr. Bates, a social work supervisor in private practice, was doing supervision with Mr. Carney who had recently begun a private practice of psychotherapy. In their first supervisory session, this private supervision had been structured in a rather secured-frame fashion, but with one exception. Mr. Bates had had only one possible hour available for their work together, and, once each month at that time, he had a commitment to attend a staff meeting at a hospital where he worked — so they would have to forego the supervision during the weeks on which that meeting fell.

In his fourth supervisory session, Mr. Carney said that he was upset with the supervision, but he had no idea why. Some of the teaching had been confusing and seemed contradictory to him, but it was hard for him to identify the exact basis for his doubts and unease. He then ventured to ask a question about a different patient from the one he had been presenting. The patient was a man in his 40s who was very depressed and had begun therapy three weeks earlier. He had asked for a change in his session because of a business trip. It was too early in the therapy — or so Mr. Carney thought — to hold him to his hours, so Mr. Carney had made the change.

In the session that followed the make-up hour (which preceded the trip and seemed empty and hollow), the patient, who was married, reported that while he was away, his flight home had been cancelled at the last minute and he had gone to a hotel where he picked up and slept with a woman whom he'd never met before. He felt terribly guilty and was thinking of terminating his therapy — he needed more direct advice than he was getting. As a child, his mother never respected his closed bedroom door and had often come into bed with him — maybe that's why he has trouble setting limits for himself.

Mr. Bates, who was using a model of supervision that mixed both classical and communicative principles, suggested that the patient had felt that he had seduced the therapist into changing his hour, and then acted out the frame-breaking seduction when his own schedule was changed (*the bridging experience and theme*). Oddly enough, even though this appears communicatively to be a valid formulation, Mr. Carney raised several manifest objections to these ideas and did not tell a confirmatory story. Instead, he spoke of other supervisors who in the past had not understood his needs and, as an aside, mentioned that the doorman to the supervisor's building had been so confused that he had told Mr. Carney that Mr. Bates did not have an office in the building.

Given that Mr. Bates remained silent, Mr. Carney went on to report that he had not intervened in the session that he was presenting, and that, towards the end of the hour, the patient spoke of how his father pretended to be blind to his mother's seductiveness, and that he felt he needed more from the therapist and would like to stop therapy for now. It was all very discouraging for Mr. Carney, who added that the loss of income from the patient, who did terminate, might make it impossible for him to continue with the supervision.

   To focus our discussion, this is a situation in which the supervision was established with many secured-frame features and one blatant frame modification. A common but mistaken argument is that this was their agreed-upon structure, and therefore this defined the ideal frame for this particular super-vision. This is a conscious-system argument, logical on that level, but it fails to appreciate the adaptive workings of the second unconscious system. The ideal frame is *not* defined by an agreed-upon conscious contract between a supervisor and supervisee; *it is defined by the deep unconscious system and its validating encoded derivatives and themes*. This supervi-sory situation therefore had a distinctly mixed frame, one that was inherently self-contradictory and therefore dysfunctional and crazy-making.

An unconscious effect of the deviant frame was seen when the supervisee modified the time of his second patient's ses-sion—frame deviations beget frame deviations. The patient then acted out the seductive, betrayal implications of his therapist's frame-change, much as the supervisee had acted out with his patient the similar attributes of his altered supervisory frame.

It seems clear that carrying out the supervisory discussion in terms of the supervisee's frame modification with his patient totally missed the contribution to this frame deviation that the supervisor himself had made. It is prejudiced and persecutory to focus on a supervisee's frame deviant needs and secured-frame anxieties when these very problems have been manifested by his supervisor — no matter how well rationalized consciously, these deeper meanings are experienced unconsciously by both parties to the basically frame-modified supervisory situation.

This approach is much like a great deal of classical psychotherapy and psychoanalysis, in which the therapist's contribution to a patient's dysfunctions are denied and overlooked, so that the treatment becomes accusatory and blaming of the patient. Doing something similar in supervision also has very destructive effects on the supervisee and evokes unconscious guilt in the criticizing supervisor as well.

Over and over again, frame-related or other types of powerful interventions in supervision unconsciously empower and drive the behaviours and interventions of a supervisee. It is inconsistent to focus on the supervisee's problems without touching on the comparable problems in the supervisor when they do exist. To do so gives supervision a biased and false foundation. In this case, the supervisee found a marginally related narrative, in the form of a patient who was not the primary focus of the supervisory work, with whom to communicate his encoded unconscious perceptions of his supervisor's deviant frame and its meanings.

It is precisely this type of narrative that is needed within the supervisory situation so that the status of the supervisory interaction, and especially its unconscious aspects, can be continuously monitored and worked with.

The key question, then, is this: Is there a way of redesigning supervision so that such material consistently is available for working through and deep insight? Is it possible to create a model of supervision in which both the cognitive learning based on the presentation of process-note case material and the im-

mediate deep and powerful experience of the supervisory interaction can be taken into account? Can the two realms of
experience be explored and worked over in some integrated
manner that offers an optimal, non-contradictory, deeply effective learning experience for the supervisee — and peace and
unmarred satisfaction for the supervisor?

The necessity of finding an affirmative answer to these
questions indicates that, contrary to accepted practice, we
must indeed find a way to both teach the student and help him
or her to access the immediate and contemporaneous workings
of his or her own second unconscious system. In the next and
final chapter of the book, I offer a proposal as to how this can be
done.

CHAPTER FOURTEEN

Self-processing supervision

I have argued that the architecture of the emotion-processing mind is such that the most powerful level of human
experience is processed by the second unconscious system.
I have indicated, too, that there are major problems with a
supervisory situation that fails to recognize and address this
critical realm of emotional interaction. We embark now on a
search for a means of integrating the two levels of experience
essential for complete, non-contradictory, and deeply effective
supervision—the conscious level which involves the case
material, the supervisee, and his or her patient, and the deeply
unconscious level which involves the supervisee and the supervisor.

THE SELF-PROCESSING PARADIGM

The communicative approach has evolved a new form of psychotherapy—*self-processing therapy*—constituted as teaching *patients* (they also are called *students*, and the *therapist* is

237

also called the *teacher*) how to do their own psychotherapy —
their own *self-processing*, as it is termed (Langs, 1992d, 1992f,
1993a). Self-processing is the communicative version of what is
generally termed "self-analysis". It has been found that teaching students, in small groups or, preferably, individually, how
to access the second unconscious system and its trigger-
encoded insights has profound healing effects — self-processing therapy is a very compelling and effective form of treatment.

The combination of supervision with self-processing —
self-processing supervision — offers a means of resolving the
dilemma posed in this and the previous chapter. This paradigm
creates the framework within which a supervisee is able to
communicate narratives and seeks contemporaneous triggers
in order to work over the supervisory interaction — the level of
experience in supervision that has primacy in the deep unconscious part of the psyche. But, in addition, the model calls for
the presentation of supervisory patient material so that the
cognitive teaching and learning also is assured. In operating in
this way, the model offers the significant added advantage of
being able to show with remarkable clarity the ways in which
*supervisory transactions unconsciously influence the work
and life of a supervisee.* In all, self-processing supervision is a
way of capturing and dealing with the two worlds of emotional
experience in a single, workable setting — consciously and
deeply unconsciously — and of showing how the two domains
interact.

THE STRUCTURE
OF SELF-PROCESSING THERAPY

Let us begin with a look at self-processing therapy, keeping in
mind that the self-processing portion of self-processing supervision is not necessarily defined primarily as therapeutic —
although it has healing qualities regardless of the way in which
it is presented. In general, the usual approach is to think of this
part of the paradigm as teaching the supervisee engaging in
self-processing in order to keep track of the unconscious pro-

cesses that are influencing his or her supervised work and other dealings in therapy and daily life.

The model of therapy that I present here can be used with small groups, although that particular setting has a number of frame alterations built into it; nonetheless, it is quite workable within limits. The same model also can ideally be used on an individual basis, in a one-to-one situation. This setting creates the *self-processing tutorial*, the potentially secured-frame and optimal form of self-processing therapy.

A self-processing tutorial is framed as a ninety-minute therapy seminar or class that is usually constituted as a series of renewable four-session segments for which the fee or tuition is paid in advance. The time is fixed for the duration of the seminars, which continue as long as the student renews them. The usual secured-frame requisites are observed: there is total privacy and confidentiality, no recording of any kind, no leakage to outside parties, the relative anonymity of the teacher, and the use of interventions that follow communicative principles — frame-securing measures carried out under the guidance of the patient's encoded material and trigger-decoded interpretations. These are the only interventions that obtain encoded or unconscious validation from the responsive student or patient, and they constitute the basic work of the self-processing paradigm.

Within this rather secured frame, which activates secured-frame anxieties of considerable strength, there is an *interior structure* to the unfolding process of each class. The student is given the first forty minutes to do his or her own *self-processing exercise*, as it is termed. The instructor is entirely silent during this period. The balance of the time is spent in active teaching designed to help the student to resolve the resistances that inevitably emerge in the course of such efforts; the enlightenment is carried out primarily via interactive, questioning methods of instruction. The process culminates in the student's own self-interpretations and frame-management efforts or comparable interventions by the instructor if need be.

There are five components to the self-processing exercise. It is essential to develop each element in sequence because conscious-system defences are such that the conscious mind incessantly veers off the singular and remarkably narrow path to deep unconscious insight. Left to its own resources, conscious-system resistances limit these efforts so that they seldom arrive at anything more than a fragment of deep insight. The structure of the exercise offers a definitive guide to the student through these treacherous waters so that he or she can *begin with a dream or comparable origination narrative*, as it is called, and *arrive at a trigger-decoded insight and deep understanding.*

The basic goal of self-processing therapy is to access the adaptive workings of the second unconscious system and its resourcefulness — and resolve a student's symptoms and interpersonal difficulties on that basis. This means that the quest is for a strong collection of disguised themes embodied in surface narratives about one thing or another outside the tutorial, which contain latently the encoded outputs that reflect the unconscious perceptions and adaptive processing of the second unconscious system inside the tutorial. This touches on the second key element of the process — the adaptation-evoking triggers that have evoked these unconscious reactions and themes. With both *triggers and themes* in hand, trigger decoding can be accomplished and deep insight experienced.

The path that must be traversed to arrive at deep understanding begins, then, with the presentation of a dream, or of a story composed on the spot by the self-processing student — it begins with an *origination narrative*, a recent dream or dream equivalent. This narrative is a unique creation of the emotion-processing mind in that it serves remarkably well as a source of associations — *guided associations*, as they are called. *Dreams are dreamt to be associated to*, not to be analysed. Each element of a dream is an exquisite source of one or more associated stories — guided associations should be *narrative* in nature (narratives are the carriers of encoded meaning). These associated stories should fan out from a given dream element into a diverse collection of tales, each of them the embodiment of a set of themes that encode or disguise the student's responses to the triggers constituted by the teacher's interventions. As noted, the latter are the contemporaneous and critical stimuli to which the second unconscious system is adapting, and they are, as a rule, frame-related. *Guided* associations are, in general, far more powerful than unencumbered *free* associations because the latter tend to move towards non-narrative intellectualizations and away from strong encoded imagery.

The student is obligated, then, to begin each tutorial session with a dream or dream substitute — an origination narrative. The second step is to generate as naively and richly as possible a strong network of diverse themes that embody reflections of deep unconscious processing — *the derivative network or narrative pool*. The themes must have powerful components because the deep unconscious system deals only with compelling and disturbing perceptions and issues that are unbearable to awareness. As noted earlier, strong themes include overt sexuality and aggression, illness and death, harm and the like; incidents that are unlikely in reality (so-called *mini-psychotic images*); allusions to rules, frames, and boundaries, including themes of dishonesty and criminality; and references to important aspects of the genetic past. Every meaningful derivative network has several such themes somewhere in their contents — themes that are available to be extracted from their manifest moorings in order to be relocated or transposed and linked to their triggers.

The third step in a self-processing exercise is the identification of what are called *self-indicators* — signs of emotional dysfunction and resistances to the process, and especially *the student's impingements on the frame of the tutorial*. The latter may be either frame-securing or frame-deviating, but they reflect the student's state of mind in a critical area of human experience — rules, frames, and boundaries. Furthermore, there is a close relationship between self-indicators and triggers — the former are reactions to and often reflect the nature of the latter.

It is essential in this process to be clear about the status of the frame of the class for both student and teacher — the second unconscious system is concentrated on such issues, and deep unconscious experience is contingent on this dimension. Indeed, both frame-securing and frame-modifying interventions have their own distinctive constellation of meanings, and each organizes human emotional experience in its own particular way.

The fourth step in the exercise is the identification of the current *adaptation-evoking triggers* that have activated the student's deep unconscious system. This is done in two ways: first, via *direct recall*— the student consciously attempts to identify all currently active triggers, and, from there, all reactivated past triggers (they are related to those that are contemporaneously active). The search primarily is for *frame-related triggers*; all other triggers are called *impression triggers,* and they tend to be secondary — often, they involve misperceptions and other types of conscious-system distortions.

The second method of identifying triggers is called the *themes-to-triggers method* in that the themes from the narrative pool are scrutinized and used as clues to active triggers (this type of search also includes a scrutiny of the self-indicators). Given that themes are a response to and therefore reflect the nature and implications of triggers, this method is quite helpful in enabling students to discover *repressed triggers*. It is not uncommon for a compelling trigger to be repressed and missed by a student; this search is a vital way of discovering over-looked emotional stimuli.

Once the key triggers have been identified, especially those that are frame-related, the fifth and final step in the exercise is taken — the *linking or transposing process*. This is accomplished by selecting a critical trigger (frame-securing triggers are in general stronger than those that are frame-modifying) and articulating its frame attributes and main implications. These qualities and meanings are then connected or linked to the themes that have been extracted from the derivative network. Linking is *not analysing*; it is a way of connecting themes to triggers to arrive at trigger-decoded insights that reflect the adaptations of the deep unconscious mind.

The result of the transposing process is stated as a logical adaptive sequence and is couched in terms of the student's encoded but valid unconscious perceptions of the teacher in light of his or her interventions and the student's unconscious reactions to these perceptions — correctives, models of frame rectification, unconscious interpretations to the therapist, and other such efforts. The model intervention is configured as follows, with the *student* speaking to the instructor:

"You did this and that in respect to the ground rules of my tutorial; I unconsciously perceived what you did in that and this way; and then, selectively, based on my own needs, pathology, genetics, and adaptive capabilities, unconsciously I saw what you did as having these and those particular meanings and ramifications. Furthermore, I have encoded this and that recommendation to secure the frame and correct the situation in ways that seem valid and necessary to me."

The student is always asked to respond, however briefly, consciously to each of his or her own interventions and to those of the teacher. But, in addition, once an interpretation or frame-rectification has been effected (most often the final touches are put into place by the instructor), the student is obligated to return to the origination narrative for a fresh guided association to some element of the initial dream or story. This new associated tale is understood to encode the student's unconscious assessment of the student's or teacher's interventional efforts. If they were valid, the images will stress well-functioning people and helpful interludes (*interpersonal validation*), and they also may add important fresh elements to the picture — a genetic link, a previously unknown aspect of the psychodynamics, and so on (*cognitive validation*). If confirmation does *not* materialize, *reformulation* is called for. By far the most common cause of error is the selection of a relatively inconsequential trigger for linking, and missing one that is far more compelling and more incisively related to the thematic material — and to the student's unconscious experience.

The experience of secured-frame moments and of trigger-decoded insights is exceedingly healing no matter what the nature of a given person's psychopathology. However, self-processing is not limited to individuals who have emotional symptoms or interpersonal or other emotionally founded difficulties. It is open to anyone with or without acknowledged emotional problems who, essentially, wants to know more about himself or herself and the human psyche. It is therefore available to any supervisee who wishes to have an optimal supervisory experience — with healing as an added reward.

SELF-PROCESSING SUPERVISION

It is a relatively straightforward step from the standard model of *communicative supervision* to a *combination of supervision and self-processing* (Langs, in press a). Before describing the process and its accomplishments, some further introductory perspectives are in order. It is well known that, with few exceptions, conventional wisdom states that a supervisee's personal therapy or analysis should be conducted by a therapist who is not, nor has been, the student's supervisor — the two experiences should be quite separate without contact between the teacher and the treating therapist. Although some training programs modify this last requirement, the essential point is that a therapist should not be the professional patient's supervisor.

The arguments in support of this position are based entirely on *conscious-system thinking and logic*. In essence, the contention is that the goals and tasks of the two situations are quite different and that the relationship between patient and therapist — "the transference", as it is called — would be contaminated and confounded by combining the two tasks into a single situation, be it done within the same session or in two separate sessions.

This position has found considerable support from the communicative approach, which has stressed the differences in the role requirements and frame of the two situations — for example, the kinds of activities engaged in, the nature of the basic communications from each party, and so forth. However, these perspectives were developed with respect to the standard communicative model of supervision, which did not take into account the architecture of the emotion-processing mind or the impact and importance of the immediate interaction between supervisor and supervisee.

As for the rare prior arguments in favour of combining supervision and psychotherapy into one relationship and situation, the general reasoning has been that placing an analyst in both roles would enable him or her to understand and analyse the supervisee better. This, too, is a naive conscious-system proposal that has no grounding in an understanding of the design and adaptive resources of the emotion-processing mind and the nature of encoded communication; it also lacks clear data to support its thinking. It must therefore be stressed that the basis for the present recommendation is quite different from earlier sources of similar proposals, and that the type of combined supervision and psychotherapy that is being argued for is also far different from forms previously connected with this line of thought.

To be clear, the present proposal stems from several distinctive sources. First, communicative supervision has revealed dramatic and strong limitations to the educational power of the standard, cognitive supervisory situation. Repeatedly, strongly motivated and seemingly skilful supervisees have been blocked in achieving any notable level of competency as communicative psychotherapists despite teachings that consistently obtained encoded validation from supervised patients. Many of these students were in non-communicative forms of dynamic psychotherapy, and they were unable to resolve the resistances and obstacles that interfered with their growth and development as effective therapists working in the domain of the second unconscious system.

Given the time constraints of the standard supervisory session, efforts to explore these difficulties consciously with these supervisees were not especially fruitful. Attempts to widen the supervisory field to include some associations and history from the supervisee also generally failed to alter these situations — time was too short to explore the supervisee's personal material adequately and also to conduct the supervision of the presented patient. The self-processing paradigm had not as yet been developed and, as a result, these more unstructured and perfunctory efforts to obtain personal material, narratives, and identified triggers did not unfold with sufficient fullness to allow for much in the way of interpretation. These early efforts seemed awkward and out of place in this kind of supervisory situation — they awaited a more formalized approach.

The main exception to these trends emerged in connection with acute frame-related interventions by a supervisor, major frame modifications by a supervisee, and other types of supervisory crises (see chapter twelve). Under these conditions, the inclusion of a moderate amount of self-processing material — an origination narrative, a few guided associations, and the identification of self-indicators and triggers — often allowed the supervisor to help the student arrive at trigger-decoded insights. Deep resolution of the issues raised at such moments was impossible without such material. This work actually revealed some striking links between a supervisee's work with his or her patients and the largely frame-connected interventions of the supervisor.

Efforts of this kind indicated that there was, indeed, a powerful unconscious interaction transpiring between supervisor and supervisee, and that the supervisory interplay and its frame were exerting exceedingly strong effects on the work and life of the supervisee — and of the supervisor as well. These emergency efforts to access the supervisee's unconscious experience of the supervisory situation also showed that such work was feasible within the supervisory situation; they also indicated that combining the two pursuits effectively would require more time than the usual forty-five- or fifty-minute supervisory session.

In all, these experiences suggested both the feasibility and necessity of a more clearly defined and consistent use of self-processing supervision. In time, observations of unresolvable supervisory resistances and crises rendered self-processing supervision more a dire necessity than an interesting addendum to the usual supervisory model.

Still another source of encouragement for the development of self-processing supervision came from experiences with self-processing therapy. This mode of treatment is constituted with an integrated frame that is both cognitive/educational and second-unconscious-system/therapeutic — a combined structure that made it easy to combine self-processing with supervision. Furthermore, work with therapists in self-processing therapy revealed the remarkable extent to which their functioning as healers was being affected by both their outside supervisory experiences and the self-processing therapy itself.

As all of this was falling into place, the evolutionary history and present architecture of the emotion-processing mind was also being clarified (Langs, 1993b, in press b, in press c) — and, with that, self-processing therapy was being forged (Langs, 1993a). The fallacy of trying to teach a supervisee how to work with the second unconscious system while ignoring its enormous influence on the supervisory couple emerged in compelling fashion. In all, there were strong motives to shift from the standard models of supervision to self-processing supervision. And, once the paradigm was put into place, it proved be quite revealing and effective in dealing with the unconscious transactions of the supervisory experience — and quite salutary as well.

THE TECHNIQUE
OF SELF-PROCESSING SUPERVISION

As I have explained, the details of self-processing therapy have been presented elsewhere (Langs, 1992d, 1992f, 1993a), so I stress here the addenda needed to conduct *self-processing supervision*. The stated goals of this process are to teach the supervisee how to do effective psychotherapy and to offer the best possible therapy to the supervised patient, to generate a deep understanding of the nature of emotionally charged communication and adaptation and to do so in the light of a supervisee's own deep unconscious experience within the supervision, and to reveal and explore the deeply unconscious effects of supervision on the professional work and personal life of the supervisee.

No explicit therapeutic goal needs to be stated, although at times, when a supervisee has raised the question of therapy, this intention should also be acknowledged — self-processing supervision is both an educational and a healing endeavour. And while the final word may not as yet have been given on this issue, it does appear that self-processing supervision must take on the responsibility of the therapy of the supervisee. Involvement on his or her part in a separate therapeutic situation is a definite frame alteration of the self-processing supervision frame — the second unconscious system is quite clear on this matter. Whenever this issue arises, the derivative material will point to the need for the exclusive use of the self-processing supervision paradigm for both cognitive learning and treatment. Thus, *self-processing supervision should be the only supervisory and therapeutic pursuit of the supervisee for as long as it lasts.*

Like no other learning or therapy situation — even communicative forms of psychotherapy — self-processing supervision affords a supervisee a first-hand experience of his or her own unconscious processes, meanings, and adaptations, and it vividly demonstrates the profound influence that these processes can exert. This model of supervision uniquely opens the world of deep unconscious experience to the supervisee, both personally and in his or her therapeutic work.

The *ground rules and framework* of self-processing supervision are almost identical to those of self-processing therapy, and it shares much with the communicative forms of secured-frame psychotherapy. All of the basic tenets of these processes — total privacy and confidentiality, a fixed time, place, and fee, etc. (see chapters four to seven) — are built into the basic ground rules of the situation and sustained for the life of the experience.

The structure of self-processing therapy is modified to accommodate the supervisory process in the following ways. The session remains ninety minutes, but the supervisee is given the first thirty minutes of each session to do his of her self-processing exercise (instead of the forty minutes used in the therapy model). During this time, the supervisor is entirely silent and the supervisee has the task of beginning with an origination narrative and arriving at a supervision-related, trigger-decoded insight (see above). As expected, a supervisor's frame-related interventions in particular prove to be the crucial triggers for the unconscious processing of the student's second unconscious system.

The patients of the supervisee, including the supervised patient, may be mentioned in the course of this exercise — often, they are a source of strong narrative material and encoded themes, as well as of important self-indicators (e.g. errant interventions and problematic behaviours by the supervisee). However, the focus during this portion of the self-processing supervision session is *not* on the supervisory teaching, but on the supervisee's deep unconscious experience of the supervisory interaction.

Once the supervisee has completed his or her exercise, the remaining hour is devoted, first, to resolving the inescapable resistances that materialize in a given self-processing exercise and arriving at trigger-decoded insights — and their encoded validation. Once these goals are achieved, the supervisee is asked by the teacher to present his or her process-note case material in the usual fashion — in sequence as prepared after the sessions. The supervision is then conducted along the usual lines, but there is an added dimension to the supervisory work: *the unconscious experience of the supervisee vis-à-vis the supervisor is available and can be made an integral part of the teaching.*

Tracing the roots of a supervisee's errors to the frame modifications and other errant interventions of his or her supervisor is a remarkable and awesome experience with proper accountability on all sides — a balance that is lacking in the highly skewed standard models of supervision. Similarly, discovering the unconscious sources of a supervisee's frame-securing and sound trigger-decoding efforts in a secured-frame intervention or trigger-decoded interpretation of the supervisor is strikingly enhancing for both supervisee and supervisor.

Another advantageous and distinctive feature of self-processing supervision is the *availability of not just one, but two principal sources of encoded validation.* The first comes, as before, from the supervised patient, while the second arises from the narrative communications of the supervisee himself or herself which are an inherent part of the new model. The confluence of validation from these two sources — and it should materialize with effective, integrated supervisory work — is an exceedingly valuable guide and means of confirmation for the supervisor's interventions and the entire supervisory process.

I have long argued and attempted to show that anyone who engages in trigger decoding can confirm that the worlds of conscious and unconscious experience are very different from each other, and that the deep unconscious system embodies extremely powerful forces that silently orchestrate our emotional lives and professional efforts with patients. The experience of self-processing supervision reveals in remarkable and often stark ways the truth and validity of these propositions. The thin red line that goes from a supervisor's frame-related intervention to a supervisee's work with a patient—and to behaviours in his or her daily life—are visualized with remarkable clarity in these efforts.

Seemingly minor incidents in supervision, most of them frame-related and unnoticed consciously, are found to evoke remarkably strong unconscious perceptions and reactions to those perceptions, as revealed through encoded images that are usually both grim and overwhelmingly strong. It is humbling to experience and realize that there is indeed a dark, deep, sometimes awful world of experience transpiring every moment of our lives—and during every second of supervision—regarding which we have virtually no idea unless we compel ourselves to engage in trigger decoding.

Doing self-processing supervision can open a window into that world that is at once disturbing to view yet awesome in its power and incisiveness. The general use of this paradigm promises to stimulate a significant advance in our means of exploring the supervisory experience as well as the emotion-processing mind and its interactions. Ultimately, self-processing supervision has the potential to expand our psychoanalytic knowledge-base, improve our ways of doing psychotherapy and supervision, and help each of us, supervisor and supervisee, to grow, mature, and have far better lives for the effort.

A final vignette

Dr. Kim, a female psychologist, was seeing Dr. Diamond, a male psychiatrist and psychotherapist, in self-processing supervision. The supervisee was presenting a female patient, Mrs. Walker, who suffered from anxiety attacks.

As mandated, Dr. Diamond began one supervisory session and its self-processing exercise with a dream of his own. He is in an operating room. He is helping a surgeon to separate male Siamese twins. The mother is standing by anxiously. One of the twins is fine, but the other one is seriously ill. The ill one is given oxygen through a nasal tube and his colour brightens.

In associating to the dream—invoking narrative, guided associations—Dr. Diamond recalled a newspaper story of

Siamese twins being separated surgically and seemed to
remember that one of them had died. When he was
younger, he'd call his mother and sister the Diamond
twins because they were inseparable. It took his sister
years to leave their mother and get married — even now
she calls her mother every day and sees her at least once a
week. It's a sick relationship and it has ruined his sister's
life — she never held a job for long and for a while she had
lived with a married couple in a ménage-à-trois that was
pretty crazy.

The operation brought to mind a story that Dr. Diamond
had read about an impostor who had done surgery at a
local hospital before he was found out. Some of his
patients did very well, but two of them nearly died because
of a serious mistake he had made — he had given each of
them the medication meant for the other patient. The drug
had suppressed breathing in one of the patients, who
nearly smothered to death.

Dr. Diamond then said that he has a patient who is a
twin — a man. This man had insisted on being given a
tranquillizer and had asked for the name of a psychiatrist
to see for the medication. Inadvertently, somehow Dr.
Diamond had given him Dr. Kim's telephone number when
he meant to give him the number of a different
psychiatrist, Dr. Kantor. Dr. Diamond found out about it
when the patient called him to say that Dr. Kim had said
she couldn't see him. He guessed that Dr. Kim had
decided to hold the frame. How could he have made a
mistake like that?

At this point, the thirty minutes of the self-processing
exercise were up and Dr. Kim intervened to ask Dr.
Diamond for his *overview of his exercise* — the standard
way in which a self-processing instructor begins the next
part of the process. Dr. Diamond realized that he had
failed to list his self-indicators and the triggers — Dr.
Kim's recent interventions. Because of that, no linking had
been attempted and no deep insight had been achieved

(insight and unconscious meaning are defined entirely in terms of linking triggers to themes).

Through queries from Dr. Kim, Dr. Diamond saw that his main *self-indicator* was his inadvertent break in the frame in giving Dr. Kim's telephone number to his patient. He could see that he was inviting a sibling into his space. When Dr. Kim intervened to point out that the first linking had to be to her interventions as the supervisor rather than to the student's own frame-related behaviours (which are, when frame-involved, secondarily processed by the deep unconscious system), Dr. Diamond drew a blank. Something must have triggered his error; it was a break in the frame, so had Dr. Kim broken the frame? (In self-processing, there is a fair proposition that states that a supervisee's frame alterations are usually triggered by a frame alteration by the supervisor.) Actually, Dr. Kim had held the frame with the referral, so where was the trigger?

At this point, a new association occurred to Dr. Diamond. He had another cousin, Grace, who had had twin boys. Suddenly it struck him — how could he have forgotten? Grace's husband had called him to tell him that he was in therapy and it turned out that he was seeing Dr. Kim! Dr. Diamond had been shocked by the revelation, but had said nothing of his relationship with Dr. Kim to the cousin.

This repressed incident reveals both the most active frame-related (deviant) triggers and a frame-deviant self-indicator as well. On the trigger side, the information was a revelation about Dr. Kim that is experienced in the second unconscious system as her own self-revelation, and the fact that she was seeing Dr. Diamond's cousin was a frame break in that a therapist/supervisor should not be seeing individuals who are known to each other in any way. Even though Dr. Diamond almost never saw this cousin, the frame had been modified in manner that would be impossible to secure fully.

Indeed, the only frame-securing possibilities were terminating the self-processing supervision with Dr. Diamond (this was not a preferred choice because he had been seen first and deserved to continue with Dr. Kim if someone had to leave) or terminating with the cousin (but Dr. Kim had already seen him in consultation and initiated therapy, and he did not know consciously of the frame modification, so it would be impossible to introduce it without violating the confidentiality and frame of the supervision). If the cousin left therapy, the frame would be relatively secured — but there was no sign that he was planning to do so. On the other hand, continuing with both situations contaminated the frame of each of them — one knowingly and the other unknowingly.

Where did Dr. Diamond's deep unconscious system stand on this complicated frame issue? The trigger is clear — it is Dr. Kim's seeing both the supervisee and his cousin. What, then, of the encoded themes — what is Dr. Diamond's unconscious perception and adaptive processing of this trigger?

In the self-processing supervision hour, Dr. Kim asked first for her supervisee's conscious feelings and thoughts on this situation (it is well to begin with the surface). In response, Dr. Diamond indicated that even though it was a frame break, he didn't feel it was that important. He hadn't said anything to his cousin and he could keep his distance — it was no big deal.

Dr. Kim next suggested that Dr. Diamond link his themes to this trigger and get a sense of his deep unconscious response as well. Dr. Diamond paused a while and then said that he thought that the dream indicated that he had acquired a Siamese twin and that the story of his sister suggested that he now felt over-involved with Dr. Kim and his cousin as if the three of them had created a ménage-à-trois as had his sister. He then hesitatingly added that the image of the impostor surgeon and the error that he had made that nearly caused the death of two patients must encode his view that Dr. Kim had broken the frame of both situations — and even though it was done inadvertently, she was now seen as a liar who had misrepresented herself and who had harmed both Dr. Diamond and his cousin.

With a good deal of prodding, Dr. Diamond completed the encoded picture of his unconscious experience by realizing that his mini-psychotic lapse (his temporary break with reality in erroneously giving his patient Dr. Kim's telephone number) was an enactment (acting out) of the newly modified, contaminated frame — of the frame-deviant incestuous three-some created by this frame break. Finally, the image of nearly smothering to death was seen, first, as a reflection of the deadly destructiveness of the frame modification and, second, as linked to Dr. Kim's holding the frame secured with Dr. Diamond's patient. There were indeed mixed triggers — frame-securing and frame-deviant.

In this instance, the frame break was inadvertent (the cousin had, of course, a different last name from Dr. Diamond and had come from an outside referral source). However, the effects of the frame deviation were in clear evidence — most striking was Dr. Diamond's peculiar mistake with the telephone numbers. His unconscious experience of a frame break by a frame-securing supervisor was that of a *mini-psychotic lapse* on her part and a betrayal of her competency. Because the incident had not as yet been subjected to self-processing, its toxic effects had led to the supervisee's lapse. Strange and strong are the effects of the frame-related interventions of a supervisor.

The questions of how the frame deviation would affect the self-processing supervision in the long run, how the frame should now be handled, and whether the supervisory situation could be continued in viable fashion under these conditions needed clear answers from the present and, if necessary, future material. At this point, the derivatives seem to indicate that termination of the supervision will prove to be necessary in light of the absence of any other viable frame-securing inter-vention for this situation.

This *corrective or frame-rectification* is encoded into the supervisee's allusions to the one Siamese twin who had died (one person needed to be terminated by Dr. Kim) and to the impostor who was dismissed from the hospital and sent to jail (an encoded commentary on the criminality of this inadvertent frame break and on the need for punishment and rectification). Because Dr. Diamond was aware of the contaminated frame, Dr. Kim would have no other choice but to terminate her work with him — thereby rectifying the frame for both her supervisee and her patient. To do otherwise was to continue to be an impostor — to claim to be a communicative psychotherapist yet to fail to do so (the claim is a lie).

These are difficult choices, but not knowing that they exist will cause harm to everyone in this situation — as it already had begun to (cf. Dr. Diamond's lapse). Everyone concerned here would benefit enormously from Dr. Kim's securing the frame of the two situations. If that action is not taken, we can be certain that these strong and insidious effects will continue to fester and lead to further harmful behaviours and symptoms in everyone — including the supervisee and his supervised patient. Consciously, you can deny what exists in nature, but nevertheless it continues to exist and exert strong unseen influence.

It is imperative to notice the difference between Dr. Diamond's conscious reaction to this frame break and his deep unconscious response. The conscious-system picture and response is enormously constricted, simplistic, general, naive, and potentially deeply hurtful to both himself and others — especially through its use of denial. The world of the conscious system is a rather empty world where most of the real action is denied or missed and the stage is set again and again for further trauma and damage.

In contrast, the deep wisdom subsystem of the second unconscious system had a profoundly complex and intricate view of the same frame deviation. The unconscious experience was rich, stark, specific, detailed, honest, uncompromising, and devastating. The second world of experience is one of truth, power, and confrontation. It is where emotional life is being lived and emotional battles are being fought — and true resolutions and triumphs are possible.

SELF-SUPERVISION

In chapter eleven we briefly considered the subject of self-supervision and outlined a few precepts for these efforts. In principle, an independent therapist should have a life-long commitment to monitor his or her therapeutic work and to discover the existence of countertransference expressions as well as to recognize validated and effective interventions and techniques. As we would expect, patients' encoded validation of all silences and interventions are the guiding lights for these endeavours. And personal self-processing (Langs, 1993a) is the best means available for discovering the deeper, unconscious (usually frame-related) roots of a therapist's dysfunctional moments.

Ultimately, sound self-supervision requires an expansion of a therapist's highly defensive efforts at self-observation, and this is best done through a mastery of sound therapeutic techniques and their underlying observational and theoretical foundations. It is here, of course, that patients' *unconscious* psychobiological needs and capabilities to automatically supervise, teach, and interpret to their therapists play a most significant role. Indeed, learning from a patient's *encoded responses* to one's frame-related and interventional errors is a primary source of knowledge and growth for a psychotherapist — if it's not happening at least weekly, something is amiss and needs to be corrected. Self-supervision should be a major source of fresh insight for every former supervisee, and the evolution of more and more effective means of carrying out this surprisingly difficult activity is a sign of a maturing and expanding psychotherapist.

CONCLUDING COMMENTS

The emotion-processing mind has evolved to shut out the richest part of emotional experience and life. For countless reasons, we need to work consciously to set right this loss and see to it that we cope and survive far better for doing so. It can be argued that natural selection paid too great a price in favouring such extreme defences to protect conscious-system functioning. Certainly, each of us, and every supervisor and supervisee, pays dearly for evolution's design.

Self-processing supervision can help us better to explore, understand, and find ways to re-configure and improve the emotion-processing psyche. The broad use of this mode of supervision should, in time, sponsor a great deal of healthy functioning on the part of both supervisors and supervisees; and it will set the fields of psychotherapy and psychoanalysis on fresh paths towards significant new growth and development. In time, both patients and therapists, and the world at large, will greatly benefit from a shift to this new teaching/ healing paradigm.

Few people know better than I how difficult it will be to create this transformation. Strangely, the first thing you learn in doing self-processing is how impossibly resistant, dense, intransigent, and uncertain conscious-system functioning happens to be. Yet, ultimately the changes defined in this book and in the future to which they point will have to be wrought by conscious minds — we need to know far more about the kinds of psyches that can tolerate deep meaning and secured frames. Nevertheless, the communicative approach is a corrective power to be respected and reckoned with — in time it is certain to prevail. And as for motivation, it seems clear that the mental health and survival of every patient, therapist, and supervisor will be greatly enhanced by these changes. At bottom, even the survival of our civilization and societies may depend on our accessing the wisdom of our collective deep unconscious minds — it may well be the only resource that ultimately can save us from ruin.

REFERENCES

Bion, W. (1967). Notes on memory and desire. *Psychoanalytic Forum*, 2: 271–280. Reprinted in R. Langs (Ed.), *Classics in Psychoanalytic Technique* (pp. 243–244). Northvale, NJ: Jason Aronson, 1990.

Dorpat, T., & Miller, M. (1992). *Clinical Interaction and the Analysis of Meaning*. Hillsdale, NJ: The Analytic Press.

Goodheart, W. (1992). On deciphering the book of nature: Human communication in psychotherapy. *American Journal of Psychotherapy*, 46: 592–610.

Goodheart, W. (1993). Between Freud and Charcot: Beginning steps from psychoanalysis and folk psychology towards an interactional science of emotional cognition and communication. *International Journal of Communicative Psychoanalysis & Psychotherapy*, 8: 3–15.

Korn, S., & Carmignani, R. (1987). Process notes as derivative communication about the supervisory field. *Yearbook of Psychoanalysis & Psychotherapy*, 2: 68–84.

Langs, R. (1975). The patient's unconscious perceptions of the therapist's errors. In: P. Giovacchini (Ed.), *Tactics and Tech-*

niques of Psychoanalytic Psychotherapy. Vol. 2: Counter-transference (pp. 239–250). New York: Jason Aronson.

Langs, R. (1978). A model of supervision: The patient as unconscious supervisor. In R. Langs, *Technique in Transition* (pp. 587–625). New York: Jason Aronson.

Langs, R. (1979). *The Supervisory Experience.* New York: Jason Aronson.

Langs, R. (1980). *Interactions: The Realm of Transference and Countertransference.* New York: Jason Aronson.

Langs, R. (1982). Supervisory crises and dreams from supervisees. *Contemporary Psychoanalysis, 18:* 575–612.

Langs, R. (1985). *Madness and Cure.* Lake Worth, FL: Gardner Press.

Langs, R. (1986). Clinical issues arising from a new model of the mind. *Contemporary Psychoanalysis, 22:* 418–444.

Langs, R. (1987a). A new model of the mind. *Yearbook of Psychoanalysis & Psychotherapy, 2:* 3–34.

Langs, R. (1987b). Clarifying a new model of the mind. *Contemporary Psychoanalysis, 23:* 162–180.

Langs, R. (1988). *A Primer of Psychotherapy.* New York: Gardner Press.

Langs, R. (1989). The transformation function in light of a new model of the mind. *British Journal of Psychotherapy, 5:* 300–312.

Langs, R. (1992a). *A Clinical Workbook for Psychotherapists.* London: Karnac Books.

Langs, R. (1992b [1978]). *The Listening Process.* Northvale, NJ: Jason Aronson.

Langs, R. (1992c). 1923: The advance that retreated from the architecture of the mind. *International Journal of Communicative Psychoanalysis & Psychotherapy, 7:* 3–15.

Langs, R. (1992d). The self-processing class and the psychotherapy situation: A comparative study. *American Journal of Psychotherapy, 46:* 75–90.

Langs, R. (1992e). *Science, Systems and Psychoanalysis.* London: Karnac Books.

Langs, R. (1992f). Teaching self-processing. *Contemporary Psychoanalysis, 28:* 97–117.

Langs, R. (1993a). *Empowered Psychotherapy.* London: Karnac Books.

Langs, R. (1993b). Psychoanalysis: Narrative myth or narrative science? *Contemporary Psychoanalysis, 29*: 555–594.

Langs, R. (in press a). Combining supervision with empowered psychotherapy. *Contemporary Psychoanalysis.*

Langs, R. (in press b). The evolution of the hominid mind in light of a science of emotional cognition. *Contemporary Psychoanalysis.*

Langs, R. (in press c). Psychoanalysis and the science of evolution. *American Journal of Psychotherapy.*

Langs, R., & Badalamenti, A. (1992). The three modes of the science of psychoanalysis. *American Journal of Psychotherapy, 46*: 163–182.

Searles, H. (1959). The effort to drive the other person crazy—an element in the aetiology and psychotherapy of schizophrenia. *British Journal of Medical Psychology, 32*: 1–18.

Searles, H. (1975). The patient as therapist to his analyst. In: P. Giovacchini (Ed.), *Tactics and Techniques of Psychoanalytic Psychotherapy. Vol. 2: Countertransference* (pp. 95–151). New York: Jason Aronson.

INDEX